SAVING THE ORIGINAL SINNER

SAVING THE ORIGINAL SINNER

How Christians Have Used the Bible's First Man
to Oppress, Inspire, and Make Sense of the World

KARL W. GIBERSON

Beacon Press
Boston, Massachusetts

BEACON PRESS
Boston, Massachusetts
www.beacon.org

Beacon Press books
are published under the auspices of
the Unitarian Universalist Association of Congregations.

18 17 16 15   8 7 6 5 4 3 2 1

This book is printed on acid-free paper that meets the uncoated paper
ANSI/NISO specifications for permanence as revised in 1992.

Text design and composition by Kim Arney

Library of Congress Cataloging-in-Publication Data
Giberson, Karl.
    Saving the original sinner : how Christians have used the Bible's first man
to oppress, inspire, and make sense of the world / Karl Giberson.
        pages   cm
    Includes bibliographical references and index.
    ISBN 978-0-8070-1251-2 (hardcover : alk. paper)
    ISBN 978-0-8070-1252-9 (ebook)
1. Adam (Biblical figure)—Influence. 2. Bible. Genesis, I–III—Criticism,
interpretation, etc.—History. 3. Christianity—Influence. 4. Theology,
Doctrinal. I. Title.
    BS580.A4G53 2015
    222'.11092—dc23

                                                    2014043788

To my wife, Myrna

CONTENTS

PROLOGUE

In midwinter 1656, fourteen years after Galileo had died peacefully in his Tuscany home, still under house arrest for his views on the motion of the earth, armed men burst into the home of another subversive, the French Calvinist Isaac La Peyrère, and hauled him off to prison. Heresy hunters had dispatched them to deal with a threat to Christianity even greater than that of Galileo. After "enhanced interrogations" La Peyrère was escorted to Rome where, after an audience with the pope, he recanted his heresy, rejected his Calvinism, and joined the Roman Catholic Church.

In midwinter 2011 as I started work on this book, another scholar, this time an American Calvinist named John Schneider, was summoned by heresy hunters and interrogated for the same beliefs that had threatened La Peyrère.

The heresy was the status of the biblical Adam. La Peyrère got in trouble for his book *Men before Adam*, arguing that Adam was not the first man. While no historically celebrated trial accompanied Schneider's interrogation, he, like Galileo and La Peyrère, still suffered serious consequences: he lost the job he had held—and loved—at Calvin College for a quarter century. His crime was a 2010 article "Recent Genetic Science and Christian Theology on Human Origins," published in *Perspectives on Science and Christian Faith*, which suggested that not only was Adam not the first man but that he never existed.

INTRODUCTION

OUR COMMON ANCESTOR

Then the Lord God formed man from the dust of the ground,
and breathed into his nostrils the breath of life;
and the man became a living being.

—GENESIS 2:7

In the fall of 2009 I visited the Creation Museum in Petersburg, Kentucky. I was in the area to speak at Xavier University, where a class taught by a Jesuit theologian was using my book *Saving Darwin: How to Be a Christian and Believe in Evolution*, a deeply personal account of my own—and America's—struggle to understand Darwin's controversial theory of our origins.

My visit to the Creation Museum was bittersweet and ironic: bittersweet because the beautiful story of creation told in the museum's lovingly constructed dioramas had once been at the heart of my religious beliefs, growing up in a Baptist parsonage among the potato fields of New Brunswick, Canada. As a youth, uncharacteristically obsessed with theology and biblical studies, I had dreamed of one day working with organizations like Answers in Genesis that had built the Creation Museum.

My goal when I enrolled at an evangelical liberal arts college in 1975 was to train in science and join the creationist cause, an ambition soon derailed when I discovered that creationism was scientifically indefensible. But now, as I explored the museum's deeply biblical displays of Adam and Eve, their temptation and sin, and their expulsion from Eden, I felt sadness. I wondered about my younger self, the debater forever defending creationism, convinced that the only origins story that mattered was the one in Genesis, that Adam and Eve were as historical as Abraham Lincoln and Winston

Churchill, that modern scientific theories of origins were without foundation and inspired by Satan to lead people away from God's truth. That younger man now seemed like someone else, a stranger I once knew.

I wondered about the families exploring the museum—wholesome, loving, Christian families like mine had been. Eager mothers lifted their children so they could see better, explaining to them that God had to expel Adam and Eve from Eden because they had sinned. Middle schoolers listened attentively as their guides explained the displays. Would these young people have faith crises in college, as I did? I knew they would, because I had been teaching them for a quarter century, spending countless hours in patient conversation with younger versions of myself, trying to dismantle years of antiscience indoctrination.

My visit to the Creation Museum was also ironic. I had been invited to Xavier University to *critique* the ideas on display in the museum, to argue that the earth is not ten thousand years old, that dinosaurs were not contemporary with humans—and that Adam and Eve were not real historical characters.

These beliefs, once at the heart of my worldview, remain central to evangelical Christians' understanding of their faith, their world, and themselves. "The denial of an historical Adam and Eve as the first parents of all humanity and the solitary first human pair," warns leading Southern Baptist theologian Al Mohler, "severs the link between Adam and Christ which is so crucial to the Gospel."[1] Most evangelicals agree with Mohler. And even those persuaded by science that the earth is billions of years old and that life evolved—propositions Mohler rejects because they disagree with his literal interpretation of the Bible—agree with him that Adam and Eve must be preserved at all costs. If science drives the celebrated first couple of Genesis to extinction, a replacement couple must be created to take their place to account for the effects of their sin.

Mohler's concern makes sense to me, although I know he is wrong. He is, after all, protecting the story with which I grew up—a story most Christians have believed ever since there were Christians, and a story that I might still believe if my college experiences had been different, although I doubt it. It's a straightforward, logical explanation for how things got the way they are: God created a perfect world. Adam and Eve disobeyed, destroying paradise, bringing death and suffering upon everyone. Jesus—who the apostle Paul calls a second Adam—redeems humanity from Adam's sin. And God brings it all to a glorious close at the apocalypse when Jesus returns, restoring the lost paradise of our first parents.

Like most visitors, I paid a twenty-five-dollar fee to visit the 30 million dollar Creation Museum, entering the facility under the watchful eyes of massive dinosaurs. It was a journey into the past on several levels: the story told in the museum is presented as the straightforward, uncontroversial history of our origins, from the creation of the universe through the emergence of Christianity and even to the future apocalypse; the story is part of the cultural heritage of the West, and Christianity in general; and the story is one that was mine a few decades ago.

The museum is well done, free of the tackiness often found in evangelical projects, like the dreadful movies based on the dreadful Left Behind novels. Professional dioramas guide visitors through the six-thousand-year history of the world, as understood by Answers in Genesis, the organization that runs the museum. The grounds outside are magnificent.

Visitors are invited to "Prepare to Believe," but I am sure that most of them already do. The museum promises to "[bring] the pages of the Bible to life, casting its characters and animals in dynamic form and placing them in familiar settings. Adam and Eve live in the Garden of Eden. Children play and dinosaurs roam near Eden's Rivers. The serpent coils cunningly in the Tree of the Knowledge of Good and Evil. Majestic murals brimming with pulsating colors and details provide a backdrop for many of the settings."[2]

I stood for some time at the Adam and Eve displays. The innocent couple stands naked in the Garden of Eden, enjoying the paradise that God made for them, tactfully covered. They know nothing of sickness, disease, or mortality. They live happily with peaceful herbivores who live happily with each other. God walks and talks with Adam and Eve like a loving parent. Friendly dinosaurs look over their shoulders, no more threatening than household pets. I so wished that this story could still be true for me.

An Edenic paradise redolent with beauty and purpose seems the only world that God would create. I could not imagine the creator saying, "Let zebras gallop across the grasslands, pursued by lions who will kill them in the most horrible way imaginable. Let humans live for a few short decades in the dark shadow of their own mortality and witness the deaths of those they love. Let the earth orbit a star for billions of years while countless species evolve, struggle, suffer, and go extinct millions of years before humans appear. And let that star grow until it incinerates all of its varied forms of life that have managed to survive."

And yet, we don't live in that paradise God should have created for us. We travel a vale of tears, surrounded by death, resigned one day to die ourselves, perhaps in great pain or humiliating dysfunction. But Christians have never believed that God created that world. That nightmare was summoned from hell by human sin, unanticipated by the first humans, unintended by the creator, destined for replacement by a new paradise where all that is good will be gathered for eternity. It's a message of hope for Christians, perhaps for everyone. It is a flickering message of hope for me, holding out the possibility that I may once again see my mother, who remains daily in my thoughts despite having passed away years ago.

I stood in front of the display where Eve, eyes cast down and looking guilty, held out a handful of fruit—red berries of some sort—inviting Adam to indulge, although God had told them to avoid those berries. Adam obliges the woman God made for him from his side. This is the point in history—a few thousand years ago and probably somewhere in what is now Iraq—when sin enters the creation. The results, powerfully displayed, are sobering: the first couple clothe themselves, ashamed of their nakedness; God expels them from paradise into a hostile world; their son Cain kills his brother Abel; animals are ritually sacrificed to atone for sin. This disaster—the worst thing that ever happened—would one day be labeled, simply and poetically, *the Fall*.

The Fall lies near the heart of Christianity, which teaches that we have inherited sinful natures from Adam, our first parent. Most Christians are taught, as I was before I could read, that our tendencies to go astray and do wrong—to sin—came from our fallen natures. We were born with original sin. Babies, I was taught, need no instruction in crying to get their own selfish way—they are born sinful and advance their own agendas before they even know what those agendas are. Toddlers are mysteriously born knowing how to lie. My adolescent temptations arose from my original sin. My inability to choose the right path throughout my life comes from my sinful nature. But hope is found in the salvation offered by Jesus—the second Adam—who empowers us to overcome sin and choose righteousness.

Christianity's central truth is salvation through Jesus—a salvation made essential by the devastation of the Fall. But what would Christianity look like if there were no Fall? What if our bad behavior is just the way we are? Or maybe we just evolved into sin, under evolution's relentless promotion of self-interest?

The Creation Museum is evangelistic. I passed carefully sequenced displays highlighting the important events in history, cleverly labeled the "Seven Cs": Creation, Corruption, Catastrophe, Confusion, Christ, Cross, Consummation. The apostle Paul, who first connected Christ to Adam, is pictured writing his famous letters that eventually became part of the New Testament. After Paul, we see Martin Luther, calling the church back to the absolute authority of the Bible, launching the *sola scriptura* Protestant tradition that would eventually spin-off the biblically literalist branch of Protestant thought that inspired this museum. The giants of Christianity prior to Protestantism—Augustine, Thomas Aquinas, Francis of Assisi—are nowhere to be seen, for they were Catholic and, at best, wayward, misguided Christians.

The tour ends at the Last Adam Theater where a museum volunteer invites visitors to commit their lives to Christ. Converting sinners, in fact, is the "ultimate motivation for the Creation Museum" according to Ken Ham, the entrepreneurial Australian who leads Answers in Genesis.[3] I passed by on the other side, wondering why this felt so strange.

The displays project scientific credibility in ways I would once have appreciated. No fairies or leprechauns peek out from behind the boulders. No cupids hover over scenes picturing Adam and Eve in love. The naked Eve is modestly presented as a normal woman, not a sexualized Barbie doll. The happy couple's ambiguous complexion seems appropriate for the parents of all human races. The display of Noah's flood explains how the animals would fit in the ark and where the floodwaters originated. Displays resembling—but not containing—actual science appear with regularity.

Viewers unfamiliar with modern science can only be impressed. Some of the museum staff have PhDs, a fact emphasized in the many publications of Answers in Genesis. One of them, Georgia Purdom, taught biology for years at Mount Vernon Nazarene University, a sister institution of the one where I taught for twenty-seven years. Purdom and the other PhDs on the staff lend authenticity to a message rejected long ago by the scientific community.

Most visitors to the museum are sympathetic to its message but aware that its claims are controversial. As compelling as the story of Adam and Eve may be to those who embrace it, explanation is needed for why so many scientists do not. The answer presented throughout the museum is "starting assumptions." Visitors are told that the conclusions people draw about Adam and Eve and other contentious issues derive from different *starting points*, rather than *evidence*. If you start by rejecting God's infallible wisdom in the Bible and instead put your faith in fallible human reason, you end up with evolution, the big bang, despair, moral relativism, and eternity in hell. And, of course, it makes no sense to reject the explanations God provided in the Bible. God created everything a few thousand years ago and told us about it in the Bible so we would not have to make irresponsible guesses about our origins.

The oft-repeated claim about starting assumptions is both wrong and offensive. It's a cheap debating trick. Like most Christians who no longer believe in Adam and Eve, I did not come to that belief by rejecting the Bible and then forcing whatever changes followed from that as though being anti-Bible was a reliable way to generate falsehoods. I came to it by trying to reconcile science with that Bible.

Saving the Original Sinner is about *Christians* wrestling with questions of Adam and Eve. Most people in this conversation—like me—have explored creative modifications to the story of Adam and Eve, prior to abandoning it. We will meet some novel conceptions of the first man in the chapters that follow. Adam fades reluctantly from the canvas of one's theology despite one's efforts to keep him there, not because of it.

ADAM AND ORIGINAL SIN

Adam's role in Christianity is so important that many Christians—and almost all of America's one hundred million evangelicals—believe their faith collapses like a teetering Jenga tower if Adam is removed from the foundation. Christian scholars noting the implausibility of the human race appearing suddenly ten thousand years ago are not greeted with cheers. They are more often met with inquisitions and in too many instances they lose their jobs.

I have friends who now are unemployed after decades of service at evangelical colleges. Slowly and steadily they were pushed to the margins of their academic communities until they were coerced or "persuaded" to leave. I was unemployed during much of the writing of this book after twenty-seven years of steadily growing discomfort at Eastern Nazarene College. The stories are eerily similar: A young professor gets an appointment at an evangelical college. Popular with students, effective as a scholar, his profile grows as he writes articles and books, emerging from the insular world of his college to join larger cultural conversations. These larger conversations provoke responses from people we call gatekeepers—self-appointed watchdogs, often poorly educated, often waving checkbooks—who demand that "their" institutions censure the scholar. I spent many unpleasant hours crafting responses to gatekeepers, at the request of my employer, explaining that evolution is not anti-Christian. I was scolded by my provost because Ken Ham, on his blog, was warning Christian parents not to send their children to a school where they might come "under the teaching of ardent evolutionist Karl Giberson."[4] One group of gatekeepers—the Reformed Nazarenes—rejoiced at my departure from "their" school, writing publically to me on their blog, "I pray that you never teach in another Christian school again, spreading the kind of Bible doubting evolutionary faith that you call Christian faith. However, I will continue to pray for you and that you will come to truly trust all of God's word."[5]

My story has a happy ending, as I now teach at Stonehill College, a Catholic school in the Holy Cross tradition that welcomes critical examination of its own traditions.

Many of the stories, however, do not have happy endings. My friend Howard Van Till was pushed out of his institution after thirty-one years for writing a book about the big bang theory. My friend Richard Colling was terminated in his midfifties after almost thirty years of service at his alma mater for writing a book suggesting that God could have created through the process of evolution. My friend Peter Enns was terminated for his book arguing that evangelicals cannot keep reading the Old Testament literally. Bruce Waltke, one of America's leading Hebrew scholars, was terminated for an offhand—and incredibly benign—comment in an interview: "If the data is overwhelmingly in favor of evolution, to deny that reality will make us a cult, . . . some odd group that is not really interacting with the world."[6] Such casualties illustrate a sobering reality: contemporary evangelical Christianity is so threatened by the onward march of scholarship that critical voices are discouraged, censured, silenced, and expelled. Nowhere is this more clearly illustrated than in the case of John Schneider, a theologian who lost his job at Calvin College after writing a paper arguing that the Genesis creation story could be read in a way that did not require a literal Adam and Eve.

Schneider's career as a tenured full professor was derailed by a paper titled "Recent Genetic Science and Christian Theology on Human Origins."[7] The paper asks, "What sort of genuinely Protestant theology could be compatible with the narrative of human evolution?" Schneider suggested that there were authentically Christian readings of the creation story, faithful to the Bible, that interpreted Adam and Eve as *literary* rather than *historical* figures. He noted, in particular, that his own tradition had been too heavily influenced by Augustine, who promoted an excessively literal approach to the Eden story in Genesis.

Schneider's approach was motivated by science. He was aware that advances in genetics had established that the human race could not be

descended from two people who lived a few thousand years ago. This unwelcome revelation has been a bombshell for evangelicals, and most simply
reject it out of hand. But Schneider could see, as he told me, that "genom-
ics will be a game-changer," and he wanted to help evangelicals—starting
with his own community—get started on a long and difficult conversation.[8]
Noting that evidence pointed to the nonhistoricity of the Genesis story, he
sought to motivate reconsideration of the theological and biblical issues.
His paper offered a helpful perspective to the evangelical struggle to make
peace with evolution—a struggle in which his institution, Calvin College,
had long been a leader. He argued—as I have—that Adam and Eve are not
theologically *necessary*, noting that some leading Christian thinkers centuries ago held this view, even before science made it expedient to do so.[9]

The response to Schneider could not have been more hostile than if he
had showed up on *Fox & Friends* waving bones he claimed were those of
Jesus. The problem for the branch of Protestantism that supports Calvin
College comes from its founding—and defining—creeds and confessions.
Protestantism's many divisions under the leadership of its many Reformers
forced each faction to define itself over against other, often similar, traditions. These definitions were often articulated in creeds, catechisms, and
confessions with little flexibility.

Such faith statements keep traditions on theological leashes, preventing
dramatic changes or steady slippage. The theological leash at Calvin was
contractually enforced by specifying that faculty members were "required
to subscribe to three historic Reformed forms of unity—The Belgic Confession, The Heidelberg Catechism, and the Canons of Dort—and pledge
to teach, speak, and write in harmony with the confessions."[10]

Gatekeepers call for the heads of those—like Schneider—who pull too
hard on their theological leashes. The Reformed journal *Christian Renewal*
warned that tolerance of Schneider's ideas would put Calvin on a "tragic tra-
jectory" that would ultimately secularize the college. Those who campaigned
to "save Christianity by liberalizing it," said the journal, "only helped to establish an atmosphere congenial to secularism and relativism." History, they
argued, showed that "acceptance of evolution inevitably led to a decline in
the belief that the Bible was divinely inspired." The article concluded with
the concern that Christians were "to let the Bible speak for itself and to let its
teachings set the bounds for our science—rather than vice versa."[11]

Schneider's dismissal made national news. Secular academics scolded
Calvin, wondering what "academic freedom" meant there, but many evangelicals were strongly supportive.[12] Al Mohler, the leading Southern Bap-

tist theologian and fundamentalism's most enthusiastic gatekeeper—he had fired several "liberal" faculty while he was president of Southern Seminary—called on *all* Christians to reject *any* science that threatened the story of Adam and Eve. "The denial of an historical Adam and Eve as the first parents of all humanity and the solitary first human pair," he wrote on his blog, "severs the link between Adam and Christ which is so crucial to the Gospel."[13] Mohler's concern is the primary reason for the controversy that swirls about the first man.

A pastor cautioned, in language all too familiar to me, "If you have children studying at Calvin College, be aware that their young minds will be molded by some professors who are themselves unbelievers masquerading as Reformed Christians."[14] Calling Schneider an "unbeliever" because he doesn't think Adam and Eve were real is, of course, uncharitable nonsense of the sort that used to be leveled at heretics whose lives were also threatened.

The controversy made the June 2011 cover of *Christianity Today*, the flagship publication of evangelicalism and a bit more moderate than the bombastic Mohler. Titled "The Search for the Historical Adam," the story ranged over the controversy, noting with an arched eyebrow that some leading evangelical scholars had apparently abandoned the idea of a first man without abandoning evangelicalism. But an accompanying editorial, titled "No Adam, No Eve, No Gospel," made it clear that Christians could hold only one position on Adam. The response is worth quoting at length:

> Christians have already drawn the line: there must be an original pair of humans endowed with souls . . .
>
> What is at stake?
>
> First, the entire story of what is wrong with the world hinges on the disobedient exercise of the will by the first humans. . . .
>
> Second, the entire story of salvation hinges on the obedience of the Second Adam. The apostle Paul, the earliest Christian writer to interpret Jesus' work, called Adam "a type of the one who was to come" (Rom. 5:14, ESV), and wrote that "just as we have borne the image of the man of dust [Adam], we shall also bear the image of the man of heaven [Jesus]" (1 Cor. 15:49, ESV).[15]

The *Christianity Today* story was picked up by *Inside Higher Ed*, the *Chronicle of Higher Education*, and even National Public Radio, whose audience is typically oblivious to in-house evangelical squabbles: "Is this another Galileo moment for the Church?" an NPR reporter asked me, recalling the confrontation between the Catholic church and Europe's most famous scientist.[16] Would scientific discoveries force the church to abandon Adam, just as they had once forced the church to abandon a stationary earth at the center of the universe?

How this "Galileo moment" will play out is far from clear. Most expressions of Christianity, from Augustine to Al Mohler, have never been without a historical Adam and Eve, despite more liberal Protestant traditions moving in that direction as early as the nineteenth century. And even as evolution was tentatively embraced by sophisticated evangelicals over the course of the twentieth century, Adam and Eve were inserted somewhere. And then, as mounting evidence made that insertion ever more implausible, theological pressures were brought to bear. Wheaton College in Illinois—the preeminent and highly selective evangelical institution—drew a line in this particular sand in the 1990s, insisting in a faith statement that faculty must sign, that "God directly created Adam and Eve, the historical parents of the entire human race . . . in His own image, distinct from all other living creatures, and in a state of original righteousness."[17] The statement dealt a significant blow to evangelical acceptance of evolutionary science. Wheaton biology faculty, with PhDs from institutions like the State University of New York, Vanderbilt, the University of California, and Purdue, must agree—or at least sign a document claiming they agree—that humans did not originate through the process of evolution. (The president who produced the document bristled when I suggested to him—as is widely believed—that Wheaton faculty were signing that document with their fingers crossed.)

Christianity Today, Wheaton College, and Calvin College are not academic backwaters populated by ignoramuses who blindly reject established science. They are staffed by intellectual elites educated at top universities. Many of their scholars have great respect for scholarship. Some have reputations that reach into the larger academic community. They are reluctant to reject scientific evidence. But they are also, for the most part, specialists, like their counterparts in the larger academic world. My former evangelical colleagues in theology and biblical studies, to take one example, can't quite imagine that geneticists have actually *proven* that the human race could never have numbered just two. Many academics from outside science think "science is always changing" so that one can simply wait for unwelcome scientific ideas to be replaced by congenial ones. Al Mohler assures his readers that the threatening science of today will turn into something friendlier tomorrow. My colleagues in chemistry and physics, on the other hand, don't see why Adam and Eve can't be fictional characters in a story about why we are sinful. They have limited interest in "systems" built to make sense of the disparate claims in the Bible. The result is a muddled conversation about the first man, the first sin, and the importance of both.

The controversy over Adam draws strength from main street America's rejection of evolution. A 2014 poll revealed that 42 percent of Americans reject the claim that "humans evolved," with or without God guiding the process, believing instead that "God created human beings pretty much in their present form at one time within the last 10,000 years or so."[18] Only Turkey ranks lower than the United States among developed nations in the acceptance of evolution.[19] The grassroots energy of this antievolutionism—close to universal in the evangelical world—empowers gatekeepers who tend to be populists with no familiarity with science. The battle to uproot Adam from history is certainly being fought uphill.

ADAM AND THE SOCIAL ORDER

Another reason why Adam maintains a hold on so many Christians, beyond his role as the source of sin, death, and evil, is his role in maintaining the social order. We see this most clearly in discussions of gay marriage where many Christians—and most conservative politicians running for office—invoke "God's plan for marriage" by pointing to the story of Adam and Eve, where we read that "For this reason a man shall leave his father and mother and be joined to his wife, and the two shall become one flesh."[20] This viewpoint is often summarized with a smirk as "God made Adam and *Eve*—not Adam and *Steve*." The story has been and is similarly invoked to assign a subordinate role for women and blacks, to authorize exploitation of nature, to condemn nudity, to maintain a holy Sabbath, and other social agendas. Notice how much of our modern Western culture is explained by this list.

The notion that God provided rules and social structures for the first humans to pass on is deeply appealing. Ken Ham calls his organization Answers in Genesis to emphasize that God created humans *and* their rules, and that this is laid out for all time in the Book of Beginnings. "We must start with Genesis," Ham says, "if we are going to teach God's people how to defend the faith in this age of unbelief and skepticism."[21]

The power of this argument, which plays out quite differently than the theological one about Adam being the source of sin, draws on our tendency to root our values in historical narratives, to understand the present social order in terms of its past. We use formative stories like that of Adam and Eve *mythologically*—although Ham would vigorously object to this characterization—to create and maintain our social order and identity. We are exploring the anthropological blueprints of our tribe.

Few of us revere the past as people in the Middle Ages and the early modern period did. They tended to assume that the more ancient the writings, the more authoritative they were. Ancient Bible stories were especially important, they believed, because God told them to human scribes in an era when the distance between the heavens and the earth was much smaller. These stories illuminate the ways things are supposed to be—insights that guided the Christian West for many centuries.

Looking to our past to understand our present is an instinct we must acknowledge if we want to understand our long conversation about the first man and our reluctance to part with him. We are attracted to our own histories. Steven Spielberg made *Schindler's List* to explore his own Jewish heritage. Brendan Fraser starred in *Dudley Do-Right*, a corny movie about a bumbling Canadian Mountie, because his grandfather had once been a Mountie, although probably not so bumbling. Charles Darwin's great-great-grandson, Randal Keynes, wrote the engaging biography *Darwin, His Daughter, and Human Evolution*.

Familial identities—our tribes—exist at many levels with varying levels of cohesion, all rooted in the past. My extended family was one of several sharing the village of Bath, New Brunswick, population six hundred. Bath was one of five villages in Carleton County, one of fifteen counties in the province of New Brunswick. Our province—with Nova Scotia and Prince Edward Island—made up Canada's Maritimes. We grew up proud to be Maritimers—a hearty tribe shaped by long, hard winters with school cancellations and electrical outages, well-defined seasons, and the changing personality of the Atlantic Ocean.

My American friends speak in reverential tones about their founding fathers, as if they are descended from them. Politicians invoke, embellish, and fabricate the ancestral wisdom of the founding fathers to undermine their opposition.[22] Children grow up with stories of George Washington confessing to cutting down his father's cherry tree; of Abraham Lincoln's birth in a humble log cabin; of Ben Franklin's courageous exploration of electricity; and Paul Revere's midnight ride—all parts of a past that tells us about the present.

Singular individuals—Washington, Mohammed, Christ—play central roles in creating tribal identities. Some cultures worship their ancestors. And Adam, embraced by Abrahamic faiths as the ancestor of the *entire* human tribe, has long played a central role in creating identity in those traditions. We should not be surprised that tribes that ground their identity in Adam and believe that God set up the social order around him defend his historicity with vigor. The story of Adam speaks directly to their contemporary concerns: marriage, abortion, evolution, the big bang theory, animal rights, and more.

Despite Adam's sometimes cosmic role, his story begins as a sort of parochial constitution for the ancient tribe of Israel rather than a blueprint for all humanity. The Hebrew version of the story—and there are others in adjacent cultures, as we will see—emerges around the time the Jews were regrouping after a long exile in Babylon and were looking to define themselves after this demoralizing disruption of their history. The account of Adam and Eve getting expelled from Eden was *their* story of losing their home—their paradise—because they had not followed God's laws. The week with its day of rest was *their* religious calendar, long practiced but now being woven into the fabric of the universe as the way the world is, because that is how God decreed it. Much of the creation story—actually, there are two stories—was shared by neighboring tribes, but these first Jews converted local stories into their own, expelling the anthropomorphic deities and local concerns of their neighbors in favor of a single creator. Monotheism—perhaps the most enduring and powerful idea in any religion—appears, fitfully and ambiguously, for the first time in these stories.

The story of the first man—destined to be revered by billions of Christians as the patriarch of *all* human tribes—thus began as a tale undergirding the identity of one small tribe of wandering nomads in the Middle East a few thousand years ago. And Adam would have remained a bit player had Paul not created a theological model making Christ a second Adam, offered by God to undo the sinful damage of the first Adam.

Two millennia of reflection on the first man has shaped our ideas about marriage, free will, the exploitation of nature, the value of farming, the place of women in society, the nature of temptation, and the place of the black race in the world. Historian Elaine Pagels argues in *Adam, Eve, and the Serpent* that the interpretations of the creation story developed in the early centuries after Christ "have continued to affect our culture and everyone in it, *Christian or not*, ever since."[23] Classics scholar Sarah Ruden argues that Paul, as he worked out his theology of Adam and Christ, Jews and Gentiles, males and females, sin and redemption, "created the Western individual human being, unconditionally precious to God and therefore entitled to the consideration of other human beings."[24] Social theorist Glenn Tinder refers to Paul's insight about the importance of every person as "the central moral intuition of the West," and argues that much of the social progress in the West has been motivated by that intuition, albeit often buried under less noble agendas.[25]

Augustine, the most influential writer of the first millennium after Paul, looked to Adam to explain the overwhelming sexual temptations that plague humans; the greatest medieval thinker, Thomas Aquinas, defended human reason by saying it was not ruined in the Fall, and in so doing he unleashed an explosion of intellectual activity that led to science; the celebrated Italian poet Dante Alighieri explored the question of the first language by asking what was spoken in Eden; Francis Bacon promoted science in the seventeenth century as a way to recover Adam's ancient knowledge, and thus partially restore the lost paradise. Early explorers debated the humanity of the Native Americans by asking if they were descended from Adam. Columbus wrote home from the Americas claiming to have discovered the Garden of Eden. Apologists for slavery argued that "the Negro" was not descended from Adam and thus could be owned like a horse or cow. Twentieth-century creationists argued that Adam's sin was the origin of the second law of thermodynamics, which says that everything tends toward decay. Subordination of women has forever been justified by the curse God placed on Eve. Gay marriage is condemned as non-Edenic.

Christians since Paul have created their own new incarnations of the first man and his world, summoned to address new questions, pressed into the service of new agendas, reconfigured to match new understandings of history. When science, global exploration, or geological history raised questions about the prevailing concept of the first man, a new one was created, one who better fit the times, like a species evolving in response to an environmental challenge. British biochemist Denis Alexander, who embraces evolution as God's method of creation, rescues Adam and Eve from a science that would destroy them by turning them into Neolithic farmers.[26] Christian apologist Hugh Ross moves the Garden of Eden into Africa, where the human race was discovered to have originated, and pushed the time frame back to one that accords with science.[27] Ken Ham insists that Adam and Eve had perfect genomes to explain their longevity. A different Adam is far better than no Adam at all.

These stories come to life in the pages that follow—how Adam went from the patriarch of a small tribe in the Middle East to one of the defining stories of the Western intellectual tradition—and is now at the center of a religious firestorm as millions of Christians contemplate the sober truth that he never existed.

FIRST MAN OR FIRST JEW? THE MYSTERIOUS PATRIARCH OF THE TRIBE OF ISRAEL

An Aristotle was but the rubbish of an Adam,
and Athens but the rudiments of Paradise.

—ROBERT SOUTH[1]

"The first man," wrote the Jewish philosopher Philo (ca. 20 BCE–ca. 50 CE), "appears to me to have been such both in his body and in his soul, being very far superior to all those who live in the present day, and to all those who have gone before us."[2] A 1663 French Academy paper specified this superiority with claims that Adam was 140 feet tall. Contemporary creationists have assigned Adam heights of 12 to 16 feet,[3] superintelligence, a perfect genome, and even supernatural powers.[4] What are we to make of such claims?

After Jesus, Adam and Eve are the most fascinating, controversial, and provocative characters in the Western tradition, producing museums full of images and libraries full of discussions. But Adam and Eve are also largely unknown. The piecemeal stories of their origins—the Hebrew Bible has two different, frustratingly brief stories—were shared by neighboring tribes in the ancient Near East. The Hebrew versions—in what Christians call the Old Testament—were adopted and modified by the emerging nation of Israel, evolving as oral traditions until writing was invented, and then taking a final form, with further changes strictly prohibited.

Adam's tale begins on the first page of Genesis, part of the story of how everything—or almost everything—originated. The familiar text greets the reader, not with the philosopher's *nothing*, but with pitch-black darkness and a churning ocean. No dry land below or sky above punctuates this darkness. No primitive human—or bird or fish or life of any sort—looks on. What exists is a deep, dark, ominous, untamed, watery mystery. The ancients called this *chaos*, the primordial enemy of life. The world, says the creation story that opens the Bible, was not created out of nothingness—that notion was millennia in the future. It emerged when the creator pushed back, but did not destroy, this chaos and imposed order on disorder.

In the span of six short days, Elohim—"God," in English, although the term can be plural—transforms this terrifying wasteland into a delightful habitat. "Let there be light," he says on Day One, sundering the darkness and turning half of it into light. On Day Two he tames the watery abyss and puts half of it behind a protective overhead dome with windows through which rain can be regulated. Sky appears for the first time. On Day Three he divides the waters below; submerged lands burst through the surface of the deep. Earth and sea share the space below the sky. A habitable world has been formed—light, sky, earth, and seas. Chaos has been pushed back—but not eliminated. Life is next.

Elohim fills the newly ordered creation with life. On the fourth day, grasses, flowers, and groves of fruit trees appear, and reach toward the new sky. On Day Five Elohim populates the once hostile waters with sea creatures. Birds fill the sky, swooping, singing, celebrating. The earth now awaits the final act.

On Day Six, Elohim makes man, and speaks to him—and his mate—directly, addressing his creation for the first time: "Multiply and fill the earth." Elohim reaches out to the newly created couple and invites them to come alongside and help rule this bountiful new creation. On the seventh and final day, Elohim rests from a job that he pronounces, in a curious act of self-congratulation, "well done." This day of rest would be a perpetual reminder for humans to set aside one day a week, to keep holy and protected from the stress and distraction of work. Elohim had ordained the *work week*, a first step in laying the foundations of an orderly society.

The creation story seems to end here. But it goes on.

The next scene is puzzling and strangely discontinuous. It opens with God—now named Yahweh Elohim, or the "Lord God"—searching for someone to till the ground, as if he forgot that he had just made a gardener and commanded him to fill the earth. Finding no one to do the work, Yahweh takes a lump of clay and shapes it into the first man. The confident "Let there be" creative power of the earlier story has been replaced with anthropomorphic crafting. Yahweh animates this lump of clay by breathing into its nostrils the "breath of life." And, finally, he names it man.

The story is written in ancient Hebrew, in which the word for man is *adam*. This eventually became a popular English name, hiding its origins in the ancient world. Yahweh puts the newly created "man"—Adam—to work tending a plot of land called the Garden of Eden. The garden teems with beautiful fruit trees he is welcome to enjoy. The lone human resident of Eden—the only man in the entire creation—has just one rule: he is not to eat any fruit from one particular tree, mysteriously called the tree of the knowledge of good and evil. Yahweh offers no explanation why this seemingly arbitrary command is so important. All Adam is told is that if he eats fruit from that tree, he will immediately die.

Along with farming, Adam is tasked with looking after the animals, all of which are vegetarian and getting along with each other. But they have no names—an indicator of confusion in this ancient world. The chaotic animal kingdom—like the watery chaos a few days ago—thus awaits the imposition of structure. So Adam, in a ritual that would come to symbolize human mastery of the animals, begins the long process of naming them. Hanging out with the newly named animals, all of which had mates, provided company for Adam but he needed a mate of his own.

Yahweh appears to agree that he overlooked the fact that every creature had a mate except Adam. So he puts Adam into a deep sleep, extracts from his side a mass of flesh and bone—a rib many would eventually call it—and makes woman. Adam—still in the naming business—describes his new partner with Hebrew wordplay, calling her *isha*, from *ish*. (*Isha* is "woman" in Hebrew and *ish* is "man." The usage suggests that they complete each other.) Isha will become known as Eve, the Hebrew term for "living."

The first man and his new mate reside happily in a paradise called Eden, located in the fertile crescent of the Tigris and Euphrates Rivers, as well as two other rivers of which we know nothing, somewhere in what is now Iraq.

THE BEGINNING OF THE END

Trouble soon finds its way to paradise. That mysterious tree of the knowledge of good and evil with its forbidden fruit stood invitingly in the midst of Eden. And a mysterious talking serpent made sure Eve had a chance to think about the odd prohibition.

We don't know why God created the serpent, or how a creation with such a creature could have been pronounced "good" by God. We are told simply that the serpent was more "crafty than any other wild animal." The serpent approaches Eve, in a scene that artists would later render with great creativity, and asks if God *really* told her, "You shall not eat from any tree in the garden." Eve explains the rule: "You shall not eat of the fruit of the tree that is in the middle of the garden, nor shall you touch it, or you shall die." The serpent objects: "You will not die," he says, suggesting that God was hiding something, "for God knows that when you eat of it your eyes will be opened, and you will be like God, knowing good and evil."

This provocative scene invites speculation about what was really going on. The common interpretation would be that Eve gave in to temptation by taking a bite from an apple, and to this day, an apple with a bite out of it connotes temptation, lust, and the lure of the forbidden. But other interpretations suggest more dramatic actions, including sexual intercourse between Eve and the serpent.[5] Whatever happened, the serpent put a different spin on the rule about the forbidden tree. Eve is intrigued. Is it possible that God made this rule out of self-interest, to avoid sharing divinity with his new creatures? Eve likes the idea of being "like God" and so she "took of its fruit and ate," wondering what glorious transformation awaits. And, being the loyal mate that she was—or perhaps seeking a partner in crime—she shares the fruit with Adam.

And so the first sin was committed in an otherwise perfect creation. Like a tiny crack in a magnificent window, this was the beginning of the end of something wonderful. Centuries later Christians would refer to this event as the Fall—a singular cosmic moment when God and humans parted ways. Yahweh is enraged at the disobedient couple. Adam and Eve had a perfect situation with just one trivial rule. They could eat the fruit of countless beautiful trees except one. And they couldn't restrain themselves.

Angered by the betrayal, God punishes the residents of Eden. He also punishes the serpent for his role in the greatest disaster of all time. Eve and her female progeny will now bear children in great pain. A divinely ordained social order will require them to submit to their husbands. Adam and his male offspring will sweat and struggle for the food they grow, challenged by weeds, thorns, drought, and difficult soil. Serpents will now eat dust and crawl on their bellies.

These are terrible punishments. But God is not done. He evicts Adam and Eve from the garden, banishing them into a hostile world beyond paradise. Curiously, he leaves Eden intact, a decision that will one day motivate intrepid explorers to search for it. He places angels and a flaming sword at the entrance so that nobody can get back in. And, finally, in the greatest outpouring of wrath imaginable, the God that used to walk with his creatures in the cool of the evening now brings death upon all creation. It descends like a dark and foreboding fog, shrouding every living thing, from the tiny hummingbird to the great whale; from the bumblebee to the elephant. From now on it will be the way of every living thing to live amid perpetual violence and eventually to die.

Humans will live under the cloud of their own mortality, a depressing reality that will shape their lives and the cultures they create. They will watch their parents and other loved ones die, often wracked with pain. Their children will frequently die in childbirth or of childhood illnesses; innumerable tiny gravestones will come to dot the weed-infested lands where humans live out their difficult lives.

God grants no immortality option to the first humans. No mention is made of a blissful afterlife to mitigate the sorrows of this one; no license is provided to imagine weed-free meadows bordered by bubbling streams and filled with songbirds, fruit trees, laughter, and eternal youth. Children become the only hope that one will not have lived in vain and perished without consequence. "Behold, sons are indeed a heritage from the Lord," wrote the psalmist, "the fruit of the womb a reward. Like arrows in the hand of a warrior are the sons of one's youth."[6] Large numbers of children would symbolize one's enduring importance, and God's favor was often bestowed in the form of large families.

The first couple's life outside Eden was filled with misery they could never have imagined. Their first child, Cain, becomes a dangerous and vengeful adult, and kills his younger brother Abel in a jealous rage. God, still intimately involved in the affairs of the troubled first family, expels Cain from his homeland to wander an unfamiliar earth. Cain, the planet's first child and first criminal, objects that people will track him down and kill him, meting out frontier justice for the murder of Abel. So God, inexplicably concerned for the cursed Cain's life, puts a mysterious protective mark of some sort on him.

The marked man settles "east of Eden" in the land of Nod (which means "wandering" in the original Hebrew). There Cain finds a wife whose origins will forever puzzle readers. He raises a family, tilling cursed soil and fighting weeds and thorns. His wife bears him children in great pain. He builds a city that houses a population that appears from nowhere.

Cain's troubled family creates civilization. Within a few generations, his great, great, great, great, great-grandson Jabal—born while Cain is still alive—becomes the "ancestor of those who live in tents and have livestock."[7]

Jabal's brother Jubal lays the foundations of music; another brother makes tools from bronze and iron. The boys' father Lamech becomes a murderer and brutal polygamist.

Adam makes his final appearance in the midst of the story of Cain's establishment of culture. At age 130, he and Eve have a third child, Seth. The grieving Eve views Seth as a replacement for the slain Abel, provided by a God who still cares. Seth's lineage—at least some of it—remains faithful to God, eventually leading to Noah. Adam dies at the age of 930 and reappears only in genealogical tables as the father of Seth and the grandfather of Enosh.

THE WAGES OF SIN

Cain's community started off poorly and never recovered; his lineage grew ever more wicked, until God became disturbed that "the wickedness of humankind was great in the earth." His once innocent creatures had fallen so far that now "every inclination of the thoughts of their hearts was only evil continually."[8]

The confident Elohim that had spoken the world into existence and pronounced it good now appears chastened and remorseful, "sorry that he had made humankind on the earth."[9] In all the earth, only Noah, the first man to be born after the death of Adam, remained righteous. And so, in a puzzling display of favoritism, God decides that all living creatures on the planet should be drowned in a great flood, save for Noah's family and a small contingent of animals to prevent mass extinction.

God commands Noah to build a great ark to protect two of every species—a male and a female to carry on the lineage—and the members of his family, to replenish the destroyed human population. Noah, now almost six hundred years old, builds the ark according to God's specifications. At no point does he raise questions about the impending destruction. Apparently satisfied that he and his family will survive, he makes no effort to mitigate God's wrath, secure his relatives, or sneak any of his friends and neighbors aboard the ark.

The flood is terrifying in its universal carnage. "Everything on dry land in whose nostrils was the breath of life died. [God] blotted out every living thing that was on the face of the ground, human beings and animals and creeping things and birds of the air; they were blotted out from the earth. Only Noah was left, and those that were with him in the ark."[10]

The flood recedes. The ark comes to rest in the mountains of Ararat, where hopeful explorers search for it to this day. Noah and his family disembark, followed by the animals. Noah is clearly in the role of another Adam, although the carnage and destruction he encountered after the flood were a long way from Eden. God reminds Noah of his exalted place in the grand scheme by giving him the same commandment he had given Adam two millennia earlier: "Be fruitful and multiply, and fill the earth." God promises Noah that there will never be another flood and seals the promise with a sign:

> This is the sign of the covenant that I make between me and you and every living creature that is with you, for all future generations: I have set my bow in the clouds, and it shall be a sign of the covenant between me and the earth. . . . The waters shall never again become a flood to destroy all flesh.[11]

The descendants of Noah's sons—Ham, Shem, and Japheth—populated the earth, as Adam's children had once done. But humanity's second chance soon goes off the rails. Noah gets drunk and something dreadful happens. The story tells us that Noah was observed inappropriately by Ham, who gets his brothers to sneak in with a cloak to cover their father, who has, by the norms of his culture, humiliated himself by lying naked. Most Hebrew scholars believe this cryptic story euphemistically describes Ham sodomizing his father. An enraged Noah takes out his wrath on poor Ham, cursing him and his descendants and consigning them, the people of Canaan, in chilling language that would roll ominously across the millennia and one day be on the lips of Christian slave owners, to be the "lowest of slaves." And Noah continues, "Blessed by the Lord my God be Shem; and let Canaan be his slave. May God make space for Japheth, and let him live in the tents of Shem; and let Canaan be his slave."[12]

But even this new world order enrages God. This time, once again grasping at divinity, humanity starts building a tower into the heavens, under the leadership of Nimrod, the "mighty hunter before the Lord."[13] To derail the project God introduces multiple languages so the various tribes working on the tower cannot understand each other. And he scatters them abroad "over the face of all the earth" so they can no longer work on their grand tower at Babel that would grant them access to the abode of the gods.

The confusion of languages at Babel is the last time that God interacts directly with humanity all at once. The nation of Israel emerges after this confusion, in the midst of other, often hostile nations surrounding it, and speaking different languages. The term Gentiles describes these other peoples and great energies are expended battling them, enslaving them, being enslaved by them, making peace with them, debating the reality of their gods, figuring out if and how they can become Jewish.

Adam-like figures—Abraham, Moses—continue to emerge throughout the history of the Jewish people, who begin to look for such singular rescuers. More than three hundred references to a coming Messiah appear in the Hebrew scriptures. Moses reports God as saying, "I will raise up for them a prophet like you from among their own people; I will put my words in the mouth of the prophet, who shall speak to them everything that I command."[14]

The original Adam fades from the biblical canvas. No stories report what he did over his long life or how many of his nine-plus centuries were shared with Eve. We don't know how many children he fathered, how much land he acquired, or what legends arose about his youth and his sojourn in the Garden of Eden before it all went so wrong. Whatever disaster was precipitated by his sin is never again invoked in the Hebrew scriptures; it plays little to no role in Judaism's emerging self-understanding, at least as it unfolds within the pages of what we now call the Bible.

THE AMBIGUOUS FIRST MAN

The story in Genesis, from the creation of the world to the origin of languages, eventually became far more than a Jewish story. For billions of believers in the monotheistic traditions, these stories became ultimate explanations. There we find the account of the origin of the universe, the solar system, planet Earth, all life, and humanity in particular. There we find the instructions given by God to Adam—divinely ordained blueprints for society, specifying the definition of marriage, gender relations, and the proper attitude toward nature. There we find the tragic tale of how it all went wrong and the explanation for why humans need salvation.

Wrestling with the text of holy books is complicated. The monotheistic religions have traditionally affirmed that God speaks to his people through their books—the Bible, the Torah, the Koran. But what are we to make of messages that come with claims of divine origin? Religious leaders from Old Testament prophets to twenty-first-century televangelists have embellished their messages by adding, "God said . . ." Christians—the focus of this book—have expended much energy figuring out what role God played in the production of the Bible and what expectations can be brought to the text as a result.

For believers today, God's involvement in the production of the biblical text makes it fundamentally different from other ancient texts like Plato's *Republic*, Homer's *Odyssey*, or Augustine's *Confessions*, for those are purely human documents. Most Christians consider that God, in some sense, is the *coauthor* of the Bible, making the Bible both human and divine, with no obvious way to adjudicate those contrasting sources.[15] In the New Testament Paul claims that "all scripture is inspired by God."[16] Although he was referring only to the Hebrew scriptures—the New Testament did not exist yet—his claim became the basis for the assertion that the entire Bible was divinely inspired. Over the centuries Christian communities often interpreted this to mean that God dictated the scriptures to the various scribes who wrote down the exact words that God wanted. This viewpoint, widely shared throughout the Christian tradition, but especially as championed by Protestant fundamentalists at the beginning of the twentieth century, removes any genuinely human element in the Bible, suggesting that the biblical authors were little more than scribes writing things that they often did not understand. In a later chapter, we will meet Hugh Ross, who claims that the opening verses of the Bible make references to the big bang that could not possibly have been understood by Moses. We will meet Ken Ham, who claims that God was an eyewitness to the creation and told Moses what occurred, in contrast to "secular scientists" who were not there and have to make inferences based on inadequate and uncertain data. Ham encourages young people to ask their high school teachers, "Were you there?" when they speak of events that occurred millions of years ago.

The view that God wrote the Bible transforms those ancient texts, with their different languages, authors, and cultural contexts, into a single book with a single author. This explains why preachers, when quoting the Twenty-third Psalm, will say, "*God says*, he is our shepherd and we will not be in want,"[17] rather than "*David says*, 'The Lord is my shepherd.'"

Christians believe that the Bible stories are there because God wanted them there. Getting the Bible stories right is important; and we must not change those stories, or suppose they contain errors. And certainly we cannot deny them. In the evangelical traditions that dominate American Christianity, children learn Bible stories in Sunday school before they can read. They play with toys based on Noah's ark, read picture books about heroes like Samson or David, watch movies about Moses, and play games measuring biblical literacy. And all based on the belief that God is the author of the Bible.

The belief that God wrote the Bible raises serious questions. Throughout the Hebrew scriptures, for example, God is quoted directly as though he were in the room speaking, as he once was in Eden with Adam and Eve. This rhetorical structure puts great pressure on the reader to comprehend God's message. If God is truly speaking, then of course we want to know what he is saying. But God says some terrible things.

God commands Moses at one point, for example, to "avenge the Israelites on the Midianites."[18] This avenging is a divinely sanctioned genocide with instructions to "kill every male among the little ones, and kill every woman who has known a man by sleeping with him. But all the young girls who have not known a man by sleeping with him, keep alive for yourselves."[19] Such passages—and there are several—have disturbed many readers. In *The God Delusion*, Richard Dawkins invokes such passages to argue, quite plausibly, that the God of the Hebrew Bible is a "vindictive, bloodthirsty ethnic cleanser."[20]

Elsewhere in the Bible, however, in messages that seem more thoughtful, God commands the Jews to care for widows and orphans and the stranger at the gate. Jesus famously instructs his followers to love their enemies. The Bible thus creates moral, as well as literary, scientific, and historical challenges.

HOLY QUESTIONS, UNHOLY ANSWERS

Complex interpretative issues run throughout the Bible but nowhere more prominently than in the creation stories. These accounts, traditionally understood as given to Moses by God, skip over difficulties that must have been apparent to the editors of the original stories. In seeking a resolution that the ancient editors did not provide, we must wonder if we are bringing inappropriate modern questions to an ancient text. Before we leave our discussion of the Genesis account we should hone in on these unanswered questions so that we can appreciate what subsequent interpreters ended up doing with the story of Adam.

First, why God would give Moses two *different* accounts that don't fit together, and with God using different names in the two accounts? Why was Adam—but none of the other creatures—made of *dust?* Is dust significant in ways that water or wood are not? What does it mean for God to breathe life into Adam's nostrils? Is this the transition to life or a divine spark passing from God to humans?

Was Adam a godlike superman or simply the first flawed human? Or was he like an innocent child, coming of age physically, morally, and sexually with Eve? Why was Adam sequestered in a garden? What was outside the garden? Where is this paradise now? Why was Adam put to work in the garden? Wouldn't the garden be more perfect if the residents did not have to work? If humans were intended to never die, wouldn't the garden have become overpopulated as the generations expanded their progeny? Why does God put the tree of the knowledge of good and evil in the garden and then tell Adam to keep away from it? Wasn't God guaranteeing that the first humans would screw up? Did he foresee the outcome? And why does God want to withhold the knowledge of good and evil from Adam in the first place, seeing that the Bible consistently holds people accountable for not knowing the difference between good and evil?

Every generation of Christians brings new questions to the text, looking for insights into *their* issues, like the role of women or the contours of marriage. Why, for example, in the second creation story did God create all the other creatures with mates, but Adam's mate seems to have been an afterthought?

What is that destructive serpent doing in the garden? Why doesn't God warn Adam and Eve about the serpent, like he did about the tree of knowledge of good and evil? Why doesn't Eve just walk away when the serpent starts talking? Why did Adam take a bite when Eve offered the forbidden fruit, when he knew better? If he was perfect, why would he disobey God so overtly? And what—or who—is that "serpent" anyway?

The greatest question relates to sin, the Fall, and the curse. Isn't death for Adam, all subsequent humans, and every other living thing unreasonable? Why was the entire cosmos wrecked by Adam's sin? Why do we have to struggle to feed our families and fight off illness in the dark shadow of our mortality because of Adam's sin? What justice permits you and me to be punished for something with which we had nothing to do? And, if Adam's sin has such dramatic consequences, why is it not mentioned when God punishes a sinful humanity by drowning almost all of them? Or confounding their languages at Babel? Or raining fire and brimstone on their heads at Sodom and Gomorrah? If these things are all Adam's fault, why is that never mentioned?

And don't the other punishments seem arbitrary? Why are serpents made to crawl on their bellies? Did they have legs before? Is the story asking us to believe in talking snakes? Why is pain in childbirth for Eve and trouble in tilling the ground appropriate punishments for eating forbidden fruit? What was Eve's original physical body like that it could have children without pain?

The perennial poser, put to William Jennings Bryan by Clarence Darrow at the Scopes trial, was, "Where did Cain get his wife?" Cain, Abel, and their parents were the only people on the planet. Whence Mrs. Cain? And who are the vigilantes that Cain fears will kill him for murdering Abel? How can there be a "land of Nod, east of Eden," if the world population was three after Abel's murder? How can Adam die at the age of 930—itself a puzzle—when God said he would die on the "day" he ate the fruit?

The biblical story tells us that God made humans in his image. And somehow this feature of the first man has been passed to all humans. The readers of this book, according to the traditional understanding, bear the image of God. This is the most important aspect of the human part of the story, but it is *never* clarified. Was this known to ancient readers?

Readers wrestling with the incompleteness of the story inevitably fill in the gaps. After I have given a talk about evolution, fundamentalist critics often state with a great rhetorical flourish, "I am created in the image of God and not the image of a monkey," as if their personal appearance is the image of God. This seems like nonsense but, without clarification, can we reject that interpretation?

The vagueness of the text invites readers to create Adam in *their* image. If Adam is the ancestor of *their* tribe, after all, why can't they work backward from the way things are—or the way they want them to be—to the way they must have been?

In the next chapter we will look at this conversation as it developed outside the Hebrew Bible, first within the Jewish tradition and then in the New Testament, where we will meet Paul, the most important interpreter of Adam. Paul made sense of Jesus's death by creating a major new role for Adam, a role so central that many Christians believe their faith depends on Adam being the ancestor of all humanity. Paul's embellishments of the Hebrew Adam are the most controversial and influential claims of any that have been made about the first man.

CHAPTER 2

THE TWO ESSENTIAL ADAMS OF THE APOSTLE PAUL

*In the history of Western Christianity—and hence, to a large
extent, in the history of Western Culture—the Apostle Paul
has been hailed as a hero of the introspective conscience.*
—KRISTER STENDAHL[1]

In 34 CE a Jewish tent maker, destined to exert great influence on Western civilization, began a long journey along a major trade route from Jerusalem to Damascus. He had been dispatched by Gamaliel, an expert in religious law and a member of the Pharisees, a Jewish sect.

The tent maker was Gamaliel's celebrated student, Saul of Tarsus, known for his birthplace—the thriving capital of the Roman province of Cilicia. Mark Antony first met Cleopatra in Tarsus, and it remains an important city in modern Turkey. Tarsus was also a major academic center.

Well-educated and deeply religious, Saul had been enlisted by Gamaliel to throttle the growing popularity of a rabble-rousing Jewish preacher named Jesus. He was traveling to Damascus with documents authorizing the arrest of any disciples of Jesus. It was a journey of some 140 miles, much of it along a well-traveled thoroughfare through the Jordan River valley. Saul anticipated returning to Gamaliel with a bounty of Christians, beaten, bound, and ready for trial. Some would have been killed and left behind to remind their communities of the dangers of following false prophets.

Sometime before arriving at Damascus, perhaps as snowcapped Mount Hermon was coming into view, Saul was blinded by a light he later recalled as "brighter than the noonday sun." A powerful voice, seemingly from heaven, challenged him, asking, "Saul, Saul, why do you continue to persecute me?" Blinded and disoriented, Saul responded to the voice: "Who are you?" His companions also heard the voice and, although they were not blinded, they saw no one.

The voice responded, "I am Jesus, whom you are persecuting." Jesus, crucified a few years earlier, instructed the shaken Saul to "get up and go in the city, and you will be told what you must do." Saul did exactly as commanded, with the help of his companions, who led him into Damascus. There he was rewarded with the return of his eyesight and a new commission to spread the gospel of the very Jesus whose followers he had persecuted for so long.

Saul's reputation was widespread. The community that feared him described him as "breathing threats and murder against the disciples of the Lord."[2] After his encounter on the Damascus road, however, Saul of Tarsus was transformed into *Paul the apostle of Jesus Christ*, a role that would make him one of the most influential people the world has ever seen and arguably as important—or maybe even more important—than Jesus in shaping the beliefs of the world's most influential religion. One of Paul's biographers credits Paul with doing more than *anyone* to shape the concept of the person who has given Western culture its central moral intuitions:

> More than anyone else, Paul created the Western individual human being, unconditionally precious to God and therefore entitled to the consideration of other human beings. . . . Broad social change did follow inevitably from the idea he spread: that God's love was sublime and infinite, yet immediately knowable to everyone. No other intellect contributed as much to making us who we are.[3]

Paul is the most important interpreter of Adam. Christians continue to wrestle with the role he assigned to the first man—a role that linked Adam to Christ in a package deal, with details that would be heavily debated by millions of Christians into the present. Unfortunately, the connections Paul drew between Christ and Adam were so tightened by subsequent interpreters that their historical reality appeared to rise and fall in unison. Christian theology became so dependent on Adam that any hint he may not have been a real historical figure became an attack on Christianity.

Paul's letters to the early church wrestle with theological questions confronted by the emerging Christianity as it struggled to understand itself.

Sin and salvation from sin were primary. The first, said Paul, originates with Adam; the latter with Christ.

In places, Paul seems to suggest that all humans have actually *inherited* sinful natures from Adam. Shaped forcefully by Augustine in the fourth century, this notion—original sin—would become the dominant view in the Christian West, and the view that would make the historical Adam so difficult to dislodge. Prior to Augustine, however, no such consensus existed and many Christians viewed Adam simply as Everyman, the first of our species, like us in many ways, tempted by Satan as we are. Adam, however, was weak and gave in to temptation, but his failure was his, and his alone. We can do better.

THE COFOUNDER OF CHRISTIANITY

Under Saul the persecutor, it is hard to see how Christianity could ever have been more than a tenuous, shaky, and heretical sect on the margins of Judaism. Perhaps it would have disappeared like other small movements at the time, such as the Essenes or the Sadducees. With Paul the apostle as its champion, however, Christianity not only survived but became the dominant feature of Western culture and a global religion that would eventually claim the allegiance of one-third of the world's population.[4]

Paul wrote a third of the twenty-seven books in the New Testament, and four or five others are misattributed to him. Most were letters to churches, such as Romans and Corinthians, or to individuals, such as Timothy and Philemon, clarifying points of doctrine and practice for a new religious movement. Paul developed most of the key ideas of Christian theology, including the divinity of Christ and the universal availability of salvation. He made ambitious missionary journeys, spreading the gospel of salvation through Jesus Christ throughout Asia Minor, Greece, Syria, and Palestine. One pundit ranks Paul the sixth most influential person who ever lived, after Mohammed, Isaac Newton, Jesus, Buddha, and Confucius.[5]

Paul saw his Damascus road experience as far more than a "conversion" to Christianity. He did not simply stop persecuting Christians, return to his tent-making shop, and join a local group of believers for weekly meetings. Paul understood his experience to be a commission from God. He had encountered the creator of the universe, and like Jeremiah, Isaiah, and other heroes of his tradition, he was now a part of God's grand plan. In his letter to the church at Galatia, Paul expressed his confidence that his part in God's great providential drama was written even before he was born:

> For I want you to know, brothers and sisters, that the gospel that was proclaimed by me is not of human origin; for I did not receive it from a human source, nor was I taught it, but I received it through a revelation of Jesus Christ.
>
> You have heard, no doubt, of my earlier life in Judaism. I was violently persecuting the church of God and was trying to destroy it. . . . But when God, *who had set me apart before I was born* and called me through his grace, was pleased to reveal his Son to me, so that I might proclaim him among the Gentiles, I did not confer with any human being.[6]

Paul's language is intentionally reminiscent of claims made by prophets when they established their credentials. Jeremiah writes, for example,

> Now the word of the Lord came to me saying, "Before I formed you in the womb I knew you, and before you were born I consecrated you; I appointed you a prophet to the nations."[7]

His credentials established, Paul goes on to play a defining role in the story of Adam, lifting the first man from parochial obscurity in the pages of the Hebrew scriptures and placing him at the center of Christianity's conversation about the nature of sin, free will, and what it means to be human. Paul's enlargement of Adam became a defining feature of Christianity, perhaps going beyond what Paul might have envisioned. Even now, two millennia later, millions of Christians, to understand themselves and their world, look to a lively tradition that began—but certainly did not end—with Paul's discussion of Adam.

Paul's engagement with Adam, however, is far from straightforward. His tradition read their scriptures with the assumption that Adam and Eve were historical figures, as real as Moses and David. But precisely because they assumed this history uncritically, it is hard to tell how important it was to them. Our historical questions were not theirs.

Paul wanted to universalize Christianity to include non-Jews, to gather all people into one unified tribe, to make everyone Christian. And what better way than to make the story of Adam the story of every man, the singular ancestor on everyone's family tree? Paul thus transforms the story of Adam and connects it to Christ's sacrificial death so that both become relevant to everyone. Adam brings sin and death into the world, and Jesus takes it away.

THE INTERPRETATIVE WORLD OF PAUL

Paul's central concern was the relationship between Christianity and Judaism. Should Jesus be understood as a new Jewish prophet, critiquing his tradition like the prophets of old and calling believers back to a more authentic practice of their faith? Or was Jesus starting something new—something post-Jewish or even non-Jewish? This is quite possibly the most serious religious question ever debated, given the history that followed.

The national identity of Israel—and its various expressions of Judaism—developed significantly during the Second Temple period, between 530 BCE and 70 CE. Israel's first temple was built by the famously wise Solomon and destroyed by the Babylonians around 587 BCE. Many educated Jewish leaders were relocated to Babylon, where they served as slaves for decades and wrote heart-wrenching poetry about being separated from the land that God had promised them. They wept at the challenges of being Jewish so far from home:

> *By the rivers of Babylon we sat and wept when we remembered Zion.*
> *There on the poplars we hung our harps,*
> *for there our captors asked us for songs, our tormentors demanded songs of joy;*
> *they said, "Sing us one of the songs of Zion!"*
> *How can we sing the songs of the Lord while in a foreign land?*[8]

The Jews returned to their homeland around 520 BCE and began laying the foundations for the Second Temple, where the heart of a renewed Judaism beat vigorously until the Romans destroyed it in 70 CE.

Solomon's Temple was the holy center of Judaism. One of the seven wonders of the ancient world, the legendary structure has long fascinated scholars, including Isaac Newton, who devoted an entire chapter to it in his little-known *Chronology of Ancient Kingdoms*.[9] The destruction of the temple and scattering of the tribes of Israel created an identity crisis for Judaism. If Judaism was not the religion of *these* people on *this* land, performing *these* ceremonies, worshiping in *that* temple, led by *these* priests and prophets, then what was it? *How can we sing the songs of the Lord while in a foreign land?*

Wrestling with these questions of self-understanding created the religious traditions of first-century Jews, including Jesus and Paul. Israel's scripture cataloged a critical part of the answers that developed as their leaders looked back into history and tried to figure out who they were. The resulting history was enlarged through timeless, complex, sometimes troubling, and often magnificent literature like the poetry quoted above.

Events like the exile in Babylon, the giving of the Ten Commandments, or the destruction of the temple became episodes in a narrative of national identity—a story that began with the creation of the world, ran through a purposeful present, and continued into a future when God would make everything right. Judaism was no longer the organic and unfolding experiences of the children of Abraham, rooted in the soil of present events, but became instead a grander narrative.

This narrative became enshrined in sacred texts. The final production of the particular texts we call the Hebrew scriptures—Christians' Old Testament—was largely an editorial process, based on existing materials. Oral traditions from preliterate centuries were written down; related accounts—like the creation stories in Genesis—were stitched together with bits of editorial thread. A final form for the collection of texts emerged in the centuries after the Jews returned to their homeland in the sixth century BCE and was completed by the third century BCE. Once the Hebrew scriptures were completed, the important, challenging, idiosyncratic, and often infuriating task of *interpretation* emerged, a task at which Paul proved quite ingenious.

People of the Book

By the time Jesus began preaching in the synagogues of first-century Palestine, those places of worship had seen centuries of teaching and reflecting on the stories in the Hebrew scriptures. These reflections had given rise to a substantial body of extrabiblical texts, the authorship, veracity, and significance of which have been hotly debated. But we cannot understand Paul apart from the interpretive context in which he worked, and this literature was an important part of that tradition. Christians today often naively assume that their first-century counterparts read the same Bible they do.

Paul's tradition explored their scriptures with a creativity that permitted fanciful extrapolations that went way beyond what the text could possibly have meant. Modern cautions about minding the original intent of authors are absent in this tradition, and all other first-century traditions for that matter. Novelties are constantly—and without controversy—being read into the scriptures to make them speak to new questions. In particular, the Hebrew scriptures were reread—some would say twisted—to make them speak repeatedly of a future Messiah who would be Jesus of Nazareth.[10] These texts also enlarged the story of Adam and Eve, adding details and interpretations, always rooting Judaism in its past, even when that meant inventing new historical episodes or embellishing and changing existing ones.

One collection of writings is known as the Pseudepigrapha, so called for its strategy of claiming authorship by famous people from the past, like Moses. The celebrity-author ploy was possibly a publicity strategy, to generate interest rather than deceive.[11] Another collection of writings is the Apocrypha. Fourteen or fifteen of the most well-known Apocryphal books are found in the Bibles used by the Roman Catholic and Orthodox traditions, often sandwiched between the Old and New Testaments. Apocrypha literally means "things hidden away," but there is nothing especially "hidden" about apocryphal literature.[12]

The Pseudepigrapha, Apocrypha, and other writings provided a substantial exploration of the Hebrew scriptures. This constant engagement kept breathing new life into the stories. Different Jewish factions produced different literatures, reflecting their idiosyncratic self-understandings. The New Testament springs from this literary cornucopia, as first-century Christians wrestled with their identity. New Testament writers cited the Hebrew scriptures hundreds of times and made more than one thousand allusions to it. They also cited apocryphal and unknown sources.

This literature shaped subsequent reflection on the scriptures, including the meaning of the story of Adam and Eve. The Jews were becoming "people of the book," increasingly defined by the social, moral, and theological blueprints provided by God in their scriptures, rather than by the organic and evolving social structures of their community. In the centuries to come, their tradition will, in fact, spend much of its energy reflecting on how the ongoing community can remain faithful to its scriptural roots.

Great tensions attend the evolution of any community, corporation, or activity that is anchored to a written charter. No matter how prescient or brilliantly conceived, texts *never* anticipate all the questions they will need to answer. Balancing faithfulness to a defining text and meaningful engagement with a changing world is at the heart of the story being told in this book, embodying the tension that makes the story of Adam and Eve so controversial.

As people of the book, their evolving religious life was anchored in ancient texts that increasingly came to define them. Defeated, their temple destroyed, relocated to a foreign land, they were decoupled from their own history. Their identity became uncertain in a time when few people could read and oral traditions carried much of the culture. When the Jews returned to their sacred homeland they looked to their history to recover an understanding of who they were. Getting their sacred texts in order was an important part of this task. Commentary, gloss, expansion, and clarification would keep the texts alive and relevant.

The Judeo-Christian tradition came to be shaped by three interwoven sources of authority. The first was the Hebrew scriptures, to which the New Testament was eventually added. The second was the more controversial collection of texts discussed above with their uncertain authority—the Apocrypha and Pseudepigrapha. And the third strand in the weave was the ongoing discussion, generally in print, by influential thinkers like Augustine, Aquinas, Luther, Calvin, and their present-day counterparts, of how to make the scriptures speak to new issues like democracy, capitalism, health care, and homosexuality. Such writings were not treated as divinely inspired, but exerted and continue to exert great influence on how the developing tradition understood its sacred texts.

ADAM AND EVE OUTSIDE THE BIBLE

The Hebrew scriptures were essentially completed by 200 BCE and collections that gathered its many books into a single document began to appear. The literature from the period after those initial compilations, roughly 200 BCE to 200 CE, relates to these scriptures in complicated ways. Stories are retold. Anonymous characters receive names. Historical episodes are fleshed out and interpreted, removing old ambiguities and creating new ones. Brief stories are expanded. We read of Eve's fifth child, a daughter, Awan, who grew up to be Cain's wife. Another tells of Adam, feeble and sick at the age of 930, gathering his children to pass on his wisdom. Seth takes pity on his aged father and offers to fetch some of that special paradise fruit from the Garden of Eden.

While this new literature engages the Hebrew scriptures at countless points, it is noteworthy in its expanded interest in Adam and Eve. Where Genesis was ambiguous, cryptic, abbreviated, and piecemeal, the new literature is expansive, rich in detail, and self-contradictory.

This new literature provides our first look at the evolving narrative of the first man and woman. The forgotten couple grow in significance as the Jews enlarge the importance of the events in the Garden of Eden. The nature of human beings, our relationship to God, the burden of sin, and other big questions are explored by considering how God created everything in the beginning. Social issues like the role of women—an enduring and contentious problem—are adjudicated by invoking the divine arrangements established in Eden. And all this eventually leads us into the most important Adam story of all—the one told by Paul.

The book of Jubilees from the second century BCE retells the story of the first couple, based on a revelation given by an angel to Moses. The retelling explains how Eve loses the equality she had with Adam in the first creation account. In the Jubilees, God gives "dominion over everything" only to Adam instead of both of them: "And after all this He created man, a man and a woman created He them, and gave him dominion over all that is upon the earth, and in the seas, and over everything that flies, and over beasts and over cattle, and over everything that moves on the earth, and over the whole earth, and over all this He gave him dominion."[13] The culturally exceptional equality of male and female in the first creation account was apparently too radical to endure.

The philosopher Philo of Alexandria (ca. 20 BCE–50 CE) is especially hard on Eve (and women in general). Eve is not merely the first person tricked by the serpent—a detail that could be of no consequence—but is in every sense inferior to Adam, *precisely because she is a woman.* Philo poses the question "Why does the serpent speak to the woman and not to the man?" Answer: "Woman is more accustomed to be deceived than man." Eve was the first to "touch the tree and eat of its fruit" because "it was fitting that man should rule over immortality and everything good, but woman over death and everything vile." By Philo's patriarchal lights, the secondary status of women in his day was simply the way God intended things to be.[14]

In contrast, the Apocalypse of Moses lets Eve explain herself. In a scene near the end of Adam's life, written with more flair than the Genesis account, Eve summons the children to pass on the story of what happened centuries earlier, when everything went so wrong:

> Then saith Eve to them: "Hear all my children and children's children and I will relate to you how the enemy deceived us. It befell that we were guarding paradise, each of us the portion allotted to us from God. Now I guarded in my lot, the west and the south. But the devil went to Adam's lot, where the male creatures were. (For God divided the creatures; all the males he gave to your father and all the females he gave to me.)

"And the devil spake to the serpent saying, 'Rise up, come to me and I will tell thee a word whereby thou mayst have profit.' And he arose and came to him. And the devil saith to him: 'I hear that thou art wiser than all the beasts, and I have come to counsel thee. Why dost thou eat of Adam's tares and not of paradise? Rise up and we will cause him to be cast out of paradise, even as we were cast out through him.' The serpent saith to him, 'I fear lest the Lord be wroth with me.' The devil saith to him: 'Fear not, only be my vessel and I will speak through thy mouth words to deceive him.'"[15]

Eve explains how the devil tempted her "through the mouth of the serpent":

"Ye do well but ye do not eat of every plant." And I said: "Yea, we eat of all. Save one only, which is in the midst of paradise, concerning which, God charged us not to eat of it: for, He said to us, on the day on which ye eat of it, ye shall die the death." Then the serpent saith to me, "May God live! but I am grieved on your account, for I would not have you ignorant. But arise, (come) hither, hearken to me and eat and mind the value of that tree."[16]

Eve acknowledges she was so eager to eat the evil fruit that she swore an oath to pass it along to Adam as a condition of having it: "By the throne of the Master, and by the Cherubim and the Tree of Life! I will give also to my husband to eat."

In this retelling, the evil comes not from simple disobedience, as Genesis suggests, but from a lustful wickedness that the devil placed on the fruit:

And when he had received the oath from me, he went and poured upon the fruit the poison of his wickedness, which is lust, the root and beginning of every sin, and he bent the branch on the earth and I took of the fruit and I ate. And in that very hour my eyes were opened, and forthwith I knew that I was bare of the righteousness with which I had been clothed (upon), and I wept and said to him: "Why hast thou done this to me in that thou hast deprived me of the glory with which I was clothed?" But I wept also about the oath, which I had sworn.[17]

By far the strangest treatment of Eve—and the one making her secondary status most explicit—is the fascinating tale of Lilith, Adam's first wife, the demanding and rebellious spouse provided for Adam in the first creation account.

Stories of a woman named Lilith appear in the same ancient Near Eastern myths that scholars believe inspired the accounts in Genesis, but it takes several centuries until this shadowy character evolves into Adam's wife.[18] She is mentioned once in the Old Testament and does not appear in all translations.[19] The prophet Isaiah warns, in a widely accepted translation, that "the Lord is enraged against all the nations"[20] and is wreaking his wrath on the land: "Thorns shall grow over its strongholds, nettles and thistles in its fortresses. . . . Wildcats shall meet with hyenas, goat-demons shall call to each other; there too Lilith shall repose, and find a place to rest." [21] In context the most likely meaning is that Lilith was some sort of demonic creature, unrelated to Adam and Eve at the time this account was penned, probably 800–700 BCE.

By the eighth century CE, however, the pseudepigraphical Alphabet of Ben Sira was juxtaposing Eve and Lilith as Adam's two wives—one evil and one good, one a role model for Jewish women, the other a warning about what happens when you don't play the role God assigned to you— which was submission, of course.

Lilith's evil nature was revealed when she insisted she was equal to Adam. After all, she had been created at the same time and in the same way. On what basis did Adam insist she was subordinate? The ensuing disagreement, according to the Alphabet, got Lilith expelled from Eden, or perhaps she left on her own in a fit of pique. She is said to have sprouted wings after refusing to be subservient to Adam—especially during sexual intercourse—and is often drawn as a woman with long hair and wings.[22] In Jewish folklore the demon Lilith came to be feared as a sinister force interfering with family life. One legend says she killed poor Job's sons. She seduces men, corrupts children created through impure sex, steals men's semen through wet dreams, torments women during childbirth, and kills babies.[23]

The Lilith mythology took on a life of its own. Medieval Jewish women hung amulets in their birthing rooms to keep Lilith away from their newborns. Nineteenth-century Scottish writer George MacDonald recast Lilith as a vampire. Twentieth-century television screenwriters named Dr. Frasier Crane's frosty, meddling ex-wife Lilith. Feminists and Wiccans continue to invoke her as a symbol of their demands for equality.

The Jewish tradition that generated the myth of Lilith was once shared by Christianity but eventually separated to run its own course. But—and here we return to the New Testament—it was this literary milieu that nurtured Saul of Tarsus and liberated him to develop the understanding of Adam that became the centerpiece of the Christian understanding of the first man.

Much of the contemporary conversation about the historicity of Adam is muddled because Paul's presentation of the Adam story is read in isolation from his literary tradition. This tradition licensed theological creativity and, as the above examples make clear, paid little attention to historical accuracy. We should thus conclude, in opposition to many conservative contemporary readers of Paul, that the apostle would certainly have felt free to use the Adam story in any way he wanted, without necessarily implying that his creative claims were rooted in history.

PAUL'S ADAM

The Jesus that Paul encountered on the Damascus road was Jewish. We need periodic reminders of this, in light of Christian anti-Semitism that became so pervasive. Jesus was born into a Jewish family and was circumcised when he was eight days old, as was the custom of his family's religion. He was raised a Jew and visited the synagogue regularly. He did not eat pork or work on the Sabbath. He studied the Torah and referenced it often.

Much of Jesus's message was familiar to his Jewish audiences. Their sacred literature encouraged care for the poor, widows, and orphans and a welcome to the foreign enemy. Appearing before a congregation in Nazareth Jesus read a familiar passage from Isaiah that he said applied to him:

> The Spirit of the Lord is upon me, because he hath anointed me to preach the gospel to the poor; he hath sent me to heal the brokenhearted, to preach deliverance to the captives, and recovering of sight to the blind, to set at liberty them that are bruised.[24]

Jesus preached consistently and powerfully, if often ambiguously, of the coming "kingdom of God," a familiar theme in Judaism. The kingdom of which he spoke seems to have been understood by both Jesus and his followers—at least initially—to be an earthly kingdom about to appear. He taught his followers to pray, "Thy kingdom come, thy will be done in earth, as it is in heaven." Later Jesus would say, "My kingdom is not of this world." Similar vagueness attended Jesus's comments about himself. On some occasions he scolded his disciples for referring to him as the promised

Messiah of Israel; on others he seems to have accepted the label. The Gospel of John reports that crowds hailed Jesus as "King of Israel," suggesting they thought he was a political Messiah.

Throughout his short but dramatic ministry, Jesus understood his Jewish tribe to be the chosen people of God. He was often quite clear that his message was exclusively for the "lost sheep of the house of Israel"[25] and not for the despised Gentiles. His audiences often interpreted Jesus as a Jewish prophet, a familiar role, comparing him to earlier prophets like Moses and Elijah. Virtually nothing suggests that Jesus had any significance beyond Judaism.

As history has made clear, however, Christianity is effective at attracting converts, and it wasn't long until first-century Gentiles were converting to the new faith. Many early converts were women, attracted in part—perhaps in large part—to a faith that treated them more respectfully than the alternatives. Many had already embraced the monotheism and some of the rituals of Judaism. Alas, things were not so simple for male Gentiles converting to Christianity because of circumcision.

Circumcision in the Jewish tradition was not a medical procedure—it was a holy act, symbolizing an ancient covenant that the people of Israel had made with God. To become Jewish was to enter into this sacred covenant with Yahweh, and circumcision was a critical part of that, a distinctive marker one would wear for life. Adult male circumcision was, understandably, a higher price than many first-century Gentile males were willing to pay.

Circumcision raised a central question: Was Christianity a part of Judaism? Was becoming Jewish an automatic part of becoming Christian, just as becoming American would be an automatic part of becoming a New Englander? Or was Christianity something different? Circumcision was not an issue as long as the new gospel was preached only to Jews, as Jesus had specified.

PAUL'S REVOLUTION

Paul was the "apostle to the Gentiles." He understood only too well that circumcision had the potential to forever keep Christianity inscribed within Judaism. And given that some had already labeled the new religion a Jewish heresy—after all, he had been working earlier to exterminate it—Christianity might not survive into the next century unless it put down roots in Gentile soil. So Paul pushed back against those first-century gatekeepers keeping uncircumcised Gentiles out of the faith. He also challenged the need to keep the oddball Jewish dietary regulations.

It would be a serious mistake, however, to suppose that Paul's motivation for these revolutionary proposals was entirely practical, as though inviting uncircumcised males into the new faith was like having a potluck dinner to encourage church attendance. The theology that Paul developed for the embryonic Christian church transcended the parochial concerns of Jewish ritualism so thoroughly that it left Judaism behind entirely.

Paul's central—and radical—theological intuition was that God had created all humanity and not just the Jewish people. It followed that, at least in the eyes of their creator, every person had value. God loved *everyone*, and God loved everyone *equally*, a concept that was hard to understand in a time of great, multifaceted inequality. It only made sense that God would redeem *all* humanity directly—as human beings created in his image, not as members of the Jewish faith. In a famous sermon to a Greek (Gentile) audience on Mars Hill in Athens, Paul spoke of God making "of one blood all nations of men."[26] In context, this was a profound statement of human unity to a culture that believed some men were naturally slaves. We must not make Paul too modern, of course, for he shared the beliefs of his century that some people were by nature slaves and that women were subordinate to men. But these were incidental differences to God, who viewed them as a father might view his different and unequal children. Paul's emphasis on the *unity of humanity*—remarkable for its time—became a distinctive feature of Christianity and the heart of its theology.

In Paul's theology, the human predicament is summed up in a widely quoted verse: "All have sinned and fall short of the glory of God."[27] Paul, however, is not entirely clear on the nature of this sin and it would be several centuries until Augustine would develop the understanding that most Christians have today. Why, exactly, do we sin? Is it because, like Adam, we give in to temptation and in so doing *become* sinners of our own free will? As we commit sins, do we fall from perfection as Adam did? If we were sufficiently righteous, could we refrain from sinning as Jesus implied when he said, "Be perfect, therefore, as your heavenly Father is perfect"?[28] Or are we born with sinful natures that make us sinners even before we have made the choice to sin? Are newborns sinful? Do they need to be baptized to cleanse them of their sin? Does hell contain a region called limbo for unbaptized infants, as Roman Catholic doctrine would eventually claim, following Augustine's interpretation of Paul? Is every human being born deserving God's wrath, destined for hell, because of sin?

Paul took sin and the resultant curse from God seriously. He viewed the physical creation as cursed, and wrote that it "groaneth and travaileth in pain."[29] God did not create things in this sad state of affairs, of course; Paul saw this disaster as entirely a consequence of Adam's sin, for which God bears absolutely no responsibility. Adam's decision to sin was his free choice and he could have done otherwise. And, in some mysterious way, the entire creation was present with Adam and involved in his decision to sin. He was genuinely guilty. But have we inherited his guilt? Are we born in a state of sin, deserving to be punished?

Paul's view of the consequences of Adam's sin is the most dramatic of any of the ancient writers wrestling with this difficult question. And it becomes even more dramatic with time. Certainly many viewed Adam's fall from perfection as catastrophic, but there was no agreement on the nature of the catastrophe. The Life of Adam and Eve lists moral corruption, change of diet, sorrow, and loss of spiritual joy as the consequences of the Fall. The Apocalypse of Moses lists loss of dominion over the creation and loss of "glory." The Jubilees report that this was when animals lost their ability to talk directly to humans. Several accounts report that death was one of the results, either prematurely, in the sense of cutting short a long life, or the loss of immortality.[30]

The early Jewish tradition did not have a well-developed concept of eternal life; therefore it would have been unreasonable to expect the Fall to be interpreted in terms of eternal damnation in their writings. But most Jews of Paul's generation believed that humans would live in eternity; therefore attending to one's salvation is the most important part of one's religious life.

Paul's Adam wrecked the world. But despite the cesspool created by Adam and into which we leap by choosing to sin, Paul asserted that God still loves us with unconditional love. He loves us so much, in fact, that he sent his son Jesus to suffer and die to rescue us from this sin. In the Jewish moral calculus of first-century Palestine, suffering and bloodshed were essential to atone for sin. Jesus's torturous death—being the undeserved suffering of God in human form—atones for all the sin of everyone who ever lived, past, present, and future, Jew and Gentile alike.

In Paul's letter to the Romans—Christianity's central theological document—he makes the case as follows:

> God demonstrates His own love toward us, in that while we were still sinners, Christ died for us. Much more then, having now been justified by His blood, we shall be saved from wrath through Him. For if when we

were enemies we were reconciled to God through the death of His Son, much more, having been reconciled, we shall be saved by His life . . .

Therefore, just as through one man sin entered the world, and death through sin, and thus death spread to all men, because all sinned, . . . nevertheless death reigned from Adam to Moses, even over those who had not sinned according to the likeness of the transgression of Adam, who is a type of Him who was to come. But the free gift is not like the offense. For if by the one man's offense many died, much more the grace of God and the gift by the grace of the one Man, Jesus Christ, abounded to many. And the gift is not like that which came through the one who sinned. For the judgment which came from one offense resulted in condemnation, but the free gift which came from many offenses resulted in justification. For if by the one man's offense death reigned through the one, much more those who receive abundance of grace and of the gift of righteousness will reign in life through the One, Jesus Christ.

Therefore, as through one man's offense judgment came to all men, resulting in condemnation, even so through one Man's righteous act the free gift came to all men, resulting in justification of life. For as by one man's disobedience many were made sinners, so also by one Man's obedience many will be made righteous.[31]

This passage addresses the meaning and significance of Adam's sin and Christ's death, both of which had been puzzling and challenging to the first Christians. Adam and Christ emerge as bookends in the drama of salvation. Christ is a second Adam, or perhaps "anti-Adam" would be a better term, undoing the damage of the first Adam. God had created a perfect world, with no death, no sin, no sickness—nothing but beauty and wonder—and gave it to us to look after and enjoy. Adam, the first of our species, was created in harmony with God. But he disobeyed.

Paul's Adam was thus not merely the first *Jew*, but the first *human*; his sin was thus the first *human* sin, and not merely a Jewish transgression. We are all Adamic in some sense. In places Paul seems to suggest, as the Christian tradition would come to believe, that we are born with that same sinful nature that mysteriously came upon Adam when he chose to disobey God. In other places, however, Paul seems to suggest that we have the same choice as Adam. The ensuing debate would rage for centuries: Are we sinners because we sin? Or do we sin because we are sinners? However we answer this question, Paul asserts that God has extended his love universally to everyone through the sacrifice of his son Jesus, the only human to make it through life without once giving in to the temptation to sin. By embracing Christ's sacrifice—a gift freely given by God—we find salvation.

Paul's theology was revolutionary. He broke down the ancient walls separating the Jews—God's chosen people—from the rest of the humanity, including the Gentiles that even Jesus referred to as "dogs."[32] And, like other theologians of his generation, he looked to the story of the first man for inspiration in how to accomplish this agenda. Paul's central point was clearly the unity of all humans and their common need for salvation. He used the Adam story to make this point; he did not use the Adam story to claim that a historical Adam was an essential part of Christian theology, although belief that Adam was a real person would certainly have been a part of his worldview.

The Christians that followed Paul were a small band of underground believers practicing an illegal religion under the threat of martyrdom. Some died for their faith, often in cruel and disturbing ways. Debating theological nuance was a luxury in the face of horrific persecution that seemed inspired by Satan himself. Could it really be, as some believed Paul had taught, that the Christians and their persecutors shared a common sinful nature? Surely the Roman guards, entertaining cheering crowds by killing helpless women and children, were consumed by sin in ways the Christians were not.

CHAPTER 3

THE DEVIL MADE THEM DO IT
Adam's Free Choice, and Ours

The line separating good and evil passes not through states,
nor between classes, nor between political parties either—
but right through every human heart.
—ALEXANDER SOLZHENITSYN[1]

Tradition records that the apostle Paul was beheaded in Rome during the reign of Nero, probably in the mid-60s CE. It was the end of a hard life. In his second letter to the Corinthians he detailed the adversity he had faced, relative to other eminent leaders:

> I have worked much harder, been in prison more frequently, been flogged more severely, and been exposed to death again and again. Five times I received from the Jews the forty lashes minus one. Three times I was beaten with rods, once I was pelted with stones, three times I was shipwrecked, I spent a night and a day in the open sea, I have been constantly on the move. I have been in danger from rivers, in danger from bandits, in danger from my fellow Jews, in danger from Gentiles; in danger in the city, in danger in the country, in danger at sea; and in danger from false believers. I have labored and toiled and have often gone without sleep; I have known hunger and thirst and have often gone without food; I have been cold and naked.[2]

Paul's story was familiar to first-century Christians. Ten years after Paul's death, during the famous fire that destroyed much of Rome, the emperor Nero—suspected as the arsonist—arrested a group of Christians, charged them with arson, hung them up in his garden, and burned them alive as human torches. Other Christians met comparably cruel fates at the hands of gladiators or the teeth and claws of various beasts in the Roman Coliseum—horrific deaths arranged for entertainment.

The first Christians confronted a challenging political reality. Their emerging faith was quite literally a "deadly superstition," as the Roman historian Tacitus wrote.[3] Nevertheless, the movement that came to be known as Christianity grew steadily more popular, helped along by treating the disenfranchised, especially women, better than the state or popular alternative religions.

Historians estimate that Paul was one of but a thousand Christians in 40 CE. By 100 CE this number had increased sevenfold, and by 200 CE it surpassed two hundred thousand. These improving fortunes did not go unnoticed. In 313 CE the Roman emperor Constantine converted to the new faith that by that time claimed almost nine million adherents—15 percent of the population of the Roman Empire. Christianity became the official religion of the empire, and by 350 CE more than half of the populace—some thirty-two million people—are estimated to have embraced the newly approved faith.[4]

Christianity at the beginning of this formative period confronted radically different challenges than at the end. The seven thousand or so Christians meeting secretly at the end of the first century lived in the shadow of persecution from a hostile Roman political system—one prepared to execute them for crimes like refusing to pay appropriate respect to the Roman rulers and their pagan deities.

Early Christians came to understand themselves as separate from the political—and sometimes oppressive—structure in which they were embedded. In their eyes the state responsible for this nightmare must be sinful and its leadership possessed of an otherworldly evil spirit; swearing allegiance to such a sinister carnival was inconceivable.

"Our contest," wrote one of Paul's followers who penned "Paul's" letter to the Ephesians, "is not against flesh and blood but against powers, against principalities, against the world rulers of this present darkness, against the spiritual force of evil in heavenly places."[5] Early Christians came to see their situation in cosmic terms—a conflict between the power of Satan and the demons possessing their enemies, and the gracious purity of their own movement, freed from such evil by its faith in Jesus Christ. The "world" and its entanglements had to be avoided. Some responded by fleeing into the deserts and living in caves.

Some Christians, unable to avoid worldly entanglements, received death sentences, often carried out in the Coliseum as part of a public spectacle that included gladiator fights, slaughter of animals by people and slaughter of people by animals, and execution of criminals. The audiences that witnessed the deaths of Christians, however, were often struck by the peace with which many of these gentle, sincere, and often illiterate believers went to their deaths. Christians about to be killed would sometimes even show concern for an executioner squeamish about killing children and young mothers.[6] Some observers were so impressed by the fortitude of the martyrs they converted to this new religion, and became influential Christian leaders, embracing the new Messiah at great personal risk. Who was this Jesus whose followers seemed fearless of death? And what were the beliefs energizing his followers, who placed loyalty to their leader more highly than their own lives, who would rather die than surrender to Rome?

The Christian communities of the first centuries were scattered—geographically, culturally, educationally, theologically. They worshiped in secret, without central organization or common texts. Faith communities were small, local, with a single leader, isolated from similar communities. Their beliefs were diverse, even on basic questions like whether Christianity was simply a new expression of Judaism.

The important theological question of sin and its origins had no generally accepted answer. What is striking, however, are the constant references in early Christian documents to Satan and demons as the sources of evil in the world, and the absence of reference to Adam and his fall into sin. On those many occasions in the four Gospels when sin rears its head—Herod's slaughter of the innocents, the modest betrayal of Jesus by Peter, the fateful betrayal by Judas, the conviction by Pilate—the explanation is always cast as cosmic warfare between the forces of good and evil, God and Satan. Satan is everywhere, even tempting Jesus in a memorable encounter in the wilderness. And this framing occurs despite Paul's "second Adam" theological explanation of Jesus's death and resurrection, which predated the Gospels by a couple of decades. Early Christians did not understand Paul's theology of sin in the same way that most Christians do today.

Christianity's transformation from persecuted minority sect to official religion is remarkable. Converts to the new religion included philosophers who came to Christianity after searching for truth in Greek philosophy, as well as the disenfranchised. Christianity freed women of all social ranks to seek the warm sun of equality and even leadership, out from under the relentless patriarchal cloud of their times. Slaves saw their lots improved when their masters embraced Christ and mysteriously turned into better people. These remarkable conversions were often treated like exorcisms. Through the ritual of baptism, Christ expelled demonic forces and came to dwell in them.

Christianity was attractive to pagans, skeptics, and, of course, Jews, although Christianity became increasingly non-Jewish and eventually even anti-Jewish.[7] New believers came with prior religious ideas, like special days, creating theological confusion. What, exactly, did it mean to be a Christian? What texts were authentically Christian? What ideas were unacceptable?

As concern about basic survival retreated, Christian leaders were pressed for various reasons—theological, social, political, biblical—to develop an *orthodoxy*. Canonical texts were identified, edited, translated, and gathered into what we now call the Bible; shared beliefs were clarified and universalized; unacceptable beliefs were labeled as heresy and their champions expelled; ambiguities in the Bible were cleared up with supplementary doctrines and creeds.

Few questions have received more attention from Christians than the origin of evil. If God created a perfect world—the only kind a perfect being could create—what went wrong? The world is filled with terrible things: people live in a vale of tears, surrounded by suffering and death, persecution and war. Such things could not have been created by a good God so they must be the result of some evil, unplanned event that thwarted God's purposes.

This chapter explores the changing explanation for sin, as it slowly diminished in the Christian imagination from a horrific evil controlling *the other* to the more universal sense that there is something wrong with all of us.

ANGELS AND DEMONS

We start with Justin the philosopher, born at the beginning of the second century. The well-educated Justin came to Christianity around age thirty, frustrated at his failure to find a satisfactory truth in Greek philosophies. Instead he found meaning and inspiration watching Christians endure martyrdom. These martyrs followed a God that seemed as real to them as the troubled world that persecuted them. They embodied the transcendent integrity of which Plato had spoken and by which Socrates calmly accepted his death sentence.

After his conversion Justin grew to despise, but not disbelieve in, Roman gods. Behind the chiseled faces of these ubiquitous statues—Fortuna, Hercules, Apollo, Dionysus, Roma—Justin saw "spiritual forces of evil in heavenly places."[8] These gods, he thought, embodied a genuine evil wholly separate from the goodness embodied in the followers of Christ. In reflecting on the cruel mechanisms used to kill Christians, he declared, echoing a popular refrain, "We know that those who invented them are demons."[9] Justin, after a significant tenure as a leader shaping the early church, would eventually join, via beheading, the martyrs he admired.

Justin used his considerable influence to argue that Christians posed no threat to the Roman Empire and were, in fact, model citizens: they paid their taxes, obeyed the law, and did more than their share of exemplary good works. Their refusal to worship the pagan deities of the empire could be overlooked. So why were they persecuted?

Justin addressed the Roman Senate in writings titled *The Second Apology of Justin for the Christians*, exploring questions of good and evil, sin and righteousness, right and wrong. Significantly, he makes no mention of Adam and Eve or the Fall to explain why the simple goodness of Christians was being met with such evil. In fact, Justin's *Apology* doesn't even mention Adam. Justin instead invokes one of the strangest stories in the Bible:

> When people began to multiply on the face of the ground, and daughters were born to them, the sons of God saw that they were fair; and they took wives for themselves of all that they chose. . . . The Nephilim were on the earth in those days—and also afterward—when the sons of God went in to the daughters of humans, who bore children to them. These were the heroes that were of old, warriors of renown.
>
> The Lord saw that the wickedness of humankind was great in the earth, and that every inclination of the thoughts of their hearts was only evil continually. And the Lord was sorry that he had made humankind on the earth, and it grieved him to his heart. So the Lord said, "I will blot out from the earth the human beings I have created—people together with animals and creeping things and birds of the air, for I am sorry that I have made them."[10]

The creatures known as Nephilim in this verse—the offspring of the "sons of God" mating with the "daughters of men"—have always been a puzzle. The King James Version that I read as a child translated this word as "giants." But a more literal translation would indicate something worse than giants, like bullies or tyrants.

Justin, consistent with the interpretive milieu of his time, embellishes the story of the Nephilim by identifying the "sons of God" as fallen angels who were supposed to look after the creation but got sidetracked by women:

> God, when He had made the whole world, and subjected things earthly to man, and arranged the heavenly elements for the increase of fruits and rotation of the seasons, and appointed this divine law, . . . committed the care of men and of all things under heaven to angels whom He appointed over them. But the angels transgressed this appointment and were captivated by love of women, and begat children who are those that are called demons.[11]

Justin then makes a most offensive claim, namely that the Roman gods—who Christians refused to worship—are the demonic offspring of fallen angels who mated with human women. The poets had mistakenly identified these demons as the pantheon of gods now worshiped throughout the empire. The Roman leaders persecuting the Christians, said Justin, were *possessed* by these demons, which accounted for their barbarism and cruelty:

> Among men they sowed murders, wars, adulteries, intemperate deeds, and all wickedness. Whence also the poets and mythologists, not knowing that it was the angels and those demons who had been begotten by them that did these things to men, and women, and cities, and nations, which they related, ascribed them to god himself, and to those who were accounted to be his very offspring, and to the offspring of those who were called his brothers, Neptune and Pluto, and to the children again of these their offspring.[12]

Justin, like his fellow Christians, takes the gods seriously. Unlike a modern Christian who would dismiss the conversation by saying that Zeus and Apollo don't exist, Justin acknowledges a supernatural—although less powerful—dimension to the powers that would eventually, as he anticipated, order his own execution at age sixty-five.

Justin's theology explained how the evil of the regime persecuting the Christians sprang from an entirely different source than that responsible for the temptations experienced by Christians. In the world of second-century Christianity, shaped by the drama of martyrdom, Christians perceived well-defined "good guys" and "bad guys." Although Justin and his fellow Christians might fall short of the perfection to which Christ called them, their failure was certainly not caused by demons. A demon would be explanatory overkill for why one was impatient, vain, or inclined to tell white lies. Only the truly bad guys doing truly bad things—non-Christians— were possessed of demons. The line separating the good Christians from the bad persecutors was clearly drawn *between* them, creating a sort of moral boundary that one could cross through repentance and conversion.

This notion of a moral boundary separating good from evil frames early Christian disputes about the meaning of Adam's sin. Was everybody evil in the same way or could sin emerge from entirely different sources? Were white lies and cruelty rooted in the same human flaw? Or could simple human imperfections account for the former, while the latter needed demons? Paul did connect Adam's sin to Christ's death, but the nature of this connection was ambiguous and admitted different interpretations of what happened when Adam sinned. It would be centuries before Augustine would explain this connection as "original sin," imputing Adam's transgression to everyone and moving the boundary between good and evil until it ran through everybody, and not merely between the good guys and the bad guys.

The key question was do we differ from the pre-Fall Adam because he sinned? Did he pass something down to us that makes it impossible for us to avoid sin? Or do we have the same chance to avoid sin as Adam did?

Early Christians were of two minds. On the one hand, we may all be like Adam and Eve in our capacity to resist temptation. The story of Adam may simply be *our* story, reflecting the real challenges—but not impossibility— of resisting temptation. Adam was a primordial Everyman, falling short despite his best intentions, a dramatization of what we would have done in his situation and what we must avoid in our situation.

On the other hand, God's response to Adam's sin was not confined to Adam. The ground was cursed. Abel the farmer must have had a harder time of it because of his father's sin, although no mention is made of this. Childbirth became painful for all women—not just Eve—and serpents were reduced to crawling on their bellies. Adam's descendants clearly lived in a different world and possibly were different from the first man. Did Adam do something that changed him in ways that were passed on to his descendants? Are we now powerless to resist temptation? Or are we still free to not sin, to live perfect lives, as the Genesis story suggests was the case for Adam?

The Hebrew scriptures suggest that Adam passed nothing on to his offspring. Subsequent sin—Cain's murder of Abel, the wickedness of Noah's generation, or the folly at the tower of Babel—is *never* described as inevitable. Adam's sin is never mentioned again in the Hebrew scriptures. Paul, as we have seen, embellishes the Adam story in ways that certainly stretch the authorial intent of the writer(s) of Genesis, but Paul nowhere suggests that Adam's unfortunate choice was made by a "pre-Fall" human. And, significantly, Paul also does not argue that subsequent human sin is *inevitable* because of what Adam did.[13]

Matthew, Mark, Luke, and John, the four "biographies" of Jesus written years after Paul's letters, all deal with good and evil, but they set up the tension as being between Satan and Christ, not between a sinful nature and the knowledge of good. Adam, in this light, is the first sinner only in the sense that Neil Armstrong was the first human to step onto the moon. Something extraordinary occurred when Armstrong took his "one small step for a man," but that event certainly did not transform humanity.

Celibacy as Freedom

Many early Christians felt empowered by the *freedom* they believed God had given to them at the creation. But Adam's sin made this freedom ambiguous. Was God's command to the first couple to "be fruitful and multiply," for example, a universal command that everyone must start a family or just a temporary mandate to get things started? Many assumed the latter, and avoided starting a family, lest they become entangled in the social order of a world they rejected.

So many aspects of this deeply personal freedom embraced by the first Christians have since been incorporated into Western society that we can easily overlook its initially radical character and thus overlook an important part of the Christian legacy. Who today considers it radical to enjoy the freedom of being single and childless? But such choices were once quite radical.

To appreciate this we must note what it meant to be a *person* in the Greco-Roman cultural matrix of early Christianity. This world was shaped by an ancient tradition that placed citizens within a social network that provided their identity and value based on their contributions to the common good. "A human being is a political animal," wrote Aristotle in his *Politics*, laying out blueprints for how people should relate to each other.[14]

People were born into social structures that defined their future roles; many believed it was in the natural order of things for certain people to be slaves, while nature intended others to be leaders. Prepubescent girls were promised to men they had not met; such marriages served sociopolitical functions; children, often many, were expected from married couples; family businesses or political offices would be thrust onto people and demand unreasonable levels of attention. This entangled web of responsibilities provided the identity of those born into it. These expectations were so universally accepted that abandoning them to chart one's own course was, quite literally, idiocy. Elaine Pagels writes, "In Greek, the term 'idiot' literally referred to a person concerned with personal or private matters . . . instead of the public and social life of the larger community."[15] In contrast, Christians saw themselves as citizens of another world, the kingdom of God. God, not the social order, gave them their identity. The significance of this otherworldly identity can be seen in the term *born again* that was used to describe one's conversion into it.

The New Testament constantly references "the world"—a world that Jesus and many early Christians believed was about to end. Jesus famously asked, "For what shall it profit a man, if he shall gain the whole world, and lose his own soul?"[16] "Do not love the world or the things in the world," commands the author of First John. "The love of the Father is not in those who love the world; for all that is in the world—the desire of the flesh, the desire of the eyes, the pride in riches—comes not from the Father but from the world. And the world and its desire are passing away, but those who do the will of God live forever."[17] Such injunctions encouraged Christians to liberate themselves from anything that prevented them from seeking God. When Jesus told the rich young ruler to "sell what you own, and give the money to the poor,"[18] he was not thinking only of the poor who would benefit from the donations. The great wealth of the young ruler was itself a prison from which he needed to be liberated.

Early Christian attitudes toward sex make sense only in the context of this call to freedom. Because Christians rejected contraception, abortion, infanticide, and homosexuality, there was no truly recreational sexual activity. Procreation and sex were intimately linked. To have sex was to invite the entanglements of parenthood. When Christians rejected sex—and most did not—it was not out of a prudish conviction that it was "dirty"; they were rejecting the larger world of responsibility that came with children and family, as well as keeping powerful and sometimes destructive temptations under control. They were, in the final analysis, not so much walking *away* from sex as they were walking *toward* personal freedom.

These early Christian attitudes were especially attractive to women, who were often born into heavily scripted lives controlled by men—lives dominated by the challenges and pains of bringing children into a world with appalling levels of infant and maternal mortality.

Consider the case of Gregory of Nyssa (335–ca. 395), who longed to escape the complex script of his life. Venerated as a saint, he was the bishop of Nyssa from 372 to 376 and from 378 until his death, and played a major role in developing the influential Nicene Creed. Gregory was married, wealthy, socially entangled—and frustrated by these barriers to seeking God. He understood the cost of raising a family, struggles experienced even more acutely by women:

> There is pain always, whether children are born, or can never be expected; whether they live or die. One person has many children, but not enough means to support them. . . . One man loses by death a beloved son; another has a reprobate son alive; both equally pitiable.[19]

The life idealized by Gregory, sought after by many and achieved by some, related ambiguously to the social blueprints God provided in Genesis. A controversy arose about how Christians should think about this. In celebrating their freedom to follow God, were ascetically inclined Christians disobeying God's command to "be fruitful and multiply"?

Celibacy for both genders was thus controversial and became even more so as the circumstances of Christians improved. After Christianity became an approved religion with significant social benefits, rejecting the world no longer had the same logical clarity. Christian commitment, in fact, required little actual *commitment*, as nominal believers joined the movement for personal gain rather than spiritual transformation. Many of these Christians began to argue that celibacy was a pointless sacrifice. One especially entertaining debate illuminates the way Christians on both sides of the celibacy question looked to the story of Adam and Eve to adjudicate the dispute.

The story takes place in Rome, at the end of the fourth century, after Christianity had become politically powerful. It had become clear that the end of the world was not imminent and, whatever Christ meant when he said he would return shortly in glory, he apparently did not mean shortly in any conventional sense. Practices that made sense in the short run—like selling all your possessions or avoiding having children—didn't seem quite so sensible for the long run. Christianity was becoming the establishment, attracting different adherents with different agendas and different levels of enthusiasm.

Ascetics and celibates, however, still retained their stature as the most authentic Christians and such withdrawal from the world continued to be widely endorsed, despite the Christianization of that world. A provocative quotation of Jesus in Matthew's Gospel supported the high value placed on abandoning the world: "For there are eunuchs who have been so from birth, and there are eunuchs who have been made eunuchs by others, and there are eunuchs who have made themselves eunuchs for the sake of the kingdom of heaven. *Let anyone accept this who can.*"[20] There was also, of course, a sense of adventure in heading off to live a life of spiritual contemplation. A few celebrated examples of wealthy Christians renouncing their fortunes and heading into the desert seeking God inspired more of the same, especially among young people. Ascetics occasionally returned to civilization with grand tales of self-discovery, spiritual engagement, and encounters with God. Not surprisingly, such tales sometimes motivated children from well-connected Christian families to renounce the plans their parents had made for them to become part of *the world*.

Something like this happened to Jerome, born around 347, who studied as a youth in Rome. Although baptized as a Christian, Jerome was reckless, with behaviors that often required dramatic repentance, which he sought by visiting the sepulchers of the martyrs. He even lived for a couple of years in a cave and returned to civilization with horror stories: "I used to sit alone, because my heart was filled with bitterness," he wrote in a letter to his friend Eustochium. "Day after day I cried and sighed."[21]

Back in Rome after his failed stint as a hermit, the brilliant Jerome became secretary to Pope Damasus I, the first pope to embrace the opulent splendor that soon characterized the Vatican. Jerome also became a spiritual advisor to some socially important women. One of them, Paula, was wealthy—and possibly Jerome's lover.[22] In a letter written in 384, Jerome encourages Paula's daughter Eustochium to view her virgin status—the symbol of celibacy—as a mark of spiritual superiority, even over her married sister Blaesilla. The letter acknowledges that celibacy brings hardship and loneliness, and Eustochium is told to "nightly wash your bed and water your couch with your tears." But note Jerome's curious attempt to ground his celibacy recommendation in the experience of Eve:

> Say to yourself: What have I to do with the pleasures of sense that so soon come to an end? What have I to do with the song of the sirens so sweet and so fatal to those who hear it? I would not have you subject to that sentence whereby condemnation has been passed upon mankind. When God says to Eve, In pain and in sorrow you shall bring forth children, say to yourself, That is a law for a married woman, not for me. And when He continues, Your desire shall be to your husband, say again: Let her desire be to her husband who has not Christ for her spouse. And when, last of all, He says, You shall surely die, once more, say, Marriage indeed must end in death; but the life on which I have resolved is independent of sex.[23]

In this passage Jerome transforms Eden into a paradise of virginity, arguing that the curse on women is actually a curse on those who *forsake* virginity and accept the spiritually inferior life of the family. The admonition "Let her desire be to her husband who has not Christ for her spouse" is especially dramatic. Jerome is stating that women must choose between Christ and a husband. In articulating this viewpoint three centuries after Paul had penned the letters linking Adam to Christ, Jerome expressed the widely held view that the consequences of Adam's sin were born by Adam himself. A woman could avoid these consequences simply by choosing a lifetime of celibacy: no children—no pain of childbirth. Everyone gets the same choice as Adam and Eve to avoid sin and the curse.

Critics challenged Jerome. Concerns grew about the spiritual value and even the wisdom of abandoning a world that few believed was run by demons. The challenges came to a head in a polemic penned by a celibate monk named Jovinian and delivered to Jerome in his austere monk's lodging. Like Jerome, Jovinian had once shaved his head and wandered barefoot in the desert, avoiding meat, wine, and women. Also like Jerome, he grew weary of that life and reentered society. But, unlike Jerome, Jovinian developed serious questions about the value of renouncing the world. Did God *really* think virgins were better than faithful wives raising children? Was avoiding good food and wine *really* better than enjoying it and being thankful to God? Was heaven *really* arranged so that those most deprived in this life enjoyed a higher place in the next?

Jovinian, as was typical for Christians navigating the world of sex, invoked the story of Adam and Eve, noting that God had commanded the first couple to be fruitful and multiply. God also appeared to bless the cycle of life in which "a man leaves his father and his mother and clings to his wife, and they become one flesh."[24] Jovinian's polemic enraged powerful leaders who had become invested in a tradition that praised celibacy. Pope Siricius excommunicated him and had his writings destroyed (we know his ideas only as quoted in Jerome's response).

Jerome assaulted Jovinian viciously, arguing that his words were those of the devil. Jovinian, he writes, says that "virgins, widows, and married women, who have been once passed through the laver of Christ, if they are on a par in other respects, are of equal merit." Calling him an "Epicurus," Jerome attacked Jovinian's claim "that there is no difference between abstinence from food, and its reception with thanksgiving." He objects to Jovinian's egalitarian claim "that there is one reward in the kingdom of heaven for all who have kept their baptismal vow." If true, this implied that there was no special divine favor for those making extreme sacrifices.

Jerome insults Jovinian's arguments as the "hissing of the old serpent," alluding to the shadowy tempter in Eden, and suggests that by arguments like this "the dragon drove man from Paradise." Jerome interprets the invitation to eat the forbidden fruit in Eden as though the indulgence signified the ending of a fast, yet another completely new—and far-fetched—application of the story: "For he promised that if they would prefer fullness to fasting they should be immortal, as though it were an impossibility for them to fall." This is certainly an ingenious defense of self-deprivation. Jerome then glorifies the primordial state of Adam and Eve, free of social and parental obligations, and calls the primordial couple "unhampered." Freedom from such "hampering," as we have seen, was a motivation for celibacy. "While he promises they shall be as Gods, he drives them from Paradise, with the result that they who, while naked and unhampered, and as virgins unspotted enjoyed the fellowship of the Lord were cast down into the vale of tears, and sewed skins together to clothe themselves withal."[25]

Jerome goes on at some length, heaping coals of rhetorical fire on poor Jovinian's head, twisting and proof-texting scripture as he builds an elaborate fence to keep these ideas away from a Christianity that had come to celebrate celibacy, self-denial, and radical austerity as the most appropriate paths to God.

THE STORY OF Adam and Eve continued to be socially normative for Christians, despite its ambiguities and contradictory interpretations. God created people to be a certain way, to act like this and not like that, to follow these rules and not those—and we get this from Genesis, argued Jerome, Jovinian, and everyone else in the conversation.

Jovinian's responses were also exercises in twisting and proof-texting scripture. His arguments ignore comments made by both Jesus and Paul affirming the ascetic life, although neither one condemned marriage. (Jesus and Paul both seem to have believed that the world was going to end shortly, which probably shaped their views of social life.)

This, of course, is the nature of the maturing Christian tradition. Charismatic leaders articulate visions that capture the imagination of a generation. New understandings emerge that must be rooted in scriptures that never spoke to those issues or did so with great ambiguity. New social considerations need new blueprints. Ambiguity quickly becomes a theologian's best friend, creating imaginative space to read new agendas into ancient texts, to make them speak with authority to new problems.

The moral chasm between Christians and the world in which they lived closed over the course of the first few centuries. The closure came from movement in two directions. The first was that a Christianity without social benefits became a comfortable religious home for the less dedicated and more opportunistic; as a result Christians were often less holy and saw little need to think of themselves as separate from the world. The second was that a state—the formerly maligned world—with no intention to persecute Christians seemed far less evil and its agents no longer possessed by demons. The line between morally upright nonbelievers and nominal believers grew increasingly hard to find in a world where belief was often convenient and rarely required sacrifice. Dramatic exorcisms no longer accompanied the conversion of new believers. Embracing a state-sanctioned religion, as Christianity came to be, was like joining a big club. For those born into it, it was hardly more dramatic than learning to walk. Gone were the days when following Jesus implied putting one's life—or anything else—on the altar. Not surprisingly, this led to new challenges in understanding human nature and how that nature was or was not affected by what had transpired in Eden.

⌒

CHAPTER 4

THE ORIGINAL SINNER

Augustine's Attack on Adam as Everyman

Lord make me pure, but not yet!

—AUGUSTINE[1]

An important part of the narrative about Adam and Eve ends with Augustine of Hippo (354–430), probably the most influential Christian in the Western church after Paul. Between the lines of the Genesis story and in the writings of Paul, Augustine sees with clarity something that few had discerned only vaguely, if at all—original sin. The doctrine of original sin, as Augustine would articulate it, was so compelling that his successors, including millions of Christians today, fear their faith would collapse without it. It would become the Genesis story's most important legacy.

Augustine's reflections are those of a mature, intellectually informed thinker. By the fourth century, Christianity had survived and become the dominant worldview, one that Augustine embraced after years of frustration seeking truth in other precincts. He labored to establish Christianity's philosophical breadth, intellectual depth, and logical coherence; to explain the significance, function, and necessity of its rituals; to reject heresies; to incorporate external philosophical notions like free will; to show how the sacred related to the secular and how the "city of God" should imagine itself; to engage questions of natural philosophy like the shape of the earth and scold those who would use the Bible to support nonsense about the natural world—in short, to show that the Christian understanding of the world was simply the way things were, superior to all other explanatory schemes, appropriately exhaustive and intellectually satisfying. The task was daunting, with lots of pieces that had to fit together, but Augustine was so successful that the leaders who followed him, both sacred and secular, used his work as a blueprint for how God intended things to be. He was a "pervasive and enduring influence well into the modern period . . . and even up to the present day."[2] We can even say that much of American Christianity's rejection of evolution can be blamed on Augustine establishing original sin and the Fall at the center of Christian theology.

The power of Augustine's argument for original sin comes from the synergy between distinct issues on which he brings it to bear. First, Augustine affirms the Catholic Church's doctrine that the salvation offered by Christ could only be found through the church, specifically through the sacrament of Christian baptism. Other routes to salvation, like good works or generous philanthropy, would imply that Christ died in vain. Infant baptism derived from this doctrine. If there was no route to salvation outside "one baptism for the remission of sins," as the Nicene Creed puts it, then even newborns needed to be baptized.

The high level of infant mortality that persisted until the nineteenth century demanded that baptisms occur soon after birth and, when the fetus's life was in danger, even in the womb. The question arises, however, about the reason why—as most people seemed to believe—God would not allow babies that died in childbirth into heaven. Clearly they had committed no sin, so they could not be condemned on the basis of their own actions. On the other hand, if they had somehow inherited Adam's sin through their parents, then God could not accept them into heaven until that sin—their *original sin*—was washed away. Original sin made sense of infant baptism.

Second, Augustine notes that babies are born with deformities and disease, and often into situations of abuse. Since God would not subject sinless creatures to such suffering, they must be born with the sin that leads to such misfortune. Original sin made sense of newborn suffering. A third, and essentially empirical, argument for original sin comes from the observation that as babies mature, sin reveals itself in their actions. They commit many sins on their own and even find themselves unable to avoid temptations when they know better, as if they were powerless to choose the good. Augustine had been promiscuous in his younger days and knew temptation firsthand. Original sin made sense of human depravity.

Finally Augustine makes a biblical argument based largely but not exclusively on an unfortunate mistranslation in the Vulgate, a Latin version of the Bible that Pope Damasus I had commissioned Jerome to translate in 382. Augustine notes that Paul wrote in his letter to the Romans that "sin came into the world through one man, and death came through sin, and so death spread to all, *in whom* all have sinned."[3] Original sin made sense of this passage. Most scholars agree with Augustine's fourth-century critics, however, that this passage should have been translated, as the New Revised Standard Version (NRSV) does today: "Death spread to all *because* all have sinned." Much turns on this difference. For Augustine, all humans are somehow *in* Adam, participating in his sin, and thus are born with this original sin rendering them corrupt and unworthy of salvation.[4] Even worse, their mental and spiritual faculties are so impaired that they cannot even seek the good on their own, but only as God selectively bestows grace on them, inexplicably inviting some but not others to salvation. This gratuitous divine election by which God plucks certain individuals off the pathway to hell was a controversial theological innovation that, despite making God appear arbitrary and capricious, took root and flourished in much of Western Christianity.[5]

The controversy about original sin was a controversy about Adam and how his descendants should understand what he did and how it relates to them. To this point, as we have seen, interpretations of Adam were varied and depended largely on how one nuanced their understanding of freedom.

Consider the case of Gregory, the influential bishop we met in the last chapter who lamented the burdens imposed by family, from which he longed to be free so that he could seek God with all his heart. Gregory described the world God created in Genesis as a palace prepared for Adamic royalty that would rule itself by its own will. He offers the following upbeat description:

> When, then, the Maker of all had prepared beforehand, as it were, a royal lodging for the future king (and this was the land, and islands, and sea, and the heaven arching like a roof over them), and when all kinds of wealth had been stored in this palace (and by wealth I mean the whole creation, all that is in plants and trees, and all that has sense, and breath, and life; and—if we are to account materials also as wealth—all that for their beauty are reckoned precious in the eyes of men, as gold and silver, and the substances of your jewels which men delight in—having concealed, I say, abundance of all these also in the bosom of the earth as in a royal treasure-house), he thus manifests man in the world . . . to be the beholder of some of the wonders therein, and the lord of others; that by

his enjoyment he might have knowledge of the Giver, and by the beauty and majesty of the things he saw might trace out that power of the Maker which is beyond speech and language. . . .

For as in our own life artificers fashion a tool in the way suitable to its use, so the best Artificer made our nature as it were a formation fit for the exercise of royalty, preparing it at once by superior advantages of soul, and by the very form of the body, to be such as to be adapted for royalty: for the soul immediately shows its royal and exalted character, far removed as it is from the lowliness of private station, in that it owns no lord, and is self-governed, swayed autocratically by its own will; for to whom else does this belong than to a king?[6]

Gregory's celebration of his "royal and exalted character" that was "self-governed" resonated with many—if not most—of the path-breaking early Christians. They considered their ability to rule themselves in a context of moral freedom to be at the heart of their faith—"virtually synonymous with 'the gospel,'" as Pagels puts it.[7] This freedom was not destroyed by Adam's actions in Eden. Adam chose to sin, but that was his choice and his alone. They were not born in sin and, while they might choose to sin, the decision was theirs to make and not forced upon them by a corrupt and fallen will. Adam lived among these early Christians as an Everyman, a moral example and encouragement to virtue, but not the ruler of their passions.

This view was far from an orthodoxy, of course. Many notions about Adam peacefully coexisted because where one stood on this question didn't yet matter. Christianity was about salvation through Christ. One cannot speak of an orthodoxy per se in the first three centuries of Christianity, for orthodoxies typically arise through the elimination of heresy, and elimination of heresy is not the highest priority for believers concerned about their own elimination.

It would be a mistake in the other direction, however, to suppose that no concerns about the content of belief troubled anyone. Paul's letters show the prolific apostle weighing in on theological disputes like the authenticity of the bodily resurrection of Jesus or accepting Gentiles into the faith. Elsewhere in early Christian writings we encounter extensive discussion about the relationship of Christianity to Judaism, the nature of Jesus, the role of women, the status of unbaptized infants, and other doctrinal ambiguities.[8]

By the time of Augustine, however, Christianity was a powerful institution with a maturing sense of its foundations and a concern to determine and enforce uniform understandings and eliminate heresies. One by one, various theological controversies erupted, often in response to idiosyncratic local issues. And so we find on the agenda at the end of the fourth century a controversy about Adam and how his descendants relate to him.

AUGUSTINE ESTABLISHES ADAM, once and for all, and in a most compelling way for the Western church, as both the *original sinner* and the *source of original sin*. In the latter role, Augustine's Adam is far more important than Moses, Abraham, John the Baptist, and even Paul. In Augustine's theology and the traditions that follow him, Christ is the only character in the entire Bible with a more significant role than Adam. In fact, the Bible becomes a story about Adam and Christ, with everyone else fading into supporting roles. Christians in the Western tradition could not read the story of Adam and Eve as anything other than the story of our species', our planet's, and all creation's fall into sin. The Hebrew scriptures become for Christians the Old Testament, no longer understood on their own Hebraic terms but only through the lenses of Christian interpretation.

Two things stand out here: first, Augustine interprets, defines, and, to a degree, even creates an Adam different from the one his predecessors found in the Genesis story. This Adam is not Everyman; he is *Über*man, with the power to spread sin to all creation. Second, the idea of a historical, happened-in-time-and-space Fall to explain the origin of sin and evil becomes such a central theological idea that Adam's role in it demands his historicity, even as the historicity of the Genesis creation story is questioned in the eighteenth century, challenged in the nineteenth, and rejected on scientific grounds in the twentieth. A historical Adam who "fell" stands like a solitary, impregnable tower secured by theological guy wires against the winds of the historical, biblical, and scientific investigation eroding the landscape around him.

Much of the attraction to Augustine's ideas about sin is rooted in the depth of his insights into the human predicament—or at least his experience of this predicament. He shares his remarkable journey in *The Confessions*, an important work written as the fourth century was coming to a close. Seventeen centuries later *The Confessions* remains on the reading list at universities around the world: volume 18 in the Great Books of the Western World, alongside Plato, Shakespeare, and Newton.

The Confessions is the story of a brilliant, educated, and restless young man searching for truth in pagan religions and philosophy, and eventually converting to Christianity at age twenty-eight. Readers cannot help but be drawn into Augustine's ruthlessly honest and introspective exploration of his struggles to choose the good, to do what he knows is best, and refrain from what he knows is wrong. If you identify with Augustine's struggles—as millions do—he seems psychologically profound. For readers who find his struggles overdone and his guilt excessive, he can seem neurotic and hopelessly prudish about sex. What cannot be denied, however, is that he convincingly explores the challenge of being human—how hard it is to follow our best instincts, how easy to follow our worst. For Augustine our best instincts call us to follow God. "My soul's house is narrow for you to enter," he writes in the opening pages of *The Confessions*, addressing God, "will you not make it broader? It is in a state of collapse; will you not rebuild it?"[9]

Augustine's confession begins with a lament that he cannot recall "the sin I did in my infancy."[10] He confesses that he "sinned in acting contrary to the commands of my parents and those of my schoolmasters."[11] But the real power of his confession emerges when he comes of age sexually and "was on fire to take my fill of hell." Uncontrollable urges caused him to be "swept over the precipices of desire and thrust into the whirlpools of vice." "I boiled over in my fornications," he recalls, and later lamented that he "should have become a *eunuch for the kingdom of heaven's sake.*"[12] He complains that nobody tried to "save me from falling by getting me married," when he was sixteen and consumed by the "madness of lust."

Such laments about the widely shared nature of sexual temptation dominate *The Confessions*. But Augustine's other comments about less salacious sins are more insightful, as he seems to see, as few had before, the moral complexity of all sorts of human motivations. Consider this anecdote about the youthful indiscretion of stealing some pears from a neighbor:

Near our vineyard there was a pear tree, loaded with fruit, though the fruit was not particularly attractive either in color or taste. I and some other wretched youths conceived the idea of shaking the pears of this tree and carrying them away. We set out late at night (having, as we usually did in our depraved way, gone playing in the streets till that hour) and stole all the fruit that we could carry. And this was not to feed ourselves; we may have tasted a few, but then we threw the rest to the pigs. *Our real pleasure was simply in doing something that was not allowed.*[13]

Or this one about the vanity of trying to impress others:

> I pursued my studies of the books of eloquence, a subject in which I longed to make a name for myself, though my reason for this was damnable and mere wind, being simply joy in human vanity.[14]

Augustine's quest, as he recalls after his salvation, was always for God, but even after finding God he was consistently distracted. Sometimes he was "moved more by the singing than what is sung," a state of affairs he described as "sinning grievously."[15] Conversation with friends could quickly spawn a "serious interest in their gossip."[16] And we are all possessed of a morbid and "dangerous" curiosity to seek out and experience the darker parts of life, which Augustine calls the *"lust of the eyes."*[17] This "lust to find out and to know" attracts us not only to the good things in life but also—inexplicably and against our better judgment—to terrible things. Perhaps recalling the sordid entertainment of the Roman forums, in which people were killed for sport, he writes:

> What pleasure can there be in looking at a mangled corpse, which must excite our horror? Yet if there is one near, people flock to see it, so as to grow sad and pale at the sight. They are actually frightened of seeing it in their sleep, as though anyone had forced them to see it when they were awake.[18]

Such insights into the paradoxical character of human nature overwhelmed Augustine. A few pages before he describes his conversion to Christianity he thanks God for giving him a look at just how twisted he was:

> But you, Lord . . . were turning me around so that I could see myself; you took me from behind my own back, which was where I had put myself during the time when I did not want to be observed by myself, and set me in front of my own face so that I could see how foul a sight I was—crooked, filthy, spotted, and ulcerous. I saw and I was horrified.[19]

Augustine was convinced he had two distinct wills within him—one pushing him to choose the right and another more powerful one pulling him to the dark side. He calls the moral dysfunctionality of these "two wills" a "sickness of the soul."[20] Hear the anguish in his voice as he recalls his struggle to accept Christianity, and his acknowledgment of Adam's role:

> I fought with myself and was torn apart by myself. It was against my will that this tearing apart took place, but this was not an indication that I had another mind of different nature; it was simply the punishment which I was suffering in my own mind. It was not I, therefore, who caused it, but *the sin dwells in me*, and, being a son of Adam, I was suffering for his sin which was more freely committed.[21]

Augustine's eventual conversion was motivated by a mysterious child's voice that called to him: "Take it and read it. Take it and read it."[22] He picked up a nearby copy of Paul's letter to the Romans and, in an act repeated by millions of Christians looking for God to speak directly to them from the Bible, "read in silence the passage upon which my eyes first fell: *Not in rioting and drunkenness, not in chambering and wantonness, not in strife and envying: but put ye on the Lord Jesus Christ, and make not provision for the flesh in concupiscence.*"[23]

Can one imagine a biblical passage that could have spoken to the troubled young man with more power? "I had no wish to read further," he writes, "there was no need to." The future bishop's heart was "filled with a light of confidence and all the shadows of [his] doubt were swept away."[24]

I HAVE DWELT at some length on Augustine's spiritual journey because of the central role it came to play in interpreting the story of Adam and Eve, the way it shaped subsequent reflection on human freedom, and the unprecedented influence of the narrative. I also think it worth noting at this point— and I will return to this in the conclusion—that the modern scientific view of the human personality resonates with much of what Augustine wrote. Although we would not speak in terms of *sin* and *fallenness* as Augustine did, scientists today would certainly affirm that the human will is deeply troubled and must be kept in check. As I write these words Islamic terrorists are posting videos of beheadings on YouTube, where vast audiences are viewing them, with the same morbid curiosity that drew Romans to the Coliseum. How are we to understand this? Do we have a better explanation than that something in human nature is deeply twisted? Can anyone claim today that following our best instincts is a simple matter of making good choices—something anyone can do?

Augustine felt possessed of a broken will that drove him in directions he did not want to go. Or worse—he wanted to go in all sorts of directions that he knew he shouldn't. In his youth he had famously prayed "Make me chaste and continent, but not yet."[25] But Augustine did not think for one moment that he was uniquely afflicted. Time after time he explains his own failings as a universal part of the human condition—the "bond of original sin whereby we all die in Adam."[26] Augustine's reflections on his condition are eerily similar to those of Paul in his letter to the Romans, and he probably understood what Paul was saying in ways others had not:

> I do not understand my own actions. For I do not do what I want, but I do the very thing I hate. Now if I do what I do not want, I agree that the law is good. But in fact it is no longer I that do it, but sin that dwells within me. For I know that nothing good dwells within me, that is, in my flesh. I can will what is right, but I cannot do it. For I do not do the good I want, but the evil I do not want is what I do. Now if I do what I do not want, it is no longer I that do it, but sin that dwells within me.
>
> So I find it to be a law that when I want to do what is good, evil lies close at hand. For I delight in the law of God in my inmost self, but I see in my members another law at war with the law of my mind, making me captive to the law of sin that dwells in my members. Wretched man that I am! Who will rescue me from this body of death? [27]

Reading this passage in Romans through the lens of human depravity that Augustine ground so fine makes it hard to conclude that Augustine pulled the idea of original sin out of thin air, or invented it, as is often claimed.[28] It may not have been the most widely embraced understanding, but it is hardly disconnected from previous reflections on the nature of Adam's sin. Perhaps it was seen "through a glass darkly" and Augustine simply cleaned the glass. On the other hand, influential Catholic Christian leaders rejected Augustine's ideas, and one vast segment of the Christian Church, the Eastern (or Greek) Orthodox tradition that today dominates Asian Christianity—and is fully separated from Catholicism—has not to this day accepted Augustine's theology of original sin.

In the Christian West, however, where our story takes place in the midst of a growing and enduring emphasis on orthodoxy, Augustine's arguments precipitated a major theological controversy that created one of

Christianity's most important heresies. The heresy is known today as Pelagianism. Like most heresies, its original champions—Gregory, Jovinian—were simply Christians trying to understand their faith and coming
to a viewpoint that, when challenged, lost and was rejected as heretical by
the winners, either formally through some official ecclesiastical review or
informally by simply being rejected by one's community of faith.

The Christian tradition is a long conversation of this sort. Beginning
in the first century—and seen clearly in the writings of Paul—questions
arise in specific contexts. In the New Testament we see discussion of things
like the status of Gentiles, the place of women in the church, the ongoing
relevance of Jewish dietary rules, and so on. These were immediate concerns brought to the forefront by circumstances. If a Gentile asked to join
a house church, someone had to decide if that was okay. Until crises force
resolutions on communities, diverse beliefs coexist peacefully. Rev. Betty
can preach without controversy until someone complains that women are
not supposed to be preachers.

The Pelagian controversy—which became the Pelagian heresy—had
to do with the question we have been exploring about human free will. Pelagius (390–418) was an upbeat, pious, ascetic, and impressive Christian
who lived in Rome and then Palestine. His ideas embroiled him in constant
controversy, making it hard to figure out exactly what he thought about
the many positions he defended before hostile interrogators in ecclesiastical
courts—circumstances where obfuscation was often prudent.

Pelagius is also just the central—and perhaps not even the most important—voice of the condemned movement bearing his name. He was actually
not that interested in dogma—many pastors are not—which accounts for
some of the difficulty in understanding what he thought. His ideas were
stated with greater clarity by a controversial priest named Celestius, who
seemed to Augustine to be "declaring openly what was Pelagius's real but
unacknowledged doctrine."[29] A more sophisticated theologian named Julian of Eclanum is actually considered the architect of Pelagianism. Julian
was a younger theologian who had been mentored by Augustine. Nevertheless, he mounted a powerful assault on his aging mentor's claims about
original sin. He was the last of Augustine's many unsuccessful challengers.

The Pelagians' central concern—reasonable and pastoral—was that
Christians not be overwhelmed with sin to the point of hopelessness, par-
alyzing despair, and defeatist resignation. The idea that Adam had turned
us all into morally helpless and thoroughly depraved creatures, and our
world into a carnival of travails, was depressing. This was hardly "good

news," as Christianity came to label its message. Nor was it Pelagius's personal experience or his vision for Christianity. The Christian faith should empower believers with triumphant joy, said Pelagius, not the sort of depression that ran down the pages of Augustine's *Confessions*. One scholar describes Pelagius as a fourth-century "motivational speaker," the "Tony Robbins of his time, full of exhortation and encouragement: 'You can *do* it! You can *be* like Christ!'"[30]

So what happened when Adam sinned? For Pelagius, Adam's sin was nothing more than a sin committed by Adam, the first man, and not all that different from sins we might commit. Just as Adam had a real choice to avoid sin and remain in a state of perfection, so we have a choice. Pelagius even believed that there probably had been people who avoided sin before Christ. Infants were not born in a state of sin but rather innocence; with proper discipline they could enjoy lives of sinless perfection. The occasional fall from perfection was not a problem, as long as one got back on track.

The Pelagians noted, quite reasonably, that the New Testament was full of exhortations to be "holy" and "perfect," and to rise to great moral heights: to "love your enemy" and "pray for those who abuse you." If such things are not possible, then why are Jesus and Paul commanding us to do them? Do we not make a mockery of Jesus's commands when we respond by wailing about human depravity, universal sin, and the impossibility of choosing the good? "To call a person to something he considers impossible does him no good," wrote Pelagius.[31]

Julian objected in particular to the claim that God would curse an innocent planet because of the sin of one man. Why should fish swim in cursed waters and birds nest in cursed trees because of what Adam did? Why would bushes sprout thorns and meadows fill with noxious weeds because of human sin? What kind of God would respond to a wrongheaded choice by one of his creatures with such hyperbole, especially since God had set up the temptation in the Garden of Eden in the first place? Surely the various features of nature that we encounter—including our own mortality— are simply the way things are. Hear Augustine reporting the views of the "abominable and damnable"[32] Julian:

> [Julian claims] "our mortality is not the result of sin, but of nature! Why does Genesis not say, 'because you sinned and transgressed my precepts'? This should have been said, if bodily dissolution were connected with a crime. But recall, what does it say? 'because you are earth.' Surely this is

the reason why one returns to earth, 'because you were taken out of it.' If this, then, is the reason God gives, that one was from earth, I think it can be assumed that one cannot blame sin. Without doubt it is not because of sin, but because of our mortal nature . . . that the body dissolves back into the elements."[33]

The Pelagians saw the creation—including the pervasive human attraction to sex that troubled Augustine—as *good* and human beings as *innocent*. But we are confronted with moral choices and called to exercise our freedom wisely. Adam chose unwisely and became the first sinner. He was a *bad* example but, as Celestius argued, Adam's sin "injured only him, not the human race."[34] In contrast, Jesus made better choices, lived a life of moral perfection, and calls us to the same. He was a *good* example. Jesus and Adam are linked, as Paul said, but only as contrasting examples, not as cosmic moral forces. Christians follow Jesus because he inspires them to make moral choices, not because he disables original sin.

The Pelagians handled the Bible like other Christians: it was God's word and normative for their understanding of their faith. But because the message of that Bible is piecemeal and inconsistent they saw different things in its pages. Like Augustine, they brought their concerns and personalities to the conversation and—also like Augustine—they read their personal experiences into the text. Where Augustine, consumed by uncontrollable lusts, found sex to be an unwelcome "diabolical excitement of the genitals,"[35] Julian, who appears to have had more manageable personal experiences, found in sex just another opportunity to freely make moral choices, which it appears he did.

Pelagian ideas were popular and embraced by many Christians at the time. The Eastern Orthodox tradition prefers them to this day over the pessimistic alternatives offered by Augustine. But in the Christian West where Catholicism and eventually Protestantism dominated and where our story is taking place, Pelagianism was rejected and with it certain options for accommodating the story of Adam and Eve to our ongoing understanding of ourselves and our origins. By attaching original sin so tightly to a historically real Adam, Augustine made it impossible for Adam to disappear from history without taking an important doctrine with him.

The rejection of Pelagianism was not, like so many of Christianity's internal conflicts, an exclusively theological affair, and it was not resolved with purely intellectual tools. Politics played a role, perhaps a large one. The quarrel between the venerable Augustine and the brash upstart Julian of Eclanum—both bishops—occurred in precincts as congenial to Christianity as much of America's Bible Belt is today. The influential Augustine enlisted the emperor's support in the conflict; as a bribe for his lobby against Pelagius, he arranged for eighty stallions to be delivered to the imperial court to ensure that the doctrine of original sin would endure.

Pelagius, Christianity's infamous champion of freedom, was excommunicated in 418, condemned by the emperor, and expelled. He died soon after.[36] Augustine's battle with the younger Julian continued but that challenge was soon dismantled until today all we know of Julian's writings are what Augustine quoted in his attacks on him. By the time the African bishop had finished with the Pelagian heresy it was relegated, at least in the West, to an ignominious historical footnote.

It is fitting that the period once known as the Dark Ages emerged at the same time Augustine's gloomy vision of both human nature and nature in general was spreading as orthodoxy throughout Western Christianity. A created order once celebrated by Christians and even affirmed by God himself as "good" became a vale of tears. The robust freedom that had empowered martyrs to choose death over compromise mutated into a twisted and perverted will that was only marginally free, if it was free at all. The sexual act at the center of both love and procreation became the locus of evil—the conduit by which the cursed Adamic nature was passed on to the next generation. The simple sound of a baby's cry ceased to be an innocent call for attention and became instead the signature of its fallen nature, demanding an immediate and unwelcome baptism.

Astronomers tell us that the climate during these so-called Dark Ages actually got a bit colder, as if the sun, on behalf of nature as a whole, was expressing its disapproval.

CHAPTER 5

THE LATE MIDDLE AGES
Adam Everywhere

*The world picture which the Middle Ages inherited was
that of an ordered universe arranged in a fixed system of
hierarchies, but modified by man's sin.*

—E. M. W. TILLYARD[1]

Augustine was frightened by the darkness he discovered within himself
and overwhelmed by the evil outside. His frustrating quest to make
sense of good and evil ended when he found in the story of Adam and Eve
an explanation for all that was wrong. Millions of Christians have read that
story through Augustine's lenses, as though that cryptic text can mean only
what Augustine said it meant. Interestingly, many Protestant fundamentalists, for whom *Catholic* is often a bad word and Augustine no hero, interpret
Genesis as Augustine taught them to, all the while denying they are doing
anything beyond reading in the most "natural" way, with no assist from a
wayward Catholic bishop.[2]

Augustine embedded Adam's original sin deeply within all of us. Adam
could never again be Everyman for Christians in the Western tradition.
The loss of that ordinariness transformed Adam into a superman destined
to grow steadily in importance.

As we enter the thirteenth century, the power and influence of the Roman Catholic Church is on the rise. The faith is secure, confident, universal; everyone that matters in the Western world is a Christian; the pope is
revered as God's representative; Christian theology—the "Queen of the
Sciences"—is the starting point from which all explorations begin. And

no part of this invigorated theology is enlarged more than the original sin of the first man. Adam's baleful influence reaches up into the heavens and down into the bowels of the earth, as theologians and artists develop an imaginative and dramatic "Christian" understanding of the cosmos. Linguists ponder the problem of languages by searching for clues to the divine language shared by Adam and God in the Garden of Eden; newly encountered global languages are inspected for clues that they might be descended from the divine language, or even be that language. Global exploration raises questions about the location of the Garden of Eden; most scholars are certain it still exists, and more than one explorer claims to find it.

Thomas Aquinas (1225–1274) is the central figure in this new chapter of our story. The greatest theologian of the thirteenth and possibly any century, Aquinas's theological revolution created space for an embryonic science by recognizing that it could be used to support belief in God. Once again the context has changed and we confront the question of Adam and what happened at the Fall. Aquinas argued that, while Adam's fall had indeed impaired the human *will*, as Augustine claimed, it had not dramatically compromised human *reason*. We can thus apply our reason to the study of nature—natural philosophy—and discern God's grand cosmic plan. Aquinas's more optimistic interpretation of the Fall, as well as new ideas about astronomy and mathematics from Islam, empowered an unprecedented creativity as artists, philosophers, architects, poets, and mathematicians engaged the world with a sense of empowerment rather than Augustinian despair. The results were breathtaking cathedrals, elaborate theological systems, and epic literature like that of Chaucer and Dante— and an even more deeply rooted conviction that the first man was the key to understanding the world.

Aristotle's Almost-Christian Cosmos

Adam's starring role in the worldview of the late Middle Ages is entwined in provocative ways with one of the most important, although ultimately wrong, ideas in Western intellectual history—the notion that the cosmos is divided into two distinct realities: a corrupt, imperfect earthly realm and a perfect, unchanging heavens.

The story begins at a school established in the fifth century BCE by Pythagoras on the island of Samos in the Mediterranean, some two thousand miles northwest of where some scholars think Eden was located. Readers may recall Pythagoras's famous theorem about the sides of a triangle.

He also discovered that music had mathematical foundations. But his most far-reaching insight grew from his reflections on the contrast between the *perfection of mathematics in the abstract* versus the *imperfection of mathematics in reality*.

Triangles illustrate this contrast. Readers who paid attention in geometry class will recall with certainty that the interior angles of a triangle add up to exactly 180 degrees. This is not an approximation or an average.

Now consider an *actual* triangle that you might draw. If you *measure* the angles inside the triangle and add them, you will get a number *around* 180.00 degrees but rarely ever *exactly* 180.00. No matter how carefully you draw your *actual* triangle, it will never be as perfect as the *abstract* triangle of geometry. Unevenness in the paper, smeared lines, imperfect rulers, and other factors conspire to make actual triangles in the real world fall short of the perfection of their counterparts in the world of abstract mathematics.

Pythagoras posited two worlds to make sense of this—a *perfect* world, accessible through our powers of rationality (by studying geometry, for example) and populated by eternal mathematical truths that we can *understand* but never *reproduce* in their flawless glory—and the *imperfect* world outside our windows and on our desks where those same entities exist in a lesser form. The ability to imagine this perfect world and freely manipulate mathematical entities within it accounts for the attraction that mathematics holds for many people.

Pythagoras's reflections on these two worlds led him to *dualism*. When taken up by Plato, four centuries before the Common Era, this dualism would become perhaps the most influential idea in all Western philosophy. The great philosopher Bertrand Russell declared Pythagoras "intellectually one of the most important men who ever lived."[3] Four centuries into the Common Era, Augustine was so enamored of Plato's dualism that he declared the pagan philosopher to be God's "apostle," convinced that God had inspired him.[4] Plato and his many followers extended dualism until the perfect eternal world expanded to include concepts of justice, love, and many other things. Platonism, as it is known, still commands the allegiance of many of our brightest minds.[5]

Plato explains dualism in his famous Allegory of the Cave. Picture, he said, people forever constrained to watch a cave wall filled with shadows cast by objects behind them they cannot see directly. They see grey shadows of chairs, tables, and other familiar objects. They assume the shadows are the things themselves, because they cannot turn around to the light, and have never seen anything but these shadows. They know nothing of the three-dimensional and brightly colored real objects casting the shadows. Their shadowy reality is a pitiful emulation of a more real world.

The nature of this perfect world and its relationship to the imperfect physical world occupied Plato and many philosophers who came after him down to the present; many novel applications were found. Augustine, to take one example, located the perfect world of unchanging ideas in the mind of God—the source of divine revelation.

Adam in the Heavens, or Not

The most remarkable expression of dualism was its application in astronomy, largely through Aristotle, Plato's more empirically minded student and tutor to Alexander the Great.

An astronomical tradition going back centuries in Greece and into ancient Babylon had charted the patterns and regularity of the heavens. The constancy of the night sky was source of great wonder; the constellations cycled through the heavens with such regularity that farmers used the appearance of spring constellations as a signal to put their seed in the ground. Turmoil on the earth had no counterpart in the heavens.

How was this to be understood? Why was the earth filled with ceaseless change while absolutely no change was ever observed in the heavens? Earthly kingdoms could rise and fall, the Nile could flood a thousand times, islands could sink into the sea, but not one constellation ever changed in any way.

This contrast was interpreted as yet another application of dualism. An unchanging heaven with its many mathematical regularities was perfect and eternal in the same way that the abstract world of mathematics was perfect. The models that Greek astronomers developed to explain the motions of the heavens reflected this perfection. Everything was composed of perfect spheres, moving in perfect circles, at constant speeds, embodying the glorious perfection of mathematics. Objects were composed of *ether*, a material unique to the heavens, rather than the mixture of earth, air, fire, and water found on the earth. Different physical laws applied, ensuring that the heavens had none of the irregularity, transience, and decay that plagued the earth. The heavens must be part of that other perfect world where geometry ruled.

The boundary between the two worlds of this dualistic cosmos was fixed at the orbit of the moon. On this side of the orbit was the earthly realm, extending down to the center of the earth, also the center of the universe.

The location of this boundary—a subject of only minor interest to the Greeks—was mentioned by Cicero (106–43 BCE), assassinated as a sinner in 43 BCE but later declared a "righteous pagan" by the Catholic Church and revered during the medieval period. The heavenly border is described in Cicero's *Republic*, where we find the story of General Scipio Aemilianus (185–129 BCE), journeying into space to chat with his father and grandfather about earthly and cosmic affairs. His father's response includes these words that resonated deeply with Christian understandings of the Fall: "While the Moon shall last forever, what lies beneath, on Earth, is doomed to wither and die. . . . Earth orbited by the planet and stars, lies at the heart of the Universe. It does not move, and all things of mass tend toward it."[6]

This astronomical tradition appealed to the Islamic religion that emerged in the seventh century, more so than to Christianity. It resonated with the Koran's emphasis on studying the creation to honor the creator—studies that Augustine had warned his fellow Christians could be distractions from seeking God. Most of Aristotle's work, unfortunately, was also lost to the West even as it flourished within Islam.

The Crusades of the eleventh through thirteenth centuries brought Aristotle's ideas about the natural world—often in distinctly Islamic packages[7]—into the Christian West. Encounters with these ideas motivated Aquinas and others to develop a Christian cosmology that included new insights into the nature and extent of the Fall. Christian thinkers, impressed with the philosophy being imported from Islam, began thinking harder about the natural world, planting the seeds that would grow over the next few centuries into the scientific revolution.

If Christianity was to be a comprehensive worldview, it needed to incorporate these new ideas. Aquinas set out to "Christianize" Aristotle, a task that occupied much of his influential life's work, the *Summa Theologica*. When he was finished, many of Aristotle's ideas about the natural world were becoming Christian articles of faith, as Galileo would unhappily discover. It was quite surprising, in fact, just how well these ideas fit within Christianity.

Aquinas's new Christian cosmology started with a spherical earth at the center of the universe and stationary, as affirmed in biblical passages that Aristotle had never read, such as Psalm 93, where we read that God "has established the world; it shall never be moved."[8] The centrality of the earth became a symbol of its importance as the locus of God's great acts of creation and redemption. The perfection of the heavens reflected God's character. The mathematically perfect orbits were divine markers.

But, most important for our story, the distinction between the earthly and the heavenly realms—the border that Scipio's father noted—was a tangible indicator of both the reality and the spatial extent of the Fall and God's subsequent curse. Plato, Aristotle, and Cicero, of course, had no notion of the Fall as a consequence of Adam's sin. Remarkably though, they had discerned that the earth and the heavens were profoundly different.

The Augustinian sense of the Fall was that Adam's sin led to God cursing him, his offspring, and his world. But the curse, as suggested in Genesis, affected only the *human* part of the creation. There would be weeds and thorns and sweat, and pain in childbirth—all of which affect human activity. Immortality is lost and women must serve their husbands, but God did not curse the stars overhead or disrupt the lunar cycle. God did not announce that the constellations would no longer serve as signs of the seasons or that the stars would fall from the sky. The winter winds would still arrive on cue with Orion, as they always had.

The dualism of the cosmos confirmed the intuitions of Christian theology. The unrelenting presence within the earthly realm of sin and the troubles arising from God's curse at the Fall could be mitigated by simply looking overhead. Oppressed Christians could look forward to death, when their soul would escape its prison by taking flight into the heavens. Some even suggested that the soul's flight through the heavens would purge it of sin and ready it for arrival in paradise. Some speculated that Eden had been in the heavens, atop a high mountain reaching to the moon, and that Adam's expulsion from Eden had been a literal descent from the heavens to the earth.

Virtually all educated Western Europeans embraced this view of the cosmos by the beginning of the sixteenth century. It was ordered, grounded in respected ancient authorities, both pagan and Christian. Its organization testified constantly, visibly, and clearly to the truth of Christianity. We can imagine a sixteenth-century thinker, demoralized by his hard life, Europe's never-ending wars and terrible plagues, looking up at the night sky and taking comfort from what he saw there.

Dante Alighieri famously described this ordered cosmos in *The Divine Comedy*. His imaginative vision grounded Christian theology in the physical details of the Aristotelian cosmos, with hell at the center, in the bowels of the earth, and God on his throne in paradise beyond the final celestial sphere at the outer boundary of the universe, the sphere of the fixed stars. Concentrically layered spheres were stacked precisely between these boundaries, like a child's toy.

Descending from the surface of the earth to its center, we climb down the terraces of hell, encountering Dante's provocative ranking of sinners, starting with the "indifferent" on the "vestibule" of hell. Continuing through the circles we encounter the lustful, gluttonous, avaricious, wrathful, heretical, murderous, pandering and seducing, flattering, simonizing, soothsaying, grafting, hypocritical, thieving, false counseling, discordant, counterfeiting, and, finally, in a move so overtly political that it should have landed Dante on his own pandering circle, *traitors* resided in the deepest recesses of hell, exactly where powerful leaders would have wanted them. Whatever we think of Dante's moral ranking, the scheme is certainly orderly.

Heading upward from the surface of the earth we encounter another set of circles, taking us ever closer to heaven—the orbits of the heavenly bodies: the moon, Mercury, Venus, sun, Mars, Jupiter, Saturn, and finally the fixed stars beyond which we encounter heaven. As cultural historian Richard Tarnas put it, "The Aristotelian geocentric universe thus became a massive symbolic structure for the moral drama of Christianity, in which man was situated between Heaven and Hell, drawn between his spiritual and corporeal natures."[9]

The journey outward from the hellish center was both a physical and a spiritual path to God, a literary motif that shows up repeatedly. In *Paradise Lost*—another artistic vision of the medieval cosmos—Milton has Raphael giving Adam instructions about his upcoming visit to paradise. Adam's response reflects the hierarchical view of the cosmos:

Well hast thou taught the way that might direct
Our knowledge, and the scale of Nature set
From center to circumference, whereon
In contemplation of created things
By steps we may ascend to God.[10]

I am sure that many readers share my skepticism that Dante, Milton, and their fellow artists actually considered hell and heaven in quite this way. If Dante had modern machinery to tunnel through mountains, would he dig his way down to the gates of hell, expecting to chat with the indifferent sinners on its vestibule? Probably not, but he would certainly have believed in purgatory and gradations of punishment in hell. He probably believed, with others of his century, that hell was inside the earth. After all, anyone who traveled into a deep cave couldn't help but notice that it got hotter as you went down. The Bible spoke of Mount Ararat, the Jordan River, and Mount Sinai—all real places associated with supernatural events that Dante's generation knew only from books. We have no reason to suppose that heaven, hell, or the Garden of Eden would not have seemed as real. On the other hand, we can certainly imagine that Dante would not have defended the reality of a hellish vestibule or the exact placement of the pandering circle with any passion. Who can say where the literal meets the literary in imaginative works?

Our skepticism arises from the challenge of appreciating the worldviews of previous eras. The scientific questions we want to pose, decoupled from their theological context, were not considered especially important to a generation for whom Christian theology was the framework for understanding everything and the Genesis creation story the foundational document for the world. Dante's description of hell was making a point about sin, not geology.

ADAM EVERYWHERE

The Christianized cosmos was the most dramatic part of the theologically charged medieval worldview because of Galileo's famous failure in the seventeenth century to convince church authorities that the earth was actually in the heavens moving around the sun. But other investigations were also guided by the assumption that the world in all its complexity can be understood only within the framework of the Genesis creation account. "The Story of Adam and Eve," notes historian Phillip Almond, "was seminal for all aspects of seventeenth century life."[1]

Three fascinating examples illustrate this point: the problem of human languages, the location of Eden, and Adam as the biological progenitor of all humans. In each case Adam is firmly rooted in the world of early modern Christians.

Adam's Perfect Language

Genesis reports that God strolled through the Garden of Eden every night, chatting with Adam "in the time of the evening breeze." This chatting implies a common language Adam shared with God. Naturally, this first language was perfect, although it may have been compromised by the Fall—we are not told. Nor do we know what happened to it when languages were confused a few centuries later at Babel. Perhaps the original Edenic language spoken by Adam and God persisted as one of humanity's many languages; maybe it disappeared; maybe it survived in a mutated and deteriorating form.

The search for the perfect language was a natural question for scholars of the late Middle Ages, enthused about order and aware of the limitations of their own languages. The flaws in existing languages—expected because they were spoken by fallen humans—were readily apparent: grammar conventions were not always followed, spelling constructions and pronunciations were inconsistent (think of the plural spelling and pronunciation of *mouse*, *spouse*, and *house*), and ambiguities flourished like weeds throughout what should have been an orderly linguistic landscape. God's conversations with Adam must surely have taken place in a language without such imperfections.[12]

Most scholars of that time presumed that Adam and Eve spoke a perfect language, now lost, that was some variation on Hebrew, since that was the language in which the story was written. Augustine and most of the early church fathers held this view, as best we can tell, but the question was of limited interest to them. They were more interested in other linguistic details like how the fish were named, since the text reports only that God brought animals and birds to Adam for naming. How were the water creatures, for example, brought to Adam for naming? How did Adam name the great whale?

Dante was the first to systematically explore the concept of a perfect language. His *De vulgari eloquentia*, written at the beginning of the fourteenth century, took a hard look at the linguistic landscape of his day, particularly the vulgar dialects of his native Italy. He rejected the idea that Hebrew—at least the version spoken in his century—was the language of Eden; he never even bothered to learn it.

"What God gave Adam," says the great Italian philosopher and polymath Umberto Eco, paraphrasing an untranslated work by Dante, "was neither just the faculty of language nor yet a natural language; what he gave was, in fact, a set of principles for a universal grammar."[13] These principles could be the basis for quite different languages but were lost at Babel. Dante wanted to build a perfect language on these principles and write poetry in it—to undo the confusion of Babel and recover the lost Edenic clarity. He was convinced that echoes of the original language must still be present, just as the perfection of the heavens was a reminder of the original paradise.

A councilor to the kings of France, Guillaume Postel (1510–1581), jump-started Hebrew studies in the wake of the Protestant Reformation. The Reformers had rejected the Catholic Church as corrupt and would not accept that it was the mediator and interpreter of biblical texts, especially since those texts were not even in their original languages. The result, driven by the *sola scriptura* ("scripture alone") refrain of the Reformation, was growing interest in Hebrew. Postel developed the concept of "divine economy," from which he argued that "there was but one human race, one world and one God," so it only made sense that there would be "one language . . . inspired into the first man."[14] This language was Hebrew, and God had given Adam the ability to "call things by their appropriate names."[15]

Grand claims were made for the divinely provided Hebrew language spoken by Adam. One scholar argued that just as all humans had descended from Adam, so all languages had evolved from Hebrew. Linguists embarked on a quixotic quest to find vestiges of Hebrew in all the languages of the world, one of the first genuinely evolutionary approaches to the past. Another scholar argued that the Hebrew names Adam gave the animals captured their natures: "The Eagle is called Nescher, a word formed by the combination of Schor and Isachar, the first meaning to look and the second to be straight because, above all others, the eagle is a bird of firm sight."[16]

In similar fashion, but unique among all languages, the Hebrew words captured the essence of the life forms to which they were attached. Another scholar argued that one could permute the letters in the Hebrew name of an animal to illustrate some of their characteristics. Some letters in the word for "lion" could be rearranged into a new word that sounded vaguely like *panting*, which lions do. Such were the remarkable powers of a perfect language.

In 1667, as Isaac Newton was preparing his greatest work for publication, Mercurius van Helmont published a book arguing that the actual sounds required to speak Hebrew were precisely those produced most easily by human vocal cords. This echoed a popular speculation that an infant who heard no language would naturally and spontaneously speak Hebrew, as God intended when he created the world.

Adam's Garden Home in the East

The French historian Jean Delumeau chronicles the changing perceptions of Eden in *History of Paradise: The Garden of Eden in Myth and Tradition*. Delumeau notes that the medieval period began with a "tenacious conviction that the earthly paradise still existed on our planet in a place rendered inaccessible by original sin," but that this belief slowly evolved into "an enduring certainty that the approaches to this earthly paradise were not beyond human reach."[17] Adam and Eve were real people who lived in a geographical location that Genesis says was arranged by God "in the east," a location that may have been lost over time. But as Christians explored and mapped the surface of the globe and its seemingly infinite vistas were brought under control, the location of paradise attracted great interest.

As with Adam, not everyone understood Eden in the same way. Philo, the first-century Jewish thinker we met earlier, thought a literal Garden of Eden was an "incurable folly."[18] In the third century Origen wrote, "What is so silly as to believe that God, after the manner of a farmer, 'planted a paradise eastward in Eden.'"[19] Eden was part of a story with both a powerful spiritual reality and a (possible) minor physical reality. Even thinkers who believed in a real Eden emphasized its spiritual significance.

And, as was the case with Adam, Augustine in *The Literal Meaning of Genesis* gets the final word for Western Christians. Written at a time when allegorical interpretations of scripture were often taken more seriously than literal readings, he provided reasons why the Edenic events really happened.

"These facts should persuade us," he concludes in a lengthy passage, "to take the first meaning of the other details of this narrative in the literal sense and not to assume that the account is allegorical, but that the facts narrated really exist. . . . A river, therefore, went out from Eden, that is, from the delightful place, and it watered paradise, that is, all the beautiful and fruit-bearing trees shaded all the land of that region."[20]

Augustine's conclusions became the received wisdom, and disputation about the reality of Eden all but ceased. Isidore of Seville (560–636), the great educator of the Middle Ages, produced an encyclopedia that informed generations of Christians about the reality of Eden. The Venerable Bede (673–736), one of the most important authorities of the Middle Ages, was equally clear: "Let us have no doubt," he wrote, "that the paradise in which the first human being was placed is to be understood as a real place."[21] The vigorous defenses of a literal Eden, however, suggest that there were meaningful arguments to the contrary.

These authorities shaped the Middle Ages and the early modern era. Aquinas and Peter Lombard, the widely read bishop of Paris, did little more than summarize and gloss the received wisdom about Eden. Lombard's major work, the *Summa sententiarum*, was required reading in the schools where so many of Europe's leaders were educated. Lombard affirms the reality of Eden and adds a curious claim about its location "at a height which touches the sphere of the moon so that the waters of the flood were unable to reach it."[22] By putting Eden at the sphere of the moon, paradise ends up on the boundary of the heavenly realm, making Adam and Eve's eviction from Eden a long climb down from the heavens. The geographical implausibility of such scenarios was far from apparent in a century long before the birth of modern science.

The late Middle Ages and early modern period had a growing interest in the natural world. This was an age of exploration, when knowledge exploded and new disciplines were born. Maps from the period evolved slowly from crude and wildly inaccurate geographies, with Jerusalem at the center of the world and *terra incognita* in most other places to more modern and accurate versions. Explorers filled in details and double-checked the grand stories told by travelers returning from exotic lands. One constant on these improving maps was Eden—not always in the same place but never missing. Even Columbus, when he stumbled onto the Americas, thought he had located Eden in Venezuela. "All this provides great evidence of the earthly Paradise," he wrote, "because the situation agrees with the beliefs of those holy and wise theologians and all the signs strongly accord with this idea."[23]

By the end of the sixteenth century, maps and globes look more modern; Jerusalem is no longer at the center, lines of longitude and latitude crisscross territories that have actually been mapped and not just described by breathless travelers eager to impress their gullible—and sometimes paying—audiences.

And Eden is missing.

The disappearance of Adam's primordial home from sixteenth-century maps is one of the first indicators that the iron grip of the Genesis creation story on the Western imagination was loosening. But we must not exaggerate the significance of this development. Eden did not disappear from the maps because its existence was questioned. Many mapmakers considered the Garden of Eden to be a real historical place that was simply destroyed by God, or perhaps wiped out in Noah's flood, claims still made by biblical literalists today.

On the other hand, geography was one of the first fields to mature at the dawn of the scientific revolution, driven by the practical realities of global exploration. It was a harbinger of things to come, as one emerging science after another cast doubt on the literal truth of the Genesis story of creation.

Was Adam the First Man?

The great age of exploration brought European Christians into contact with tribes around the globe. These contacts, although not always peaceful, were certainly meaningful and led to engagements with new cultures—cultures with histories longer than that of Europe and sometimes even longer than Judeo-Christian history. European histories at the time were simple extensions of the biblical chronology, beginning with Adam, running through genealogical tables in the Old Testament, and then gradually connecting to their own history. The typical chronology, developed by analyzing the ages of people in the Hebrew scriptures and when they were born, placed the creation of the earth—and the first man—around 4000 BCE. Two things followed with certainty from this: First, no tribe could have a history that ran farther back into the past than this. Second, every tribe on the planet must have broken off from some group in the Old Testament at some point, with the earliest possible time being contemporary with Adam's family, but the more likely time being after Noah's great flood.

Europeans mastered the languages of the new tribes and learned their histories. And sometimes these histories—which often included their own genealogies and creation stories—were incompatible with the biblical chronology. In particular, it was often difficult or even impossible to show how the various tribes could trace their origins to Adam.

Such anthropological concerns will occupy a large part of our story in subsequent chapters, but I want to note here the assumption underlying the concerns: all human beings are descended from a literal Adam and Eve, and this fact determines both their biological and their theological status. The stakes in such considerations could be very high.

In 1550, for example, a papal junta was convened at the Colegio de San Gregorio in Valladolid in Spain to address this issue directly for the increasingly important "Indians": Did the primitive, naked residents of the Americas, as many viewed them, possess the image of God? Or were they another species? Perhaps they were bestial, or barbarian, or intended for slavery, or all these. Their biological kinship to the Hebrew-speaking Adam who lived in Eden in 4000 BCE would shape and determine the conclusions, for better or worse, often worse.

Adam thus stood, fixed and immovable, at the center of Europe's understanding of anthropology, just as the earth stood fixed and immoveable at the center of their understanding of the cosmos. One listens in vain for a whisper that Adam may not have been a real, flesh-and-blood character. The empirically discernible effects of Adam's sin could be seen everywhere, and if everyone had not descended from a first man, where did they come from?

The Beginning of the End of the First Man

The Christian worldview at the dawn of the seventeenth century was profoundly ordered and deeply rooted in the Bible, in Greek science, and in centuries of theological reflection. Everything connected to everything in mutual support. The worldview was grounded in authoritative ancient texts, but it also explained the world in which they lived—the regularity of the seasons, the struggles with childbirth, the messages astrologers found in the heavens. The insights of the key thinkers of the Christian tradition—Augustine, Isidore, Bede, Aquinas, Lombard—were woven into the tapestry that was medieval Christianity. It was the worldview that birthed the modern world.

But this was also a world being slowly dismantled. Copernicus and his successors proposed to lift the corrupted earth into the heavens and relocate the sun in its place. Newly discovered cultures claimed histories far older than that of Christian Europe. Ancient authorities were found to disagree with observations of the natural world and with each other.

We are far removed from this world, and much of it now seems incomprehensible. I taught astronomy for many years and was constantly rattled by drawings of the "revolutionary" sixteenth-century, sun-centered models of the solar system being advanced to challenge the traditional Aristotelian representation. These drawings—cutting edge for their day—typically pictured the sun with a face on it at the center of the cosmos and cherubim around the outer sphere of the fixed stars. Were these not pictures of the breakthrough inaugurating the scientific revolution? Copernicus used equally alien arguments to justify moving the earth from the center of the cosmos and putting the sun there: he described the universe as a "beautiful temple lit by the great, all-seeing lantern at its centre."[24] One cannot begin to imagine a scientist using such an argument today.

Such developments lit a slow-burning fuse. Centuries would pass before the medieval worldview gave way to our modern replacement, and the revolution is not over yet. But, with the birth of science, a quiet conversation on the margins of Christianity was starting. And although science would be done primarily by Christians for a few centuries, its loyalties lay in territories far removed from those of Augustine and Aquinas. New discoveries would no longer be expected to fit naturally into the Christian worldview. In fact, the reverse was the case: the Christian worldview was expected to adjust to fit the new discoveries.

CHAPTER 6

THE ORIGIN OF MRS. CAIN (AND THE POSSE THAT CHASED HER HUSBAND)

*Skeptics of the Bible have used Cain's wife time and again
to discredit the book of Genesis as a true historical record.
Sadly, most Christians have not given an adequate
answer to this question.*

—KEN HAM[1]

Historian Anthony Grafton describes the century beginning in 1550 as one in which "Western thinkers ceased to believe that they could find all important truths in ancient books."[2] Seven years earlier, the Polish polymath that we met in the previous chapter, Nicolaus Copernicus, had published *On the Revolutions of the Heavenly Spheres*, a book destined to transform the Western worldview. Copernicus the man, however, was in his grave when the century that dethroned the authority of the book began.

Copernicus, a canon in the Catholic Church, made the argument that the earth moved in the heavens, referencing the writings of ancient authorities Pythagoras and Aristarchus. Their view was a minority report lost in the glare of Aristotle's cosmology, but nevertheless retained the authoritative character of ancient wisdom. Copernicus had little need for new arguments; it sufficed to recover old ones. He was, as one biographer has called him, a "timid canon," retiring and uneasy about the reception of ideas that, if not exactly new, were certainly challenging.[3] The timid canon delayed publication for decades, receiving a copy of his work only on his deathbed.

In recovering the ancient view that the earth moved about the center of the universe, Copernicus cracked open a door; whether the new light flooding in was from the past or the future would take a century to determine. But for many long decades, Christians would be troubled by the implications of the new astronomy: Copernicus placed the sinful, fallen, and cursed earth in the incorruptible heavens—that perfect other world untainted by the sin of Adam and Eve.

A second book appeared that same year, written by a brash young anatomist named Andreas Vesalius (1514–1564). Whereas Copernicus articulated a new anatomy for the solar system, Vesalius's focus was closer to home. The book, titled *On the Structure of the Human Body*, critiqued the anatomical tradition inherited from Galen, the second-century physician, philosopher, and reigning authority on human anatomy. Galen's followers defended their authority. Vesalius, one of them charged, was a "madman," stating in ways that make no sense to our ears that "an advance beyond the knowledge of Galen was impossible." If Vesalius's drawings of the human body were more accurate than Galen's, outraged critics insisted that it was because the human body must have changed, not because Galen erred. Another critic declared he would rather "err with Galen than accept the truth from the innovator." His enemies called Vesalius a "grave-robber," some going so far as to claim that he had dissected a body with the heart still beating, and thus was a murderer. The epithet *atheist* was hurled at him— sometimes a death sentence in those troubled times, although no evidence suggests that he was not a faithful Roman Catholic.[4]

Vesalius's critique of Galen was shared by his fellow anatomist Paracelsus (1493–1541), who wrote in the midst of these anatomical controversies that, "every little hair on my neck knows more than you and all your scribes, and my shoe buckles are more learned than your Galen and Avicenna, and my beard has more experience than all your high colleges." Paracelsus declared clearly but impoliticly what some were beginning to think privately.[5]

Copernicus and Vesalius stand astride the chasm separating ancient ways of thinking from those that guide us today. Copernicus's thinking was more typical of scholars of that time. In not seeing his work as a rejection of the old, his work was a completion, a transformation, an elaboration of the past. It was a past that still inspired and defined the present, a past to be protected at all costs, a past with a treasury of wisdom and truth to guide scholars exploring a world growing larger and more complex. And even those who presumed to challenge ancient authorities often did so by appealing to even more ancient authorities. The great Aristotle, wrote the fiery English preacher Robert South (1634–1716), was but the "rubbish of an Adam, and Athens but the rudiments of Paradise."[6] A leading seventeenth-century scholar wrote that Copernicus and Vesalius were the "Luther and Calvin of natural philosophy," charged with restoring Adam's ancient knowledge—the divine wisdom that began disintegrating after the Fall. Genesis was mined for evidence that Adam possessed encyclopedic knowledge of everything from medicine to metallurgy. The first man's naming of the animals was understood to mean that he had detailed knowledge of their natures and could perhaps even see into their interiors. Some thought Adam must have known of the Trinity and the Incarnation, making him the first Christian.[7] And, as the first Christian but not a part of the Roman Church, he must have been justified entirely by his faith, making him the first Protestant.[8]

The ancient texts—the Bible in particular but also Aristotle, Plato, and others—originated in a time when humans were wiser, closer to God, and in touch with ultimate truths in ways that had gotten lost over the centuries. God had revealed truths to Adam directly, to the biblical authors, and even to the pagan Greeks—truths that guided their lives, their thoughts, and the ships that carried them to new lands. This knowledge was uncontroversial to fifteenth-century Christians.

Christopher Columbus is a case in point. He embarked on his epic voyages expecting to find a biblical Eden as real as the Atlantic Ocean on which he sailed. When, on August 1, 1498, he stumbled upon a portion of the New World in northeastern Venezuela that was lush and verdant, he announced, matter-of-factly, that he had found the paradise where Adam and Eve once lived. As expected, it was high up in the craggy mountains, out of reach of the floodwaters of Noah that had inundated the rest of the world.

The New World was, of course, new, but it also provided answers to old questions raised by the patchwork and puzzling "history" in the Bible. The Americas, as they became known, were populated with exciting new creatures, including human tribes of mysterious and uncertain origins. Explorers encountering these mysteries used them to dispel mysteries in the Bible; the mysterious origins of the people Cain feared would kill him for murdering Abel, for example, was resolved by the discovery of tribes that did not appear to have descended from Adam.

Always there were new lands, populated with other tribes. They spoke other languages, confirming the confusion of tongues at the tower of Babel. Linguists inspected each new language to see if it might be closer to the lost dialect of Eden. The English author Sir Thomas Browne (1605–1682) suggested that the ancient language of Eden might still be spoken by a tribe that was not part of the linguistic chaos created by God at Babel. The Chinese seemed likely candidates, being so far away, so ancient, and with such an unusual language. "The Chinoys," he wrote in his essay "Of Languages," "who live at the bounds of the earth, who have admitted little communication . . . may possibly give account of a very ancient language."[9]

The new tribes worshiped other gods, like Israel's neighbors in the Hebrew scriptures. They told other tales of creation, often in a past more ancient than permitted by a strict biblical chronology. They were, ventured Paracelsus, "from a different Adam," a speculation destined for controversy.[10] Europe was soon awash in updated new maps, new imported goods, new tales of far-off places, new puzzles about the eclectic character of the human race, and even new people brought back by the explorers to be civilized, Christianized, exploited, enslaved.

Christian Europe's relation to its traditions became complex, even strained. Not only was there diversity within the tradition, as Copernicus had exploited in his critique of Aristotle, but many of the canonical texts of this great "Age of the Book" had been copied and translated so many times that they were no longer faithful to the originals. A new generation of scholars warned that the scriptures had been corrupted over the centuries. The Catholic scholar Desiderius Erasmus Roterodamus, known today simply as Erasmus (1466–1536), produced a new translation of the Bible in 1516 in which he showed repeatedly that the church had built doctrines and developed practices based on mistranslations of key biblical passages. Some of these were significant. The command to "do penance," which the church had turned into a sacrament motivating confession, absolution, and even mortification of the body, was one such example. Erasmus showed that the Latin Vulgate had mistranslated a Greek word as "do penance" that meant, more benignly, "repent."[11]

In 1517 the renegade priest Martin Luther (1483–1546) went public with his charges that the church had invented teachings and practices with no biblical foundation. His initial efforts were aimed at reforming the church from within, delving into the past like Erasmus and Copernicus to recover truth for the present. But Luther's stridency soon got the better of him, and in 1521 the pope excommunicated him for challenging the authority of the church. The event split the Western church, inaugurating the Protestant Reformation—a movement that began as an attempt not to move Christianity ahead but to return Christianity to its roots. The movement would bring a cornucopia of new theological perspectives to Christianity and raise difficult questions about the received wisdom of the past. Erasmus, John Calvin, Ulrich Zwingli, and a host of others (both inside and outside the Catholic Church) pressed for expressions of the faith that were more firmly rooted in the authority of the Bible and freed of dubious, self-serving, and even lucrative theological innovations. The net effect of these developments was an enhanced emphasis on understanding exactly what the Bible said, on the eve of a revolution that would slowly begin to raise questions about the reliability of the Bible.

William Shakespeare, John Donne, Leonardo da Vinci, Michelangelo—the roster of new minds in a new time, doing new things, is a *Who's Who* of trailblazing geniuses. But these innovators were at best ambivalent about the new things coming into focus on the horizon, as they squinted to see whether they were observing the past or the future. As a young man, Michelangelo (1475–1564) marketed his first accomplished sculpture by antiquing it to fool buyers into thinking it a Greek relic.[12] Donne (1572–1631) wrote these memorable lines about the "new philosophy" in *An Anatomy of the World*, expressing his reservations about the emerging worldview that was imprudently shaking the ancient and venerable foundations of his world:

> *And new philosophy casts all in doubt*
> *The element of fire is quite put out.*
> *The sun is lost, and th'earth, and no man's wit,*
> *Can well direct him where to look for it.*
> *And freely men confess that this world's spent,*
> *When in the planets and the firmament*
> *They seek so many new; they see that this*
> *Is crumbled out again to his atomies.*
> *'Tis all in pieces, all coherence gone,*
> *All just supply, and all relation; . . .*

Donne's lament that the earth and sun were "lost" captured the anxiety of an age resting on trembling foundations. If the accursed and sinful earth was a planet—and thus not unique and not different from the other planets, long thought to be perfect as befit their location in the heavens—then what had happened to the world when Adam and Eve sinned?

Less than a decade after Donne died another English poet, steeped in tradition but drawn to the revolutionary currents swirling about, embarked on a highly symbolic journey to see Europe's most celebrated architect of the new philosophy, a scholar who had labored heroically to launch the earth into the heavens. The poet was John Milton (1608–1674), and the visit was to the Florence home of the aging and blind Galileo. Milton needed permission for the visit, for Galileo was under house arrest, having been condemned in 1633 on "vehement suspicion of heresy" for having violated an agreement he had made with the church to refrain from promoting Copernicus's idea that the earth moves about the sun.

Milton's masterwork, *Paradise Lost*, captures the dissonance of a tradition coming apart. His epic poem contains a grand tale of how things went wrong, from the fall into sin of the angel Satan to the transgression of Eve and then Adam, and on to the fall of humanity in their disobedience. Rich in cosmological references, Milton subtly acknowledges the new astronomy that the aging Galileo had been imprisoned for promoting. In one scene Adam interrogates the angel Raphael about the solar system, posing his question from a geocentric perspective that references a "sedentarie Earth" that "attaines Her end without least motion."[13] Raphael does not contradict Adam on this point but in his response refers to "Planet Earth." This innocuous sounding reference, so familiar to us today, would have clanged like a gong in the ears of Milton's generation. The earth was most certainly *not* a planet and had never been one. *Planet* means "wandering star" and there were but six of them—the moon, Mercury, Venus, Mars, Jupiter, Saturn. Planets were bodies in the heavenly realm that moved across the sky independently of the fixed stars. A stationary earth was certainly not a wandering star.[14]

Paradise Lost, published in 1667, was the finale of centuries of literary elaboration of the story of Adam. Written to justify "the ways of God to man," it was the last major literary work that began—as countless histories in previous centuries always had—with the powerful story in the opening pages of the Bible.[15]

THE FADING OF ADAM

I have introduced this critical period with snapshots of the giants of the Western intellectual tradition, familiar names and familiar ideas that populate our high school and college curricula. We must remind ourselves, however, as we reflect on this great era of change that new ideas often need centuries to dislodge old ideas. New and old, of course, share the stage for a while—sometimes a long while—and Adam is no exception. Copernicus published his heliocentric theory in 1543 after circulating it privately for three decades. Milton published *Paradise Lost* in 1667 yet was still unwilling to cast his poem within the new sun-centered astronomical paradigm championed by his hero Galileo. As Milton was composing *Paradise Lost*, Isaac Newton was studying at Cambridge University and about to announce his theory of universal gravity. The Cambridge curriculum was still entirely traditional with a heavy focus on the Bible, Plato, Aristotle (with his geocentricity), and Galen, rather than Copernicus, Vesalius, and Paracelsus. Newton wrote more pages explicating the Bible than he did explaining the heavens, indicating the enduring stature of ancient wisdom. The Lutheran Church—Missouri Synod, the most conservative bastion of biblical literalism in America, continued to reject Copernicanism until 1905—the year Einstein published the theory of relativity.[16]

Alongside these central conversations were the smaller, quieter conversations taking place on the edge of the cultural radar. In casual communications, letters, safe classrooms, and not-so-safe inquisitorial investigations; in emerging empirical investigation of everything from human anatomy to lunar craters; in lesser known books, obscure tracts, and anonymously published literature, scholars engaged each other on everything from the actual size of the earth—Columbus had it wrong—to the relationship of all the newly discovered animals to the carrying capacity of Noah's ark.

As this conversation developed over the next few centuries and into the present a recurring pattern emerged: New information was initially just inserted into the biblical account under the assumption that the Bible is completely reliable. Contrary information was either modified to fit—the history of the Chinese people isn't as old as they claimed—or rejected simply because it cannot fit. Arguments undermining the biblical stories about the first man were consistently denounced as unorthodox and suppressed— often with deadly consequences for their champions—until the arguments grew strong enough to require a proper response. Such responses often entailed creative expansion or reinterpretation of the biblical stories to match external realities. The guiding assumption was always that the biblical version of history was the correct one but, thanks to the piecemeal structure of the biblical narrative and the ambiguity of its literary genres, there was room for interpretation.

The biblical stories, to take a difficult and familiar internal problem, contained characters of unknown origin, the most famous being Cain's wife and the people Cain worried would hunt him down for murdering his brother. After his crime, Cain headed off to the land of Nod, where he built a city populated by people who came from God knows where. We read

about the "sons of God" who mated with the "daughters of men." We read
that there were giants in those days. These obscure cameo appearances had
long puzzled readers, for they all had to have descended from Adam, at least
in the traditional picture.

Adam, however, was not like us. He began his life in Eden as a perfect
human being; he talked to God directly and had more than nine hundred
birthdays. He and Eve may have had hundreds of children. The residents of
Nod may have been a tribe of Adam's early descendants who had been gone
for centuries before Cain was banished. Cain's wife was probably a distant
relative. Such explanations, while strained and not based on the text itself,
were far from impossible and the alternative—that Adam was not the first
man and biological parent of the entire human race—was unthinkable.

Other tribes reporting more ancient histories than the Bible cast
unfavorable light on the chronologies of Genesis. Fantastic, but widely
accepted, tales of monstrous races on the margins of civilization raised questions about the definition of humanness. Tribes in far-flung corners of the
globe or on isolated islands raised questions about human migrations. Tribes
with different appearances raised anthropological questions about the definition of humanness. The number of questions, while not all new, grew
during the great age of exploration and exploded as new sciences developed.

Incompatible histories associated with other tribes posed the first challenges. As far back as the fourth century, Augustine had protected the
biblical chronology from contradictory accounts by simply claiming the
Bible was true and the other accounts were not. The Egyptians, he writes
in *The City of God*, have a "mendacious vanity" in that they "ascribe to
their science an antiquity of a hundred thousand years." Their historians
"babble with most empty presumption" and thus deserve only to be "rid-
iculed rather than refuted." Christians, he concludes without elaboration,
need have no doubt about the veracity of their story of "the first man, who
is called Adam," because they are "sustained by divine authority" and thus
have "no doubt that whatever is opposed to it is most false."[17] In short the
challengers are simply wrong because they are wrong. Ignore them.

As engagement with nonbiblical chronologies increased, glib dismissals
of their timelines became less tenable. By the sixteenth century, alternative extrabiblical histories were sufficiently well understood and common
enough that a few scholars realized the gravity of the problem. The biblical
chronology, for example, was being laid alongside that of the Egyptians,
Persians, and Babylonians and reconciled, often successfully, by finding
ancient episodes common to each and then compressing or stretching to

make the intervening intervals fit. But we must note the revolutionary character of such investigations: it is not the growing awareness of puzzling discrepancies with the biblical chronology that is remarkable but that the Bible is being read as though it were a book—like other books.

The slow gestation of interest in history on its own terms drove the project of understanding the past. As long as "history" was viewed as a set of stories addressing questions of morality, social order, and ultimate origins, its details were all but irrelevant. But even the most mythically infused history makes claims about the world that can, in principle, be checked. At issue is the claim that Adam was the first man and that all humans were descended from him. Could the history of *every* tribe on *every* far-flung island on the planet be traced back to a pair of humans, living alone on the planet, probably in the Middle East, some six thousand years ago? And could this history account for their language, skin color, religion, location and other distinctive qualities?

The brevity of the biblical account served it well as it engaged increasingly broader ranges of phenomena from the seventeenth century to the present. The story of Adam and Eve, the Fall, the curse, Noah's flood, and the tower of Babel were little more than skeletons to be creatively fleshed out to make sense of anomalies. Take the anthropological challenge of the Chinese. Some early seventeenth-century scholars became convinced that there must have been people living in Asia before the flood, a conclusion demanded by the data. But, if the Chinese were descended from Adam, they should have been speaking Adam's language—Hebrew—which they were not. Or were they? Since nobody knew for sure what language Adam spoke, maybe Chinese *was* the original Hebrew. This thesis was creatively defended by John Webb (1611–1672), an English scholar and architect who wrote Europe's first treatise on the Chinese language, titled *An Historical Essay Endeavoring a Probability That the Language of the Empire of China Is the Primitive Language*. To make this scenario work, Webb exploited an ambiguity in the biblical story—the location of the mountain where Noah's ark came to rest after the flood. If Noah's ark came to rest in China, not on Mount Ararat in modern Turkey, then an ancient tribe speaking the primitive language God gave to Adam could have flourished in Asia. And, since they were too far removed to have participated in the ill-fated construction of the tower of Babel, their language would not have been "confused" by God.[18] Webb, remarkably, didn't even speak Chinese. His work was based on the popular travelogues of Jesuit missionaries working in Asia.

Scholars like Webb stretched the linguistic and geographical boundaries of the biblical story to encompass regions far removed from the Middle East—regions that, by any reasonable standard, could not possibly have been a part of that original story unless God had told Moses about it directly. Far-fetched tales of human—or not—monstrosities from around the globe stretched other aspects of the biblical story. With a gullibility that confounds us today, educated people during the centuries prior to the scientific revolution accepted at face value the tales told by explorers of their encounters with exotic creatures: people with faces on their chests or feet so large they could shade their owners by being lifted into the air, people with two heads or dog heads, with one eye, without noses. The less provocative end of this pantheon shaded imperceptibly into human group like Pygmies and dark-skinned Ethiopians. But all were accepted as real and—if human—descended from Adam, living in sin, and in need of salvation. Labeling them properly was profoundly important, although largely an imaginative exercise, since most of them didn't exist. But such labeling became all too real when a physically deformed infant was born and parents had to decide whether or not it was human and needed to be baptized.

Stories of exotic and strange creatures grew even more fantastic as explorers made contact with the New World. Sir Walter Raleigh received—and believed, as near as we can tell—reports of "a nation of people, whose heades appeare not aboue their shoulders." Was this tribe, with "mouths in the middle of their breasts," human?[19] If so, they needed to be converted to Christianity. The tribes encountered directly in the New World raised questions, created in part by geography. Adamic ancestry was a central part of the meaning of *human*. Human beings were defined *theologically*, not biologically, as creatures descended from Adam. Definitional problems arose when tribes were discovered that appeared geographically isolated from the Middle East. How could such people be descended from Adam if there was no geographical bridge to carry them to their present homes from the Middle East? The stakes were high in these deliberations.

Such controversies strained Christian anthropology and its biblical worldview. The oriental scholar Jacob Palaeologus (ca. 1520–1585) was beheaded for claiming that not everyone had inherited original sin. The (apparently) human tribes nestled in far-flung corners of the planet could not possibly have descended from Adam and Eve, argued the hapless and eventually headless Palaeologus. Paracelsus protected the prevailing biblical criteria for humanness by suggesting that these isolated tribes had no souls and were thus not fully human. "These people," he wrote, "are from a different Adam," an initially casual claim that would come to have greater—and eventually sinister—meaning.[20]

Solutions like those of Paracelsus were erected around the biblical story of Adam and Eve, the flood, and Babel, guarding the Genesis history like sentries against the incursions of new discoveries. Perhaps, argued some, Noah was an intrepid sailor who dropped off some of his passengers in North America. Or maybe the Native Americans were the ten lost tribes of Israel spoken about in the Bible. The Spanish Jesuit Jose de Acosta, at the end of the sixteenth century, insisted that Native Americans had migrated to the New World across the frigid wilderness of Northern Asia. What was not demonstrably false was often claimed as true in the service of biblical veracity. What was clear to all, at least initially, was that biblical truth was not to be lightly challenged. The great Age of the Book came to a close when this was no longer true—a revolution inaugurated by a brilliant, eccentric, entertaining, and unlikely French Calvinist.

THE STRANGE CASE OF ISAAC LA PEYRÈRE

Isaac La Peyrère (1596–1676), although unknown today, was the Galileo of biblical exegesis—boldly going where others had gone only timidly. Like Galileo, he said clearly, publicly, imperfectly, and ahead of his time what others were only thinking. And like Galileo, he got smacked down by the church. If Galileo was famous for discovering moons around Jupiter, La Peyrère was (in)famous for discovering where Cain found his wife.

La Peyrère's exegetical revelations began when he was a boy growing up as a Calvinist in the south of France. At a time when his peers were focusing on finding mates, he was puzzling over where Cain got his. "I had this suspition [sic] also being a Child," he wrote in his *Theological System upon That Presupposition That Men Were Before Adam*, "when I heard or read the History of Genesis: Where Cain goes forth; where he kills his brother when they were in the field; doing it warily, like a thief least it should be discovered . . ." And, of course, the perennial conundrums: "Where he fear punishment for the death of his Brother, . . . where he married a wife, . . . and where Cain 'builds a city.'"[21]

La Peyrère's aha moment came when he realized the book of Genesis has two creation stories. The juxtaposition of the stories and the uncritical approach of most readers to the text had merged the two accounts into one. Somehow La Peyrère, with no relevant scholarly training, became convinced that the two creation stories were so completely independent of each other that they actually referred to two unrelated historical events.

La Peyrère was also pushed into his pre-Adamism by his reading of verses 12–14 in Paul's letter to the Romans, one of the enduring theological treatments of Adam: "As by one man sin entered into the world, and by sin, death: so likewise death had power over all men, because in him all men sinned. For till the time of the Law sin was in the world, but sin was not imputed, when the Law was not."[22]

La Peyrère interpreted this passage to mean that if Adam had sinned in any meaningful sense—if sin was "imputed" to him—the Law that Christians had traditionally assumed started with Moses must have been in place long before Moses's celebrated encounter with God on Mount Sinai. The Law thus did not originate with Moses. But why would the Law be in place if there had never been any sin? There would be no need. Lawless people must therefore have preceded Adam and were identified as sinners when God gave Adam the first law. The existence of this law, according to La Peyrère's reading of Paul, made it possible for Adam to sin.

In 1640, two years before the seminal year that witnessed the death of Galileo and birth of Newton, La Peyrère produced an elaboration of his boyhood exegetical revelations. He observed that the first creation story of Genesis—which does not mention Adam—described the creation of the universe, the earth, and the larger human race—a race created without law. The second creation story described events that occurred much later: the origins of the Jewish people, whose history—one small chapter nestled in the larger story of a planet populated with countless other tribes—was then unfolded throughout the Hebrew scriptures. Adam was not the first man, concluded La Peyrère; he was the first *Jewish* man and the representative to whom God gave the Law that would judge the rest of the world. Countless tribes had existed on other continents and remote islands for millennia before Adam and his famous first family began their distinctively *Jewish* story in the Middle East. These other tribes provided wives for his sons, posses to chase murderers, and occupants for cities and towns.

In one fell swoop, La Peyrère's proposal solved problems internal to the Bible—Mrs. Cain and the population of Nod—and external as well: any history longer than that of the Jews was comfortably rooted without difficulty in that first creation. God created Native Americans in the distant past—no need to insist they had migrated there from the Middle East on a nonexistent land bridge or made an impossible trek across the North Pole. Ancient Chinese history could now be accepted at face value, thanks to

La Peyrère, and not rejected out of hand simply because it was older than Jewish history. And he did all this without twisting the biblical text. It was a tour de force of hermeneutical brilliance, or at least a brilliant adolescent insight grown to maturity.

La Peyrère's ideas fell on many ears; a few were sympathetic, but most had doubts and many were hostile. All were intrigued by the possibility of "men before Adam," or "pre-Adamites," as they become known. Marin Mersenne (1588–1648), a French scholar active in many fields but mainly in mathematics, praised La Peyrère's work, strangely titled *A Southerner's Dream of Men Before Adam*, for making "several passages in Scripture easier to understand."[23] Mersenne, however, was theologically trained and understood that separating Jewish history from overall human history would disconnect Adam and his original sin from the larger human race.

I emphasize that La Peyrère was not bringing *external* problems to the Bible and insisting that, since the Bible had gotten it wrong, we had to change our reading. There were such problems, of course, but they were not taken too seriously by Christian scholars just yet. He was motivated by problems *within* the text—problems that had been obvious for centuries and continue to plague those who insist on reading Genesis today with the same simplistic literacy as the average sixteenth-century reader.

La Peyrère's solution had the happy consequence of solving more problems than those that had motivated it. As his ideas and rumors of his ideas circulated, however, the theological consequences of demoting Adam from father of humanity to father of the Jews moved to the fore and, in a pattern that has yet to be resolved in much of American Christianity, the theological issues trumped everything else. The guardians of the tradition insisted that Adam's theological role as the original sinner responsible for the fall of humanity had to be preserved. Otherwise, Christian orthodoxy would collapse.

Anticipating controversy, La Peyrère anonymously published a revised version of his work in Holland. It was reprinted four times and translated into English and Dutch. Holland was the most liberal culture in Europe, but opposition mounted from all quarters. Dutch Calvinists condemned it, as did the Catholics in conservative France—one of a tiny number of things on which they agreed. The book was publicly burned in Paris. Refutations appeared, nineteen of them in 1656 alone and more than forty within a century.[24] The Inquisition, guardian of orthodoxy, arrested La Peyrère in Brussels and would have put him to death, but an influential advocate worked out a deal: La Peyrère would convert to Catholicism which, in the

peculiar logic of the Inquisition, meant that he was absolved of errors committed and heresies embraced while a Protestant; and he would publish a
retraction of his subversive theory of men before Adam.

La Peyrère died a pauper in a seminary outside Paris, where he had lived
for the last few years of his life. Popular imagination of the time joined the
troubled misfit, who was technically still a Catholic, to Baruch Spinoza,
whom he influenced, and to Thomas Hobbes, who inspired him, making
a "triumvirate of devils incarnate in an age that knew Satans when it saw
them."[25] His struggles had undermined his lifelong, if evolving, religious
commitment, and it is reported that when his deathbed confessor informed
him that his soul was ready to depart for the next world, the aging former
heretic asked irreverently, "Where do you want it to go?" One of his epi-
grams reads:

> *Here lies La Peyrère, first a good Israelite,*
> *Then Huguenot, Catholic, Pre-adamite:*
> *Four religions he tried, till, perplexed with so many,*
> *At eighty he died, and went off without any!*[26]

La Peyrère was an intellectual giant, linked with Descartes and Newton
as the architects of a new order. The sheer volume of firepower summoned
to wage war on him testifies to this judgment. And his approach to the Bible
inaugurated dramatic, even revolutionary, new ways of reading Genesis
that are still with us. Fundamentalist Bible scholars to this day feel com-
pelled to dismantle his ideas. But, for reasons that are not entirely clear, the
father of pre-Adamism has largely faded from history. He was, for those
who no longer approach the Bible as a serious historical document, far too
traditional in his religious beliefs. On the other hand, in his willingness to
break with tradition, he certainly alienated those who presumed to referee
that tradition.

Pre-Adamism, however, now part of the Christian conversation, could
not be excised despite the assaults on La Peyrère. To this day it remains
the most controversial point of contact between science and evangelical
Christianity: was there a first man who sinned and brought death upon all
humanity? A good proportion of American Christians respond enthusiasti-
cally in the affirmative and look for creative ways to save the biblical Adam
from dilutions of the sort proposed by La Peyrère.

This chapter began with Copernicus, the scholar credited with starting
the revolution in astronomy that would lead to Newton, modern science,

and the transformation of almost every field of knowledge. La Peyrère was in many ways the Copernicus of biblical criticism. Like Copernicus, he was inspired to seek solutions to long-standing problems that puzzled his predecessors. Also like Copernicus, his work was condemned and then eventually became a template for all related discussion. But perhaps the greatest similarity was that he worked within a tradition he took very seriously and, whatever his religious state of mind when he died, his life was dominated by significant—albeit shifting—religious commitments.

La Peyrère died in 1676. Native Americans, whose relationship to Adam had been under discussion for a century, were fighting to survive in North America. This was the year that the Nipmuck tribe attacked Lancaster and the Wampanoags attacked Northampton, both settlements in Massachusetts. In February of that year the Massachusetts council met to consider building a protective wall around Boston and to discuss what they should do with the Christian Indians they had exiled to Deer Island. Providence, Rhode Island, was destroyed by a coalition of Native American tribes. Other towns in the colonies met similar fates. In July, troops swept through New England, capturing Algonquians and exporting them out of the colonies as slaves. Whatever theological status they may have received from sympathetic European commissions, their treatment in North America was driven by the practical realities of conquest and economics.

The year 1676 also saw Ole Roemer of Denmark make the first quantitative measurement of the speed of light. Lost amid the political turmoil of his time, it was a quiet reminder that the scientific study of nature was underway. Isaac Newton and Gottfried Wilhelm Leibniz were inventing calculus, and Newton was but a decade away from finishing his classic work on gravity, the *Principia*—probably the most important science book ever published and one that would secure a central role for science in Western culture. The new sciences being born—astronomy, geology, geography, chemistry, zoology—would eventually transform our understanding of the world. Not surprisingly, the new sciences—each in its own way—offered up a seemingly unending set of challenges to the traditional understanding of Adam and Eve.

CHAPTER 7

∽

THE FIRST MAN AND THE FIRST MINUTE

Adam and the Age of the Earth

*In matters that are so obscure and far beyond our
vision, we find in Holy Scripture passages which can
be interpreted in very different ways without
prejudice to the faith we have received.*

—AUGUSTINE[1]

God created the world in 3928 BCE, on September 21, the autumnal equinox, at nine o'clock in the morning, said Bishop John Lightfoot (1601–1675) in 1642, the year Newton was born. Titled *A few, and New Observations upon the Book of Genesis. The Most of them Certain, the rest probable, all Harmless, Strange and rarely heard of before*, the brief scholarly work combined biblical studies, astronomical observations, secular history, and theological analysis to establish the date of the creation.[2] Today Lightfoot's spurious precision invites ridicule, but in seventeenth-century England it was a scholarly exercise performed by a respected graduate of Christ's College, Cambridge.

The most (in)famous of the seventeenth century's squad of biblical chronologists—and there were scores of them—was Bishop James Ussher, Ireland's leading archbishop. In his multivolume work, Ussher produced one of the great projects of the seventeenth century—a full chronology of human history from Adam and Eve to Noah's flood, to the dispersion of the human tribes and the confusion of languages at Babel, to Jesus and the development of Christianity. Contemporary scholars, unaware that such chronologies were respectable at the time, ridicule Ussher's achievement as the product of a regressive superstition holding back science, a trivial genealogical research project consisting of nothing more than poring over tables of "begats" in the Old Testament.

But Ussher's project was more sophisticated, engaging over the course of some two thousand pages a range of historical issues reaching far beyond the biblical text. And even the textual issues were complex, requiring informed comparisons of multiple texts and translations—many with serious discrepancies in the tables most relevant to the project. Astronomy and secular history figured prominently. Jesus's birth, for example, was pushed back to 4 BCE based on extrabiblical evidence that Herod, who in the biblical account tried to kill Jesus by slaughtering all the baby boys in Bethlehem, died that year.

Ussher's chronology had thousands of dates, but his most famous was 4004 BCE—the creation of the world. Millions of twenty-first-century Protestants, myself included, encountered this number at the top of the center column in our Scofield Study Bibles, just to the right of the text's opening line: "In the beginning God created the heavens and the earth." Ussher's date for the creation fits with a popular schedule in which God carries out his plans on a millennial timetable. We read in 2 Peter 3:8, for instance, that "with the Lord one day is like a thousand years and a thousand years are like one day." Putting the creation exactly four thousand years before the birth of Jesus appealed to those attracted to this millenarian paradigm for understanding history as an orderly sequence of equally spaced divine interventions in human affairs. Noah's flood conveniently fell around 2000 BCE and, by assuming that the six days of creation symbolized six millennia of theologically driven history, Jesus would return around 2000 CE.[3] This was one of several reasons for the substantial but short-lived apocalyptic enthusiasm exhibited by biblical literalists as that date approached.

Ussher is the most renowned chronologer in a long tradition. Scholars heaping ridicule on his benighted head should take note that the chronological arts were also practiced by Isaac Newton, who dated the creation to 4000 BCE, and Johannes Kepler, who used astronomical arguments, among others, to place the creation on April 27, 3977 BCE.

Lightfoot, Ussher, Newton, Kepler, and others in their century believed that God had inspired a Bible without error, even in its references to history, geography, and the natural sciences. They no more expected a conflict between the Bible and other sources of knowledge than modern-day chemists would expect that the truths of their discipline would conflict with those of the biologists down the hall. But the growing interest in the natural world during the sixteenth and seventeenth centuries forced new interpretations and even an unanticipated abandonment of the Genesis account of God's creation of the world, for those prepared to accept the evidence. This new vision emerged like a landscape appearing through a mist, visible not because it was new or closer or viewed with a novel technology but because an obscuring fog was dissipating. That fog was an interpretative tradition that assigned layers of meaning to things—biblical passages as well as natural phenomena—that made it hard to tell what those things were in and of themselves.

The tradition of assigning multiple meanings to the same thing had long guided the study of both the Bible and nature. The third-century theologian Origen formally inaugurated this approach, although he was not the first to use it. Origen spoke of three "senses" to look for meaning in a passage. "For as a man consists of body, soul, and spirit," he wrote, "so in the same way does Scripture." These senses were the *literal*, the *moral*, and the *allegorical*; the literal was the *least* significant, the only one that a spiritually unenlightened mind could grasp, and the only one that did not even exist for many biblical passages. The moral sense was the "soul" of scripture, discerned by more spiritually advanced thinkers. The allegorical sense was the highest, revealing theological insights that shone with a grandeur that overwhelmed the literal meaning of the passage to which the allegory was attached by the thinnest of exegetical cords.[4]

A millennium later Dante summarized the widely used ideas in language that could have come straight from Origen. Speaking of the exodus, he identified the literal meaning of the story as the historical "exodus of the children of Israel from Egypt," an account of a tribal migration that even a pagan could understand. The moral lesson was the "turning of the soul from the sorrow and misery of sin to the state of grace," a mystery that would be lost on a pagan reader. And the allegory contained in that story of God rescuing his people is the "Redemption by Christ."[5] Making things even more complicated, medieval theologians added a fourth layer of meaning, the *anagogical*, which referred to a passage's revelation about heaven or the afterlife. Jerusalem, to which the freed Israelites returned in the story of the exodus, was often taken to refer to heaven. The literal text in this approach lay buried beneath more important ideas.

The natural world—understood as God's other book—received the same interpretative treatment, based on the belief that everything God created was in some sense *for* human beings. Objects in the world—rocks, rivers, rhubarb, rabbits—had an inconsequential literal meaning in and of themselves. Rocks were real, of course, and one could stub one's toe on them or sling them at a giant enemy. But one could also understand rocks as barriers, blocking spiritual growth just as they blocked forward motion. Or they could be taken as strong foundations. God placed rocks—and everything else on the earth—to *signify* important truths. Such lessons were common in Scripture: we are admonished in Proverbs 6:6 to "Go to the ant, you sluggard; consider her ways, and be wise." In this reading of nature, the ant provides a lesson of greater importance than zoological details. Jesus even encouraged such approaches, referring to himself as a "vine" and exhorting his followers to be "salt," "light," and "fishers of men." Fruit trees bear fruit, but they also remind us of beauty and the importance of being rooted. Cows provide beef and milk, and lessons about moral uprightness: "Take care not to be bent over like cattle," counseled Ambrose. "See that you do not incline—not so much physically as they do, but morally."[6] Ambrose even found a moral lesson in the barking of dogs. "To dogs is given the ability to bark in defense of their masters," he wrote, "you should thus learn to use your voice for the sake of Christ, when ravening wolves attack His sheepfold."[7]

Nature and scripture were interpreted in mutually reinforcing ways. Just as a series of letters (t-r-e-e) could *signify* an actual tree without being in any literal sense tree-like, so an object in the world (an actual tree) could *signify* the importance of, say, striving toward the heavens, without having a soul that would aspire to do so. "The whole sensible world is like a book, as it were, written by the hand of God," wrote Hugh of St. Victor's in the twelfth century, "that is to say, created by divine power and each of its creatures are like forms, devised not by human effort, but rather to be established by the divine will in order to make manifest the wisdom of the invisible things of God."[8]

This interpretive method, creatively applied, brought order to the twin worlds of scripture and nature—God's Two Books. Portions of the Bible with no theologically useful literal meaning—like the R-rated Song of Solomon with its salacious celebration of sex—could be read as *entirely* allegorical, without any literal meaning. The Song of Solomon is not an erotic tale of two lovers; it's the story of Christ's love for his church. Passages that, taken literally, contradict common sense or the "science" of the day—like how Adam and Eve had their spiritual eyes opened by eating a piece of fruit, or how Adam could name every animal in one day—were interpreted without assigning a literal meaning to them, the interpretation floating almost entirely free of the actual text.

Origen's interpretive creativity was available to all who embraced Christianity, for once illuminated by the Spirit of God, they would be "easily able to aspire to grasp even deeper truths which are concealed in the Bible." The idea that important truths were *hidden* by God in its pages opened the Bible to a search for interpretative novelties that might speak to new concerns, like the perennial "Who is the Antichrist and when will he appear?" Or the more recent "Will the world end in a nuclear holocaust?"

In this world of signification, two seemingly unrelated things had fossilized together beneath thick layers of interpretive sediment—the literal biblical text and the empirical details of the natural world. But this world began to be exposed as sixteenth- and seventeenth-century thinkers looked more closely at their texts and discovered, to their delight and dismay, that these texts—and their interpretation—had complex and troubling histories.

Such concerns were not new. Christian thinkers had long been aware, for example, that the various translations of the Bible did not agree with each other in many small details. Old Testament genealogies, for example, did not match each other when laid side by side. But this occasioned no great consternation since the real significance of these passages lay in their *interpretations*, not their literal meanings.

But scholars now wanted to understand texts in their original form—to escape the received wisdom by looking at the text as *text*, not as the inspiration for speculative gloss. One such scholar was Martin Luther, who had become disturbed by what he thought were indefensible interpretations of the Bible that were being exploited to extract money from the faithful. In a highly symbolic move, Luther ordered the printer in Wittenberg to prepare a text of the Psalms for his course—and to print the text with wide margins left blank. Luther's students would study the actual text of the Psalms, undistracted—and unconstrained—by the copious commentary that normally crowded the margins of such texts. The naked text, in all its literal glory, invited new and careful consideration of the words on the page.

With this pedagogical strategy, the not-yet-Protestant Luther severed the centuries-old link between the Bible and the interpretative tradition that had grown up around it. "Scripture without any glosses is the sun," he wrote, "and the whole light from which all teachers receive their light."[9]

GOD'S OTHER BOOK

Luther's approach was mainstream Renaissance—*re-naissance*—in his conviction that scripture (inerrantly inspired by God, transcribed by biblical authors from a time when humans were closer to their creator) was a much deeper truth than the interpretations placed on scripture by later thinkers, no matter how well intentioned. Reading the text directly—and literally—brought believers into closer contact with the Author of scripture than when they were guided by human authorities like Origen, Augustine, and Aquinas.

An identical approach to God's other "book" encouraged the direct inspection of nature itself, rather than a reliance on theological explanations for why God created planets that orbit, birds that fly, and bees that sting. And if Luther was the champion of the new biblical literalism and an apologist for a new understanding of the Christian faith, Francis Bacon (1561–1626) was his scientific counterpart. Bacon called for a similar intellectual upheaval in the approach to the natural world. In 1605, almost ninety years after Luther nailed his ninety-five theses to the door of the Wittenberg cathedral and with Luther clearly in mind, Bacon wrote:

> In the age of ourselves and our Fathers, when it pleased God to call the Church of Rome to account for their degenerate manners and ceremonies, and sundry doctrines obnoxious and framed to hold the same abuses; at one and the same time it was ordained by the Divine Providence, that there should attend withal a renovation and a new spring of all other knowledges.[10]

Bacon, eager to defend the emerging natural philosophy of people like Kepler and Galileo, the vanguard of a growing community in the early stages of its own revolution, warned that the Christian religion had been corrupted because the church had been "inclined to leave the oracles of God's word." In the same way, in the "inquisition of nature they have ever left the oracles of God's works."[11] Such comparisons were commonplace throughout the seventeenth century, even to the extent of calling Aristotle the "pope in philosophy" to be dethroned, just as the Reformers dethroned his religious counterpart in Rome.[12]

In a fascinating study, *The Fall of Man and the Foundations of Science*, historian of science Peter Harrison notes that Bacon championed a highly empirical approach to knowledge precisely because he was convinced—with Augustine and Luther—that the Fall had profoundly impaired human reason. Harrison challenges the received wisdom that science was born of an expanded view of the powers of human reason: "The birth of modern experimental science was not attended with a new awareness of the powers and capacities of human reason," concludes Harrison, "but rather just the opposite—a consciousness of the manifold deficiencies of the intellect."[13]

The details of these reformations in the reading of God's Two Books are beyond the scope of the story I am telling here. They were also far beyond the horizons of the Lutherans and the Baconians, who did not foresee that their attempts to read God's Two Books more faithfully would eventually pit those books against each other, raising troubling questions about how God could be the author of both or either. I want to note at this point only that this new literal reading of God's Two Books rooted those "texts" in separate but not incompatible soils.

The Bible was to be read as straightforwardly as possible and the most natural meaning of the verses was assumed to be authoritative. Animals, plants, rocks, and rivers were also not to be read primarily as signs or metaphors pointing beyond themselves. They were to be understood on their own terms. This was more complex, however, because animals and plants were, well, more complex. These approaches, of course, were not embraced all at once by everyone and should be viewed more as the emergence of two communities of scholars: those with primary focus on the meaning of the Bible and those with primary focus on behavior of nature. Kepler, as a counterexample, aspired in his youth to be a theologian and retained deep theological intuitions even as he advanced the Copernican Revolution. "Behold," he wrote to a friend, "how through my effort God is being celebrated in astronomy."[14] Newton similarly retained great interest in theological matters.

This interpretative revolution grew steadily stronger. Much of it played out as Protestantism defined itself in protest against Catholicism. As hostilities grew between the rival Christianities, Protestant leaders denounced the Roman Church, labeling it the Great Whore of Babylon, an evil apocalyptic institution from which the Antichrist would arise. Pope Leo X, said Luther, was this Antichrist. "I call upon you to renounce your diabolical blasphemy and audacious impiety," he thundered in response to the papal bull of Leo X, "and, if you will not, we shall all hold your seat as possessed and oppressed by Satan, the damned seat of Antichrist."[15]

As tensions mounted, the marginalia that Luther the Catholic priest had scrubbed off his text of the Psalms came to be seen by increasingly strident reformers not as the flawed wisdom of human interpreters but as the scribblings of Satan. God had written the original text and men, under the influence of Satan, had obscured it. *Sola scriptura* became the increasingly narrow refrain of the Reformers. God's truth was to be found only in unglossed scriptures. "Necessity forces us to run to the Bible," wrote Luther, "with the writings of all teachers, and to obtain there a verdict and judgment upon them."[16]

At its heart, however, the revolution—a *renaissance* to the elite occupants of ivory towers, a *reformation* to those in humble Protestant pews, a *counterreformation* to Catholics—sought to recover the most ancient and perfect wisdom, the wisdom of the first man who talked directly to God with faculties uncompromised by sin, an *Über*man whom everyone should emulate.

Widespread belief in Adam's superior understanding inspired a closer reading of God's books. Stripped of foggy gloss, the story in Genesis emerged as actual history; its author, Moses, became "the sacred historian,"[17] chronicling an inaccessible and prehuman history originally told to Adam by God. Adam's knowledge passed to Moses via the patriarchs— Seth, Enoch, Noah—who God blessed with long lives to minimize the chances of the story becoming corrupted along the way.

The Bible could thus be studied like other history books, only with absolute confidence in its accuracy. Genesis records God commanding Adam to "fill the earth and subdue it, . . . and have dominion over every living thing." Taken literally, this mandate called for a mastery of nature that required a thorough knowledge of its details. Such mastery could possibly recover Adam's original knowledge, to undo the damage of the curse, to partially restore the lost paradise of Eden.

Adam was thought to have had vast knowledge of the natural world, knowledge imparted directly from God, acquired when the earth was new and all the footprints on its uncursed soil were his own. "In the state of innocency in the first creation," wrote seventeenth-century theologian George Walker, author of *The History of the Creation*, "man had perfect naturall knowledge of all naturall things, arising and springing immediately from his naturall soule."[18]

Two investigations were thus unleashed, one into each of God's Two Books. Uncovering the correct text and precise meaning of the scriptures using new historical scholarship proceeded along one track. Along the other track was the investigation of nature, using the emerging scientific method. These projects came together like two separate strands of nucleic acid to form DNA, breathing new life into the investigation of nature.

BURNET'S SACRED HISTORY OF THE WORLD

The projects started well enough. Just as ancient biblical chronologies could be lined up with those of other civilizations, as we saw earlier, so the Bible's references to nature could be aligned with nature itself. God's Two Books could hardly disagree. The history that God had communicated directly to Adam was simply another version of the history uncovered by inspection of the natural world. But, most important, the stories told in the Two Books could be *combined* to provide a more complete understanding. Just as the Bible specified where one might look for Eden, Babel, or Noah's ark, so the new understanding of nature would illuminate what the Bible meant when it said that God placed lights "in the firmament" or created animals to reproduce "after their kind." Difficult biblical claims—like God causing the sun to stand still, or Jonah living for three days inside a "great fish," or the origination of the waters for Noah's flood—could be understood using insights from the natural world.

Read as one, the Two Books were more than the sum of their parts; they were like two partial collections of puzzle pieces that, when combined, contain enough information to figure out what the overall puzzle should look like. The best example of this—though far from atypical—was Thomas Burnet's *Sacred Theory of the Earth*, a synergistic merging of biblical and natural histories.

Burnet was a prominent Anglican and private chaplain to the king of England. His history begins with a plain, literal reading of Genesis that would have warmed Luther's reforming heart. This reading occurs within the frame of an inerrant Bible and a confidence that God's Two Books will agree. "We are not to suppose," wrote Burnet in *The Sacred Theory of the Earth*, "that any truth concerning the natural world can be an enemy to religion." He added, "Truth cannot be an enemy to truth, God is not divided against himself."[19]

Burnet assumed that everything in the Bible happened as described, but that the events should, whenever possible, be understood as the result of *secondary* causes—natural processes employed by God, rather than miraculous intrusions into the natural order. This was consistent with the emerging view of God as a divine clockmaker whose clocks ran without constant tinkering. Bacon had written in *Advancement of Learning* that it was "certain" that "God worketh nothing in Nature but by second causes." To claim that God worked directly in the natural order through miracles was not—as some confused souls would have it—honoring to God; it was "to offer the Author of Truth the unclean sacrifice of a lie."[20]

This approach was consistent with the biblical creation story where God does not zap plants into existence but commands the earth to "bring them forth." When God destroyed everyone except Noah's family, he did it with a flood, not by magically flinging the sinful multitudes into the sun. So Burnet's new questions about the waters of Noah's flood, to take the centerpiece of his example, were entirely appropriate. The floodwaters were not created by one miracle and then removed by another—they were, as the biblical text implies, existing waters, redistributed by natural processes to produce a global flood, and then redistributed again to restore dry land.

Burnet calculated that, as things—such as mountains—stand today, the earth's water supply was inadequate for a global flood. So things must have stood differently at the time of Noah. The earth, he inferred, must have been perfectly smooth, with no mountains, and there must have been a layer of water under the smooth shell of the earth's crust. The flood occurred when the smooth shell cracked and the underlying waters burst forth. The flood ended when the waters receded, leaving a damaged and fractured surface with enough holes, cracks, and grooves to hold the waters that remained. Prior to the flood the earth had been an upright egg, which Burnet said caused waters to run smoothly from higher to lower latitudes and evaporate in the tropics. The earth stood upright, with no tilt—why would God make a tilted earth?—and Eden enjoyed a perpetual spring at midlatitude. The paradise climate facilitated the great ages of the patriarchs. The flood destroyed paradise by tilting the earth onto its present axis, inaugurating the unhealthy cycle of the seasons, and shrinking life spans to their present values.

Burnet's *Sacred Theory* strikes us today as fanciful and driven more by biblical literalism than anything resembling science, but it symbolizes a new approach sprung from the union of a "natural" reading of God's Two Books—two intertwined sources of truth underwritten by the same author.

In this emerging interpretive scheme, biblical references to nature were brought into agreement, or *concordance*, with what was known of nature directly. God inspired the biblical authors so as to *anticipate* scientific advances in the future. Bacon had declared that a careful reading of the book of Job would find it "pregnant and swelling with natural philosophy," including ideas about the earth's suspension in space, the sphere of the fixed stars, the poles, and the "roundness of the world."[21] Facts of nature could thus be used to illuminate mysterious biblical passages containing scientific insights too advanced for their time. This approach views scripture as a science text (among other things). Known as *concordism*, the approach remains vital and has become the source of much of the trouble that the Bible has confronted from science.

Burnet was a quintessential concordist: he estimated the total amount of water on the earth—a detail not mentioned in the Bible—and used that information to provide more detail for the story. Similar measurements of the mountains of the earth let him envision what the earth must have been like at the time of Noah—another relevant detail not mentioned in the Bible. He imagined a terrestrial rationale for the Edenic paradise that would let Adam and his preflood progeny live for nine centuries and a comparable explanation for the plummeting in life expectancy of Noah's postflood progeny.

Burnet was friends with Isaac Newton, who expressed approval of his sacred history, even suggesting that portions of it were "more probable" than some of his own work. Newton thought his own theory of gravitation implied a gradual deterioration of the solar system, from irregularities like comets and planetary moons, and suggested that the deterioration predicted from his theory would lead to the destruction of the world implied in the Bible.[22]

I mention Newton in this context not because of his influence on this new concordist approach to the Bible but to make the point that Burnet's approach—and that of Ussher, Lightfoot, and others—was not that of a religiously motivated thinker making an argument *outside* the scientific mainstream but was rather the approach of those in the vanguard of the scientific revolution, few of whom anticipated any conflicts between God's Two Books.

Concordism *motivated* the investigation of nature for thinkers/scholars of this era. Fossils of sea creatures found on the tops of mountains were thought to have been carried there by Noah's flood. The entombed animals dug up during excavations were drowned in the flood. Animals in North America had migrated there from the region around Eden, implying a land bridge at some point. Concordism begins with the Bible as the primary authority: the approximate date for the creation of the world or a general description of a flood comes from the Bible, and science fills in the details. If the details didn't align perfectly, both the Bible and the extrabiblical information were pressed for an accommodation that everyone anticipated was possible. Science was an exciting new activity in the seventeenth century, just getting off the ground, and many sciences—geology, for example— barely existed, and were not about to challenge scripture in any substantial way. Few had any notion that a history of the earth could be developed by examining its present features. But this was about to change, as Burnet's concordist approach to history gave way to histories that were more and more about the book of nature and less and less about the Bible.

EPOCHS AND AGES

In 1778 Georges-Louis Leclerc, Comte de Buffon (1707–1788), a prolific French naturalist with modest religious zeal, published a groundbreaking work titled *Epochs of Nature*, one of several dozen volumes summarizing what science had discovered about the world. One of the twentieth century's greatest evolutionary biologists, Ernst Mayr, describes Buffon as the "father of all thought in natural history in the second half of the 18th century."[23] Buffon anticipated the nineteenth century's discovery of the grand history of everything on earth, from plants and animals to mountains and rivers. He even speculated about evolving life forms, wondering if the *inferior* quadrupeds in North America might have degenerated from Old World ancestors, perhaps migrating there from their Edenic origins via a land bridge. Buffon's exploration represents one of the first dramatic reconstructions of the earth's history, one with only modest—and largely cosmetic—biblical content, and one with meaningful departures from strict biblical literalism.

Buffon's history describes a series of originating epochs.[24] The first occurred when a comet crashed into the sun and ejected molten material that became the earth, which has been cooling ever since. The second epoch saw the surface solidify and mountains form. Water condensed in the third epoch, cooling to the point where life spontaneously appeared; the water retreated in the fourth epoch to expose hills and valleys, and land animals appeared. In the fifth epoch giant animals, like elephants and rhinoceroses, appeared at the poles, which were the first parts of the earth to cool enough for such life forms. Polar creatures migrated toward the equator in the sixth epoch and crustal collapse placed a vast ocean between the Old and New Worlds. Humans appeared in the seventh. Significantly, to explain the presence of humans on both continents, Buffon had originally located human origins in the era before the Old and New Worlds were separated. At the last minute, however, as the book was going to press, he identified a seventh epoch as the originating point for humans, a move that had two important effects: it placed a clear divide in natural history between the human and prehuman eras, and it allowed for interpretations that humans were the intended goal or endpoint of the epochal process.[25]

Remarkably, Buffon's *Epochs of Nature* all but ignored the Bible. The age of the earth was determined by measuring cooling rates: from a molten beginning, Buffon calculated it would take three million years for the earth to reach its present comfortable temperatures. No biblical chronologies were consulted to arrive at this number. The earth was not created before the sun, as Genesis clearly stated. The animals appear in a nonbiblical order. Humans did not appear near the beginning, as they did in the Bible; and when they did appear it was not in an Edenic paradise but a threatening environment populated by terrifying beasts. The world would end in a freeze as the earth kept cooling, not in the fire St. Peter wrote about in the New Testament.

Nevertheless, Buffon had a response to those concerned that his history was too secular. His scheme entailed *seven* epochs, one for each creative day in Genesis. If each day in Genesis corresponded to an epoch, then perhaps science was simply correcting and enlarging the revealed account in Genesis. Buffon also noted that many of the already ambiguous verbs in Genesis were in the imperfect tense, allowing that the processes described were of long duration.[26] But perhaps the most significant aspect of Buffon's scheme was its clear *developmental* character—a paradigmatic understanding that would come to dominate. Buffon did not see the world as an old-fashioned, mechanical Newtonian clock, wound up by a deistic God in the beginning and left to unwind slowly across the millennia. It had a narrative; a history; a beginning, middle, and end; and most important for his readers, a way to incorporate a teleological goal into nature. Buffon's epochs were God's preparatory work, as the earth was transformed to accommodate humans. What better way to exalt the first man than to discover that the creator spent millions of years preparing his home?

Buffon's approach is now known as the day-age theory, and countless variations of it were proposed by Christians committed to the Two Books approach. It remains popular among concordists who take natural history seriously but insist that it correlate with the Genesis chronology. Millions of evangelicals believe that some day-age scheme aligns the Genesis account with history. The biblical legitimacy of the day-age theory has been defended with so much ingenuity that its most important contemporary advocate, Hugh Ross of Reasons to Believe, has become convinced that it is the clear teaching of the Bible and *not* a compromise forced by geology.

The day-age accommodation of Buffon and others was joined by another flexible scheme, an approach known as the gap theory, that harmonized Genesis and geology by postulating an original creation before the one leading to Adam. The most influential promoter of the gap theory was Thomas Chalmers (1780–1847), professor of theology and leader of the Free Church of Scotland, who has been called "Scotland's greatest nineteenth-century churchman."[27]

The gap theory takes its cue from grammatical ambiguities in the first two verses in the Bible commonly translated as, "In the beginning when God created the heavens and the earth, the earth was a formless void." The passage can also be rendered, "When God began creating the heavens and the earth, the earth was at first a shapeless, chaotic mass."[28] The latter version is justified by the conventions of the Hebrew language, but raises questions about the ultimate origin of the earth. An eighteenth-century German scholar even translated Genesis 1:2—the verse after "In the beginning God created the heavens and the earth"—as, "Afterward, the earth became a waste and desolation."[29] If we assume that God is the creator of everything, we can exploit this ambiguity and, on entirely biblical grounds, propose a prior creation that was destroyed—perhaps in a catastrophe like the flood—after which God re-created the earth and everything in it. There is thus a gap between the first and second verses of Genesis, corresponding to a (possibly) significant geological break between a previous creation and this one.

The gap theory was an ingenious concordist strategy that, like Buffon's day-age proposal, solved scientific problems, but, unlike Buffon's proposal, was faithful to a more natural reading of Genesis, including the account of Noah's flood. In particular, the gap theory addressed scientific problems posed by the growing awareness of extinction.

The story of extinction begins—or actually does not begin—with the discovery of fossils. The word *fossil* originally meant simply "dug up" and included interesting rocks and crystals.[30] And even what we now label fossils, the petrified remains of animals or plants, were initially misunderstood as unrelated to anything organic. Rocks—like snowflakes and sand dunes—were thought to sometimes just grow into interesting shapes, and sometimes those shapes resembled living things. However, as the natural world was inspected more carefully, the match between fossils and the bones and teeth of existing animals became undeniable. Fossils were then interpreted as a legacy of Noah's flood, which entombed countless creatures in sediments where they could fossilize. But as more became known about fossils, this interpretation raised more questions: Why, for example, were the fossils stacked in a specific order, with different, and apparently *simpler,* organisms in lower strata? How did Noah's flood sort them like this? And why, if all life except the inhabitants of the ark were drowned together, were no humans ever found in the lower strata? Why were no human fossils ever found with dinosaurs, for example?

The fossil record revealed that many species had gone extinct prior to the appearance of humans. If Adam had named all the animals, and they were all created, in some sense, *for* humans, how could species have gone extinct *prior* to the arrival of Adam and Eve? Why did the fossil record suggest that the earth had a vast history prior to the arrival of humans? Gap theory provided an answer: the earth *did* have a prior history, just as the fossil record revealed. The story in Genesis, with its human focus, begins *after* the destruction of a previously created order—an order that witnessed the flourishing and extinction of countless species with no counterpart in the present order. The gap allowed naturalists to sort fossils—and other artifacts—into two boxes. If they seemed ancient and unrelated to humans, they went in the prior creation. If they fit into the present order, they belonged to the creation described in Genesis.

Geology was in an embryonic stage when Buffon and Chalmers wrote their major works. All that was about to change, and within a few short decades, the discipline would mature and attract the young Charles Darwin. The first geology textbook written in English was the *Introduction to Geology* by Robert Bakewell (1768–1843). Published first in 1813, the book went through several editions and was translated into other languages. Bakewell, also an important popularizer of geology, paid lip service to concordist strategies to accommodate Christianity to new discoveries in geology.

Bakewell's text, written shortly after the birth of Darwin, is an ordinary geology text with endless discussion of rock formations, riverbeds, volcanoes, and so on. The text is remarkable, however, for its straightforward—but provocatively brief—endorsement of a theological context for its subject, using both the gap and the day-age schemes. Bakewell references a "particular definition given of the word *day* as applied to the creation," and suggests that a day is a "period of several thousand years." The work of the six days is a "renovation," not a creation out of nothing (*creatio ex nihilo*): "The six days in which Creative Energy renovated the globe, and called into existence different classes of animals, will imply six successive epochs of independent duration." This renovation was "directed by the same wisdom which regulates every part of the eternal universe."[31] The leading North American geologists—faculty at Yale, McGill, and Princeton (then called the College of New Jersey)—embraced Bakewell's approach that, with nothing more than a tip of the hat to the Genesis creation story, prepared the way for American Christians to accept the great age of the earth. The first of the new historical sciences had been defanged by a calm assurance that it fit within an acceptable theological framework.

Yet a third concordist scheme was popularized by the Scottish evangelical and writer Hugh Miller (1802–1856), which also influenced the day-age theory. Miller argued that the Genesis days were also days of successive revelations. God gave the biblical writer a "prophetic vision" of each creative epoch over a sequence of days, corresponding to the chronology in Genesis. Miller was ahead of his time in harboring reservations about the gap theory, convinced on empirical grounds that the geological record provided no neat divide between a previous order and the present, a scientific detail completely lost on less informed concordists.[32] The devil of science, of course, is precisely in those details, but many Christians ignored such details, confident that the big picture provided by science was in harmony with their faith.

Bakewell's concordism tilted strongly toward the book of nature and, in fact, made no real use of the biblical creation account. George Hawkins Pember (1836–1910), the most significant gap theorist, tilted strongly in the other direction, paying only lip service to the science. Pember populated the period before the Genesis creation story—Bakewell's "unrenovated" earth—with all manner of events, including the fall of Satan and other angels from God's grace, which is mentioned in several places in the Bible but not located in time, and with countless extinctions that ensued from God's violent response to Satan's fall.[33] Absent such a prehistory, it is hard to figure out when Satan became the evil tempter that tricked Eve in the Garden of Eden. Pember was sure that the fall of these angels into sin must have occasioned some global catastrophe on earth that would be preserved in the geological record. Pember's ideas, articulated in his influential book *Earth's Earliest Ages*, were immortalized in the notes of Scofield's popular study Bible, which first appeared in 1909.[34]

Pember has been described as "one of the foremost theologians of prophetic study in the Victorian age."[35] His books were wildly popular among Christians, promoting approaches and intuitions to natural history that remain influential today. *Earth's Earliest Ages* went through five editions in his lifetime and got a fresh new printing in 2012, with a back-cover blurb noting that the book "has been touted worldwide as a classical masterpiece."[36]

Pember embodied an important approach to the relationship between the Two Books and natural history, an approach that still influences evangelicalism. His exposition makes it clear that he accepted the broad outlines of geological history but had no real interest in those details. For example, after he makes his case for a great geological gap between the first and second verses of Genesis, he writes:

> It is thus clear that the second verse of Genesis describes the earth as a ruin; but there is no hint of the time which elapsed between creation and this ruin. Age after age may have rolled away, and it was probably during their course that the strata of the earth's crust were gradually developed. . . . There is room for any length of time between the first and second verses of the Bible. And again, since we have no inspired account of the geological formations, we are at liberty to believe that they were developed just in the order in which we find them. The whole process took place in preadamite times, in connection, perhaps, with another race of beings, and, consequently, does not at present concern us.[37]

The phrase "at liberty to believe" is key. Pember is saying, in effect, that Christians need not worry about supposed challenges from geology. It can all be accommodated. Geology can be safely ignored. Earth's "earliest ages" are theological. In the course of some four-hundred-plus pages, Pember barely comments on anything the geologist might have to say about the earth's earliest ages.

A second feature of Pember's theological history is his emphasis on the end-times. Since the first-century Christians have looked for the apocalypse and often imagined they saw signs of its arrival in their own time. Pember's theological history begins with the original creation and then describes an episode in which Satan and his followers fell and were cast from heaven, followed by whatever geological disaster(s) ensued. Subsequent chapters include the creation story in Genesis, the fall of Adam, the curse, the flood, the tower of Babel, the first coming of Jesus, and now the long wait for the second coming. These historical episodes dominate—but also *accommodate*—whatever the geologist might bring to the table. Christians embracing this view of history were content to dismiss geological deliberations about the Precambrian era, for example, as just technical details of little interest.

Concordism, as we have seen, is ambiguous and inexact. In *Earth's Earliest Ages*, theological history takes precedence over natural history, exactly the opposite of the approach taken by Buffon and Bakewell. For nineteenth-century religious believers engaging with the emerging sciences there was, of course, *one* history exposed in the geology of our planet. But there were *two* complementary paradigms for understanding that history, which could be weighted very differently in whatever scheme was bringing them into concordance. The dinosaurs, for example, went extinct, and we can all agree on that. Vast migrations of animals and human tribes occurred. Ancient landmasses disappeared into the ocean. Mountains arose; mighty rivers were carved by flowing waters. Concordist strategies interpreted these historical convulsions as either divine actions (theological history) or the outworking of natural processes (natural history) or both in some sense. The data were there for all to see, but data does not interpret itself. Increasingly, however, religiously motivated writers like Pember paid limited attention to the details, assuming that everything fit together somehow. And writers from the developing field of geology gave only a cursory mention of the supposedly biblical framework for their conclusions.

It would be a mistake to splinter the academic discussion along the lines that exist today, when the typical theologian writes with no knowledge of geology and the typical geologist has never taken an introductory course in the Bible. Scholars like Chalmers, nominally a theologian, and Bakewell, nominally a geologist, would have had training in both disciplines. Many scholars we think of as scientists were also clergy. Leading biblical expositors and theologians, in Europe and America, strongly endorsed the new concordism, especially the view that the days of Genesis were not ordinary days. Inspired by the geologists, biblical scholars looked more closely at the texts related to creation, both in Genesis and throughout the Bible. The American theologian Taylor Lewis (1802–1877) even claimed to be uninfluenced by science in his conclusion that the days of Genesis were not ordinary twenty-four-hour periods, a claim repeated today by Hugh Ross.[38]

Concordist strategies like the day-age and gap theories became almost universal among conservative Christians. The strategies were flexible, acknowledged the Bible, and at least took notice of science. At first pass, they seemed to resolve conflicts between God's Two Books. In contrast to Pember, however, for whom natural history was simply wedged into a gap between some Hebrew verbs, practicing geologists were more inclined to wedge theological history into whatever space they could find between their rock layers. The goal was the same—to maintain a concordance between God's Two Books. But the latter approach had the benefit of a steady increase in relevant knowledge of those rock layers and just what could and could not be inserted between them.

These concordist strategies were uncontroversial. They were not perceived as compromises forced on the Bible by science. The Christian tradition had never emphasized the most *natural* reading of Genesis as important.

Nothing was really at stake. No creed, for example, had ever enshrined twenty-four-hour days or a young earth, and some important figures like Augustine had even argued that the creation week was an anthropomorphism, pointing out the absurdity of God needing any time at all, and the even greater absurdity of God taking a rest after six days. There was also the problem of fitting the events of Day Six into a twenty-four-hour period: Adam's creation from the dust of the earth, naming all the animals, becoming lonely because they had mates and he did not, and being put to sleep by God for the rib surgery to create Eve—quite a busy day, even for the sinless first man. Surely all this took more than twenty-four hours.

As the nineteenth century headed toward a close, God's Two Books sat together, for those who still took the metaphor seriously in an age of increasing secularization. Liberal scholars who approached the Bible as a purely human product found error and primitive worldviews in its pages. They saw no need to take seriously the idea of a first man, a fall into sin, or any other historical event not supported by science. Secularism was also growing in a scientific community freeing itself at last from ecclesiastical constraints. But for conservative Christians in science, in theology and biblical studies, and on Main Street, the new science was not yet threatening, especially as Darwinian evolution had not yet been embraced by the scientific community.

As disciplinary specialization developed, the Two Books were pursued independently of each other. Pember's facile embrace of geology was about as much as most religiously motivated thinkers needed to assure them that their faith commitments were credible, and a few Bakewellian theological glosses on natural history were adequate for most scientists of faith.

But there were two other books to worry about.

CHAPTER 8

TOO MANY ADAMS?
OR NONE AT ALL?

O man of Shuruppak, son of Ubartutu:
Tear down the house and build a boat!
Abandon wealth and seek living beings!
Spurn possessions and keep alive living beings!
Make all living beings go up into the boat.
The boat which you are to build.
—EPIC OF GILGAMESH[1]

It's a familiar story: a man is divinely created from the soil. He lives naked and innocent among the animals, all friendly save for a mysterious talking serpent going on about immortality. Things go well until he meets a woman who proves to be a temptress. He takes food from the woman, and disaster ensues. Suddenly his nakedness is a problem and he fashions some clothes to cover himself. He is expelled from his paradise.

This familiar story is not from the Bible, but rather from the Epic of Gilgamesh, one of our earliest surviving works of literature, possibly dating as far back as 1150 BCE, approximately two-hundred-fifty years before the book of Genesis was written. It was discovered in 1853. The story in the epic or an older story from which it derived was well known to the Hebrew writers. The author of the book of Daniel seems to have drawn inspiration from it and portions of Ecclesiastes were based on it as well.[2]

In similar fashion the book of Ezra references a King Atrahasis, whose name means "exceedingly wise." The wise Atrahasis was a celebrated hero in the ancient world who has his own legend told elsewhere, in the Epic of Atrahasis, another text outside the Hebrew tradition. Fragments of this epic were discovered in the mid-nineteenth century, shortly before Darwin published *On the Origin of Species*. Over the next century more fragments were assembled and we now have a remarkable story.

The story tells of the creation of protohumans, fashioned from clay mixed with divine blood. These creatures, male and female, are instructed to marry and raise families, which they do. But they misbehave and anger their creators, who punish them. Unfazed by the divinely ordained droughts and famine, they continue to irritate the gods who become so annoyed they decide to drown them in a great flood—all except Atrahasis, who is warned to build a boat to save himself and other creatures. After the flood, Atrahasis and his fellow survivors are tolerated by the gods, who turn them into normal humans, with normal life spans, and we are now their descendants.

Two characters in this story should sound familiar: a first man made from clay who annoyed his creators and had his life made harder by the gods, and a wise boat builder who saved his race from extinction by drowning. Were these men Adam and Noah by other names?

In 1849 fragments of yet another creation myth, the Babylonian Enuma Elish, were discovered. Believed to date from the eighteenth to sixteenth centuries BCE, the Enuma Elish describes the creation of the world in terms similar to those used in Genesis, a point made in 1876 by George Smith (1840–1876), who first published the story.[3] The cosmology matches that of Genesis, with creation started by separating water above and below a firmament.

The Epic of Gilgamesh, the Epic of Atrahasis, the Enuma Elish, and other literature from the ancient Near East came to light for new Western audiences in the late nineteenth century. These tales overlapped with the Genesis creation stories in many ways. What did this mean?

The most natural explanation was that these ancient stories, including the ones in Genesis, had a common literary ancestor. Perhaps they were all based on, say, the Epic of Gilgamesh. Or maybe they all draw on an even older common cosmology, with the newer ones—like Genesis—making more explicit use of the others.[4] The term *pan-Babylonianism* appeared in the late nineteenth century to refer to the emerging conviction that the Genesis creation story comes from much older Mesopotamian (Babylonian) mythology. As a common framework defining the worldview of the ancient Near East, it shows up in variant forms, adapted to local religious contexts.

Pan-Babylonianism raised serious questions. How could the biblical Adam be the starting point for the genealogies of so many different tribes?

Assuming that Adam is the shadowy first man at the heart of all these stories, when and where could he have lived to accommodate all the histories that included him?

A BOOK WITH NO ADAM

As Christians wrestled with a literature that had too many Adams, a new origins narrative with no Adam emerged.

That narrative was launched in 1859 with Charles Darwin's *On the Origin of Species by Means of Natural Selection*. In England, where secularism was finally triumphing over religion, the challenges to the traditional story of Adam were met with a resigned capitulation from many traditionalists and joyous enthusiasm from secularists and liberals eager to break with orthodoxy. If the anemic British Christianity survived at all, it would do so without Adam.

American Christians, however, were far more enthusiastic about their faith, and even convinced that the new sciences would strengthen that faith. Adam, in their eyes, needed no defense. In retrospect, however, one can see the divide appearing between traditionalists defending Adam and modernists learning to live without an Adam.

On the Origin of Species arrived in America in 1860 to a complex reception, both scientifically and theologically. Several of Darwin's key ideas—most significant, natural selection—received limited support from the scientific community, complicating the discussion. *Evolution* thus had a variety of definitions, only one of which was Darwin's, so it is difficult to determine whether someone affirming evolution is necessarily supporting Darwin's theory. Darwin's theory taken at face value was full of holes, some of them literal. His theory implied that the fossil record should be packed with transitional forms documenting the history of life. The record should provide evidence for how reptiles evolved into birds, birds into mammals, and simple mammals into primates like us. It did almost none of these things.

Natural selection was another large hole. How, exactly, did natural selection work? Darwin speculated that organisms competing to survive and reproduce in nature would struggle and nature would *select* those most fit—smarter, faster, taller. This was trivially obvious, but it was also trivial. Of course speed would be important to cheetahs chasing gazelles. But where did cheetahs come from in the first place? It was one thing to imagine natural selection improving the species by pruning the less fit, like the familiar dog breeders had done for centuries. It was quite another to imagine natural selection producing eyes from sightless creatures, legs from the legless, and ears from the earless. Natural selection was just an editor. How did the novelties originate in the first place? Darwin, unaware of genes and their capacity to generate novelty, simply assumed some amazing wellspring of hidden creativity. But endowing nature with such capacities strained the imagination. Most thinking people, including his fellow naturalists, thought natural selection far too feeble to lift a slug out of the mud and onto the pulpit of Westminster Abbey.[5]

Evolution was hardly new in 1860. In one form or another it had been on the edge of the scientific radar for decades. And the idea of an ancient earth with a dynamic history was widely accepted, even by traditional Christians. The smart money, however, was elsewhere.

The geologist Charles Lyell (1797–1875), author of the influential *Principles of Geology*, was an important precursor to Darwin, who considered Lyell his mentor. Lyell believed the *evidence* indicated that God had created species at multiple locations and times.[6] Harvard's Louis Agassiz (1807–1873) believed that God had created species in large numbers, progressively repopulating the earth after extinction events like Noah's flood. Lyell and Agassiz expressed the consensus of their scholarly communities when they argued that the great design in nature points clearly to a supernatural creation—not a slow winnowing of the unfit. In fact the design that Lyell and Agassiz saw in nature—the celebrated natural theology of the eighteenth century and the reason traditional Christians were enthusiastic about science—was Darwin's primary target in *On the Origin of Species*. Darwin's work explicated a mechanism—natural selection—by which life forms that looked ingeniously designed could be produced without a designer. But skepticism about materialistic processes producing design was already in place by 1860. The wreckage of an earlier proposal testified clearly to those sentiments.

In 1844 Robert Chambers (1802–1871), a well-known Scottish journalist, anonymously published a thoroughgoing evolutionary historical narrative titled V*estiges of the Natural History of Creation*. (His authorship was acknowledged in 1884 with the publication of the twelfth edition.) The book speculated that the solar system had begun as a swirling cloud of gas out of which the sun and the planets congealed—the so-called nebular hypothesis. Life arose spontaneously on the earth and evolved steadily into the diversity we see today. Humankind was simply the endpoint of these purely natural processes. Chambers's well-written book was wildly popular and outsold

Darwin's *Origin of Species* into the twentieth century. Prince Albert read it to Queen Victoria; Alfred Wallace, the codiscoverer of evolution, affirmed that it inspired his work, calling it an "ingenious hypothesis" awaiting support from "more facts and the additional light which more research may throw upon the problem."[7] *Vestiges of the Natural History of Creation* threw a gauntlet into the face of the prevailing natural theology, with its claim that the wonders of nature arose naturally and not through the "wisdom of God." God, for the anonymous author of *Vestiges*, did nothing more than endow the material world with a progressive spirit of the sort animating Victorian social reformers—who, not coincidentally, loved the book.

Many American Christians were quite put off by *Vestiges'* deism—as well as its amateurish science—and rejected it. Wallace was one of the few scientists, however, who did not dismiss the oddly anonymous work out of hand. Cautions about *Vestiges* were soon rewarded as the scientific community turned its attention to this eccentric work of popularization. The condemnations were scathing. The Reverend Adam Sedgwick (1785–1873), who held a chair of geology at Cambridge University, wrote that he could find no value in the "foul book." "All other scientific men," he claimed derisively, "are indignant" about it. "If the book be true," he stated, speaking for most educated Americans in the emerging conversation about evolution, "the labours of sober induction are in vain; religion is a lie; human law is a mass of folly, and a base injustice; morality is moonshine."[8] His eighty-five-page response, with point-by-point refutations, appeared in the July 1845 edition of the *Edinburgh Review* and insisted that the anonymous author was attempting to seduce his readers, writing with the "serpent coils of a false philosophy," asking them to "stretch out their hands and pluck forbidden fruit."[9] This wily serpent, hiding behind the protective cloak of anonymity, "would have his readers believe their Bible is a fable when it teaches them that they were made in the image of God—that they are the children of apes and breeders of monsters—that he has *annulled all distinction between physical and moral.*"[10] Few scientists were as colorful in their condemnations as Sedgwick, but virtually all of them shared his dim view of the science in *Vestiges*. Sales, however, were brisk.

Watching *Vestiges of the Natural History of Creation* crash and burn confirmed the theological instincts of American Christians skeptical of the creative power of mindless processes. Their faith was true, science was trustworthy, and the former had nothing to fear from the latter.

On the Origin of Species thus arrived in America as an echo to *Vestiges*, itself an echo of earlier speculations about evolution that had fared even worse. Darwin offered yet another hypothetical outline of natural history at odds with the Bible, incompatible with natural theology, and only weakly rooted in empirical observations. And, sure enough, the response from the scientific community was negative. America's leading biologist, Louis Agassiz of Harvard, was especially critical of the *naturalism* of evolution, arguing that science, properly practiced, should lead the seeker to "recognition of the existence of God . . . from the study of His works" and "the importance of the study of the animal kingdom with reference to its manifestation of the power, wisdom, and goodness of God, is very great."[11] Darwin's speculation that natural selection acting on small variations could produce the grandeur of the natural world was pernicious nonsense.

Agassiz concluded his influential review in the *Atlantic Monthly* in 1860 with a description of Darwinian evolution as "a scientific mistake, untrue in facts, unscientific in its methods, and mischievous in its tendency."[12] Such critique from a leading authority—Agassiz was "a charming, brilliant lecturer and the most popular scientist in the land"[13]—provided Christians with genuine scientific reasons to reject both aspects of evolution, the claim that all life had descended from a common ancestor and natural selection as the mechanism of change. Darwin simply got it wrong. This worked well until around 1875 when the scientific community began to accept Darwin's claim that all life had evolved from a common ancestor,[14] but they thought Darwin was still wrong about natural selection. Common ancestry, however, threatened the uniqueness of Adam, so theologians engaged and began to grapple with the implications for Christian doctrine. It is significant that scientific arguments were used ahead of theological ones, reflecting the high view of science held by most educated Christians in America.

The conversation became complex and remained so for decades: the *historical reality* of evolution—understood as change over time accomplished by God—as an account of past history was becoming accepted by many if not most Christians; negative voices were on the margins, and widespread rejection of any form of evolution was years in the future. Few Christians, in particular, objected to claims that the earth was far older than six thousand years. Nor were they necessarily put off by the idea that life had evolved—*progressed* would be a better word—over long periods of time from a common ancestor. The idea that life had a history—either continuous or punctuated—leading to human beings was a conclusion finding increasing scientific support: fossils indicated that life at least jumped in complexity, if not changed smoothly, through history; the geographical distribution and comparative anatomies of life forms also suggested that species of today had evolved from common ancestors of yesterday. But how did this change occur?

Various mechanisms, all with meaningful support from at least a few scientists, competed to explain how species evolved. Life on earth had clearly progressed over time in the direction of humans, and the only explanation that made sense was that God guided the process, or at least set it up. One could thus claim—as late as a half century after Darwin—to believe in evolution without accepting the claim that purposeless processes were the engine of change.

One possible evolutionary mechanism was the "inheritance of acquired characteristics," in which a parent could pass to his or her offspring traits developed during his or her life—muscles, speed, a longer neck. Developed by the French naturalist Jean Baptiste Lamarck (1744–1829), the idea resonated so well with nineteenth-century intuitions that hard work produced progress that it would be a century before biologists had fully expunged its heresy.

The idea seemed like common sense: organisms develop useful adaptations. A blacksmith, for example, develops large muscles, which aid him in his work. And, as everyone could see, the blacksmith's young son working at his side was also muscular. Lamarck proposed that father's muscles were passed on to his son. Similarly, if an industrious mother giraffe stretched her neck to reach food at inconvenient heights, her offspring, when mature, would have longer necks. In this way, species experienced genuine progress as they made their way toward humanity.

Many Christians were attracted to the *moral dimensions* of Lamarck's theory, inferring that "the virtue of one generation is the gain of the next."[15] Such progress was good in every way—the reward for diligence and hard work, whether it be a blacksmith working at his anvil, a finch pecking for seeds on the Galapagos, or a capitalist growing his business. Humanity was "a slowly rising race, with a native tendency to outgrow faults."[16] Conversely—and perversely—the inheritance of acquired characteristics also accounted for the universality of sin. Humans had perverted their natures long ago with evil moral choices and their descendants inherited their "predispositions to the wrong."[17] Given that man had "fallen," wrote the well-educated nineteenth-century clergyman William Rupp, "the doctrine of evolution in its law of heredity . . . shows how the sinful tendency of nature could become persistent in the race: and hence to explain the fact of original or hereditary sin, the theologian need no longer to have recourse to any artificial notion of federal headship or to the monstrous doctrine of an arbitrary imputation of sin."[18] Lamarck's explanation, especially in the decades before the genetic basis for inheritance was understood, was deeply intuitive, and most naturalists, including Darwin, accepted it. And many assumed—quite correctly—that it could be applied more broadly to culture and society. Lamarck's idea seemed exactly like the sort of plan God would put in place.

Another alternative to natural selection was *orthogenesis*, which literally means "evolution in a straight line" and refers to the idea that species evolve along a predetermined path, according to God's plan.

Orthogenesis drew on the analogy between evolution and human development. Human beings, for example, begin as fertilized eggs and grow in complexity, first in the womb and then outside. They reach adulthood, enter a period of stability, then deteriorate and finally die, following a plan laid out at conception. With evolution, species come from simpler ancestors, increase steadily in complexity until they reach a period of stasis, and then go extinct. The similarities were provocative.

Lamarckism, orthogenesis, and other non-Darwinian mechanisms provided alternatives to natural selection, especially for audiences obsessed with progress. Such ideas were compatible with religion, viewed from the right angle. The blueprints guiding orthogenesis originated *somewhere*, and God was the obvious answer. The progress of organisms under Lamarckism *could* be viewed as moral imperatives, with every creature investing in its own purposeful advance for the good of its offspring, which was how God might do it.

Historian Peter Bowler examined the evolutionary options at play in the decades after Darwin published his theory. He concludes that the popularity of the alternatives to natural selection "originated in a long-standing tradition that organic development must be an orderly process controlled by laws inherent in life itself." Understanding these laws would make biology rigorous and mathematical. Darwin's emphasis on blind, purposeless natural selection was "moribund and incapable of furthering biological research."[19]

The non-Darwinian mechanisms resonated with both the scientific and the religious communities. The former considered Newtonian mechanics the model for science and sought to cast all other sciences in its image; the latter had a strong tradition of discerning theologically friendly designs in the insights of science. Adam and Eve had been intentionally fashioned by God, crafted over time rather than all at once.

Such nuances precluded unanimity in the response to evolution. The scientific community, of course, was most strongly proevolution and the religious community most likely to reject the theory, but the many exceptions make this little more than a caricature. The greatest scientific foe of evolution was the Unitarian Louis Agassiz. The greatest supporter of evolution was Agassiz's Harvard colleague Asa Gray, an evangelical Christian and friend of Darwin.

THREE RESPONSES TO EVOLUTION

In the early twentieth century three Christian responses to evolution can be discerned, all growing into movements that are still alive and well. For *modernists*, evolution and biblical scholarship had undermined tradition, motivating the need for a new post-Enlightenment Christianity. In complete and self-conscious contrast, *fundamentalists* circled their wagons around Christian "fundamentals"—miracles, Adam and the Fall, the resurrection—and rejected any scholarship that challenged those fundamentals. A middle group, which I call *traditionalists* for reasons explained below, emerged out of fundamentalism, trying their best to embrace science, making modest theological adjustments, while avoiding the modernist slide into a liberalism that many considered not merely post-Enlightenment but post-Christian.

The quietest response was that of modernism, which came to understand the Bible as a purely human book, not divinely inspired and certainly not inerrant. Convinced that Christianity's essential truth was "Love your neighbor," the modernists rejected scientifically impossible claims of miracles, like the virgin birth and resurrection. The Genesis story about the first man, created in the image of God, was viewed as just a bit of mythology, a morality tale at best.

Modernism was driven partly by the science and biblical scholarship discussed above but also by aesthetics. Modernist Christians stripped their faith of its bloody and judgmental aspects. They wanted a God that would not be so inscrutably unfair as to punish every living creature for one person's sin. Nor would their preferred deity *save* people via a bloody crucifixion. The Bible for modernists was a book from the Bronze Age, filled with myths and miracle stories, mangers and angelic choirs like other religious documents from that time. A Christianity that tried to bring such ancient notions into the modern world would surely die of implausibility.

Evolution played only a minor role in the emergence of modernism, and Darwin was just one soldier in a battle that began long before he published his theory. Take the case of Charles Dickens as an example. Dickens wrote a biography of Jesus for his children—a work that reflected the new sanitized Christianity. Titled *The Life of Our Lord*, it said nothing of Jesus's atoning sacrifice—the central theological emphasis of the historic Christian tradition. "Because he did such Good, and taught people how to love God and how to hope to go to Heaven after death," wrote Dickens, "he was called our Saviour."[20] The theology associated with such a faith had no need of a first man. Adam evolved into a metaphor—a way to talk about the human condition but certainly not the source of that condition, and certainly not the reason why every human being is born with a sinful nature.

The fundamentalists occupied the other end of the spectrum. Their strategy would, over the course of the twentieth century, evolve into an elaborate anti-intellectual mixture containing a rejection of mainstream science, a simplistic biblical literalism, and a quixotic attempt to create an alternative "creation science." The fundamentalists are now so reactionary that they reject anything that disagrees with their reading of the Bible, no matter how well established. I will look at this movement in the next chapter, as it remains an important voice in the American conversation.

Many Christians found themselves caught between the rock of liberalism and the hard place of fundamentalism. And just as the fundamentalists were born out of a concern to protect the truths of the Bible, so a third group, the traditionalists, emerged out of fundamentalism as it grew ever more anti-intellectual and opposed to science. Committed to keeping up with science while remaining faithful to historic Christianity, they are the true descendants of Paul, Augustine, Aquinas, La Peyrère, Miller, Buckland, even the young Charles Darwin—all those who tried to integrate new knowledge with their Christian faith. Their energy came from a commitment to protect traditional Christian beliefs without resorting to the intellectual isolationism of the fundamentalists. I call this group traditionalists because of their solidarity with the attitudes of those who went before them. Their developing story will occupy the rest of this chapter.

This three-part speciation of Christianity is an oversimplification; Christians are arrayed along a continuum from extreme fundamentalism to extreme liberalism, not clumped into three groups. And even that continuum, being one dimensional, is too simple. Other emphases like social justice, holiness, and liturgical styles are needed to properly catalog the players. But these are secondary concerns. These three groups correspond roughly to the three positions that the Gallup Poll uses to identify where people stand on origins: (1) God created humans in their present form; (2) humans evolved with God's guiding; (3) humans evolved but God had no part.[21]

The traditionalist response is important for the insight it provides into the future of Christianity. I would go so far as to say that the success or failure of this response determines the long-term future of Christianity in the developed world.[22] It seems unlikely that a naïve fundamentalism that rejects science can survive long term in a modern secular world, despite its surprising health in the United States and the developing world (it's already dead in most of Europe). And liberal Christianity has long struggled, in terms of both adherents and identity, although its decline is being mitigated by people transferring from conservative traditions.[23]

The traditionalist conversation about the historicity of Adam exploded into prominence in 2011, appearing on the cover of *Christianity Today*, on NPR, and even on *The Colbert Report*.[24] Unfortunately, this conversation is the same one that started in the nineteenth century; it shows no evidence of an emerging consensus and there is even less reason to be hopeful that one might emerge.

Traditionalists initially approached the Darwinian adventure with a multilayered confidence that contrasts dramatically with the anxious uncertainty we see today among conservative Christians wrestling with evolution. The nineteenth century had been good to American Christianity, for the most part, and there was no knee-jerk defensive reaction to new scientific ideas. The challenges created by the emerging sciences had been met with simple adjustments to the reading of Genesis. The expanded understanding of nature had provided a foundation for a secure natural theology, and Christians had become accustomed to science uncovering "the wisdom of God manifested in the wisdom of the Creation."[25] Many scientists were clergy who saw little conflict between their science and their faith (Darwin had even studied for the ministry in his younger days). Nature was widely embraced as God's other book, and most educated Christians, while mindful that the Two Books were not always in obvious harmony, nevertheless saw science as a *friend* rather than an enemy.

Benjamin Breckinridge (B. B.) Warfield (1851–1921) is a classic example of a traditionalist who accepted evolution, before that put one's job in jeopardy. Warfield was professor of theology at Princeton Seminary from 1887 to 1921, at which time he developed the concept of biblical inspiration widely accepted by evangelicals today, coining the term *inerrancy* to describe the level of veracity of the Bible. Warfield rejected the modernist view that scripture was primarily a human product. He also rejected as anti-intellectual the emotional and highly personal approach to scripture embraced by the holiness and revivalist movements. Warfield's view was that God worked through the individual writers of scripture so that their writings were simultaneously their own but also free from error.

During Warfield's time at Princeton, the seminary followed the conservative Westminster Confession of Faith, drawn up in 1646 to be a confession of the Church of England. When the seminary split in 1929, the departing faction created Westminster Theological Seminary, insisting that its faculty continue to embrace the seventeenth-century confession.[26] The Westminster Confession covers every area of Christian theology. Here is what it says about human origins, the Fall, and original sin:

> I. Our first parents, being seduced by the subtilty [sic] and temptation of Satan, sinned, in eating the forbidden fruit. This their sin, God was pleased, according to His wise and holy counsel, to permit, having purposed to order it to His own glory.
>
> II. By this sin they fell from their original righteousness and communion with God, and so became dead in sin, and wholly defiled in all the parts and faculties of soul and body.
>
> III. They being the root of all mankind, the guilt of this sin was imputed; and the same death in sin, and corrupted nature, conveyed to all their posterity descending from them by ordinary generation.
>
> IV. From this original corruption, whereby we are utterly indisposed, disabled, and made opposite to all good, and wholly inclined to all evil, do proceed all actual transgressions.

All this language was to be taken literally. Such statements were developed to avoid the ambiguities that made biblical interpretation so difficult. It is easy to see why evolution, polygenesis—the claim that the human race has multiple, separate origins—and the solidarity, uniqueness, and origins of the human species might be controversial.

Remarkably, however, Warfield's embrace of the Westminster Confession did not lead him to reject evolution, although he certainly wrestled with it.[27] Significantly, Warfield even lamented that evolution should not have corroded Darwin's faith. In an 1889 review of *The Life and Letters of Charles Darwin*, he writes, "There have been many evolutionists who have been and have remained theists and Christians."[28] Warfield also found hints of evolution in the theology of John Calvin. In a 1915 article *Calvin's Doctrine of Creation*, he writes, "It should scarcely be passed without remark that Calvin's doctrine of creation is, if we have understood it aright, for all except the souls of men, an evolutionary one."[29] Warfield notes that Calvin did not have a *theory* of how evolution worked, but that was an issue easily separated from a belief that evolution had occurred. Calvin, he concludes, "very naturally thought along the lines of a theistic evolutionism."[30] On many occasions Warfield presented a popular lecture on evolution at Princeton in which he stated, "I do not think that there is any general statement in the Bible or any part of the account of creation, either as given in Genesis 1 and 2 or elsewhere alluded to, that need be opposed to evolution." Warfield found "no necessary antagonism of Christianity to evolution," provided we allow for "the constant oversight of God . . . and his occasional supernatural interference." With these concessions, said Warfield, we can embrace evolution and still "be Christians in the ordinary orthodox sense."[31]

Warfield was scientifically informed, theologically orthodox, and widely respected as one of the great Christian scholars of his era. He was probably the most important conservative theologian at the turn of the century. It is certainly significant that he did not oppose evolution.

The other thinker I want to look it is George Frederick Wright (1838–1921), whose career ran parallel to Warfield's. Wright was a respected amateur geologist at a time when much good science was done by amateurs. (Even Darwin was an amateur by the standards of today.) Wright's scientific work led to significant insights into the geology of the area around Oberlin College, where he spent time as a student and then a professor of New Testament language and literature. Eventually he held the first chair in the Harmony of Science and Revelation.

Alarmed that antireligious polemicists were bashing Christianity with Darwin's theory, Wright set out to show that Darwin's theory was compatible with Christianity, especially the theology of John Calvin. From our perspective, after decades of nonstop culture wars and failed attempts at reconciliation between traditionalists and evolution, it's all but impossible to appreciate that Wright found Darwin's theory not merely *compatible* with Christianity but also theologically *helpful*. Anyone trying to make sense of America's enduring controversy over evolution needs to understand this.

Wright believed that evolution mitigated some long-standing challenges to Christianity. These theological problems related to origins emerged long before Darwin; and in the century preceding him—before evolution was receiving much attention—they mounted steadily. Take the age of the earth, which we looked at in chapter 7. If the earth was very old with a long history prior to humans, then what was the purpose of this prior history? Why, for example, did God create dinosaurs only to have them go extinct before humans appeared? What accounted for the bad design in nature (think human knees) and the many creatures (think mosquitoes) that seemed to serve no purpose beyond making our lives less enjoyable? What about the different races of humans? If, as leading Christian biologists like Louis Agassiz claimed, God had created different races, some of which preceded Adam, where was the unity to the human race? How could Adam's sin be universally shared if some human tribes were not descended from him? And what of slavery? Was there a non-Adamic human tribe created by God to be enslaved?

Not one of these problems was created by evolution. But Wright believed he could solve some of them with evolution. He called attention to the progressive character of evolutionary change, noting that God's sovereign will was to be found in the grand scheme of things, not the details. As Calvin and others had long taught, God's ultimate purposes often included short-term evils. Judas's betrayal of Jesus was terrible, but it advanced God's plan of salvation. Likewise the extinction of dinosaurs was terrible, but it was part of the process leading to human beings. Darwin's theory *unified* natural history so that earlier events, no matter how tragic, could be understood as part of a larger divine plan. "The language of Genesis," he wrote, "may properly be regarded as the language of theistic evolution," noting in particular that phrases like "Let the earth bring forth," in contrast to the more definitive "Let there be," suggested developmental processes.[32] Wright was convinced that Genesis contained scientific insights far beyond what its nominal human author could have possessed. "No unaided human intellect could, in the period when the first chapter of Genesis was written, have framed a cosmogony with which modern science could find so little fault."[33]

Most significant was that Wright resolved a challenge polygenesis—to which many creationists subscribed, including Agassiz—posed for the traditional concept of sin. Wright noted that Calvin had referred to the "viciousness of human nature" as being "natural" and universally received by "hereditary law." Wright understood Calvin to be pushing back against claims that humans were not born depraved but simply born into a depraved situation from which they acquired depraved habits.[34] (Not surprisingly, a key Calvinist doctrine is known as total depravity.) Wright quotes Calvin where he sounds most like Darwin: "When Adam corrupted himself, 'he transmitted the contagion to all his posterity.' From the 'corrupt root' of our first known progenitor, 'corrupt branches proceeding transmit their corruption to the saplings which spring from them.' And so the 'corruption commencing in Adam is by perpetual descent conveyed from those proceeding to those coming after them.'"[35]

Evolution for Wright was simply God's method of creation, an enduring claim still found among the traditionalists. If God commanded the earth to "bring forth" life in all its abundance, then evolution was simply the description of that bringing forth. As long as evolution embodied the intentions of the creator it was not merely compatible with Christianity, it was also Calvinist theology applied to natural history. Wright and many of his generation were convinced on scientific—not theological—grounds that the evidence ruled out purely naturalistic interpretations of evolution. It was thus congenial to see it as God's method of creating.

Wright made an important contribution to *The Fundamentals*, a set of essays that came to define fundamentalism, about which I will say more in a later chapter. In an essay titled "The Passing of Evolution," he argued that attempts by scientists to remove God's providential guidance from natural history were not only counter to Christianity but also at odds with the evidence. And, in explaining the origin of humanity, the only viable scenario is the one in Genesis:

Everything points to the unity of the human race and to the fact that, while built on the general pattern of the higher animals associated with him in the later geological ages, he differs from them in so many all important particulars, that it is necessary to suppose that he came into existence as the Bible represents, by the special creation of a single pair, from whom all the varieties of the race have sprung.[36]

Wright was scientifically and theologically informed. His ideas on evolution had been shaped by a long relationship with Asa Gray, America's leading evolutionist and another conservative Christian.

A leading historian of religion has labeled Wright "the last of a species."[37] By the time he died in 1921, four years before the Scopes trial, he was a lonely voice in the scientifically barren wilderness of American fundamentalism. Scientists, for the most part, had lost interest in the theological issues raised by their work, not because they had rejected theological truth—although many had—but because it was no longer relevant to their work. Whatever their personal faith positions, their science had become secular. And their community paid less and less attention to the concerns of Christians worried that the biblical Adam might be going extinct.

In a most unfortunate irony, however, scientific investigation and biblical literalism, despite have fully diverged onto separate tracks, retained a shared agreement on one important issue deeply embedded in the larger culture: race relations. And, although they traveled completely unrelated paths to get there, they converged on the conclusion that the white race was superior to all others.

CHAPTER 9

MARK OF CAIN, CURSE OF HAM

Is God a Racist?

*White folks and colored folks, you listen to me. You cannot
run over God's plan and God's established order without
having trouble. God never meant to have one race. It was not
His purpose at all. God has a purpose for each race.*

—BOB JONES SR. [1]

Martin Luther King Jr. famously said in 1963, "It is appalling that the
most segregated hour of Christian America is eleven o'clock on Sunday morning." Fifty years later this remains true as America's churches lag
behind its schools, businesses, military, and almost every other institution
in escaping old taboos about mixing the races. [2] Compare the diversity in the
pages of *Christianity Today* to that of *Sports Illustrated*. The greatest humili-
ation of American Christianity is its long endorsement of slavery, and even
longer endorsement of racism—a dark cloud still clearly visible at eleven
o'clock on Sunday mornings. And many other places besides churches on
Sunday morning as well: open any issue of *Christianity Today*—the flagship
magazine of evangelical Christianity—and you will see almost exclusively
white faces, most of them male.

In yet another centuries-old context extending into the present we find
Christians looking to Genesis to make sense of race, even questioning the
humanity of tribes that did not appear to be descended from Adam. How
did the corners of the earth become populated with so many different tribes
if humanity began with two people in the Middle East fewer than ten thousand years ago? How was the earth populated so rapidly that Adam's son

Cain could travel to Nod and build a city? And how could Adam's descendants in a few thousand years have turned into Eskimos, Pygmies, Aryans, and Aborigines?

The unwelcome answer that emerged in the nineteenth century was that the received biblical history was not history at all. The early chapters of Genesis were ancient Near Eastern myths, bearing no relation to the origin of humanity. The earth was much older than the Bible suggested; humanity did not originate in the supernatural creation of Adam and Eve; and Noah's ark never held every living human. Wrestling with these concerns, however, was a task embraced by few Christians of that period. Even today, most evangelical denominations avoid the conversation, with disastrous results. One of these disasters is the wholesale rejection of science by young-earth creationists, which I will look at in the next chapter. In this chapter I want to look at an even more unfortunate disaster, that of racism and slavery; I want to engage the disturbing truth that white Christians once appealed to the Bible to justify owning, whipping, and lynching black people.

The story begins with a biblical explanation for the planet's rapid population growth based on the great ages assigned to the first generations. "Adam," we read in Genesis 5, "lived a total of 930 years, and then he died." That eulogy creates the puzzle of human longevity before the flood. Eve, we presume, enjoyed a comparably long life, although the Bible omits this information for her and for other women. Adam was a typical antediluvian patriarch in terms of his longevity. Noah's grandfather, the venerable Methuselah, lived to be 969 years old.

Almost three hundred years ago, the London minister Thomas Ridgley (1667–1734) used these great ages to counter emerging claims that Adam was not the first man. In a massive work titled *Body of Divinity*, published in 1731, he targeted the "bold writer" (La Peyrère, whom we met in an earlier chapter) for suggesting that Adam was not the first man.[3] To protect the biblical story from charges of implausible claims about population growth, Ridgley argued that Adam and Eve were incredibly prolific. If they had children at the typical rate of one every two years or so, and did not lose their procreative prowess until late in life, say forty years before they died, they could have produced hundreds of children. By the time Eve was pregnant with her tenth child, for example, her first daughter could be pregnant with the first child of the third generation. Her hundredth child would be born into a gigantic extended family. Such "hyper-fecundity," as historian of science David Livingstone calls it,[4] could populate the entire

Middle East in no time, and account for the origins of Cain's wife, the posse that chases him when he murders Abel, and the citizenry to populate his city in Nod. The incestuous character of all this gave some pause, of course, but this was Adam and Eve, the first humans who walked with God in the cool of the evening. Surely their offspring could have borne children together without complications.

Primordial fecundity, then, eliminates the need to invoke other non-Adamic tribes. But what of the *variations* cataloged by the explorers? How do we account for white Northern Europeans, olive-skinned Mediterraneans, and black Africans? They can't all be descended from the same white Adam, can they? Some argued, of course, that not all these people were descended from Adam; but most Christians insisted on the universality of the human condition implied by their theology—the "brotherhood of man," which would become a key emphasis of the abolitionists.

Climate was invoked to explain the different-toned races. Descendants of Adam in hot regions were blackened by the local climate. Just as an individual grows darker by exposure to the sun, so a tribe grows darker after generations of such exposure. The skin of the African was in fact a darkened skin—*colored* would become the standard term—that had once been white when the tribe had migrated from the Middle East. Those in cooler regions retained their primordial white skin. And those in temperate regions like the Mediterranean were in between.

The process that darkened Adam's white offspring was quite mysterious. Dark tans were presumably passed on to offspring through Lamarck's "inheritance of acquired characteristics" explained in the previous chapter. Although the details are obscure, many believed that as women were more attracted to the darker skin of their mates, they psychically influenced the lives in their wombs so they were born darker still. The mysterious mechanisms were powerful: "It is not improbable that people of the fairest complexion, when removed into a very hot climate, may, in a few generations, become perfect negroes."[5]

The French philosopher Montesquieu (1689–1755) used climate to explain everything from courage to cunning, from the tendency toward alcoholism to a preference for different religious practices. Montesquieu claimed without foundation that heat affected the "fibres" in human cardiovascular systems, altering the blood flow in ways that made white Europeans robust, energetic, and successful, and black Africans lazy, dull, and inclined toward drunkenness.[6] The influential French naturalist Buffon also argued that climate was responsible for human diversity: "It is the same identical being who is varnished with black under the Torrid Zone, and tawned and contracted by extreme cold under the Polar Circle."[7]

The claim that all the human races were climate-modified tribes descended from Adam grounded the "brotherhood of man" understanding of humanity. Everyone is related to everyone else, since Adam is at the top of everyone's family tree. This encouraging view of human *unity* could have given birth to a paradigm of human *equality* if Christians had not understood human diversity within the racist imperialism of Western Europe. This unshakeable, deeply rooted, racial prejudice led Christians to interpret the distinctive African, Asian, Indian, and American races as *deteriorations* rather than *variations* of a superior white race. Humans may all be biologically related but some of the distant cousins had serious problems. The hot sun not only made the Negro darker; it made him lazy and stupid as well.[8]

THE BELIEF THAT Adam was the biological father of a human race baked by the sun into different tribes was known as *monogenesis*, for its rejection of separate creations of the different tribes. Abolitionists embraced this view, as it undermined—but did not refute— arguments that some tribes were different in ways that justified enslaving them. And while the influential climate hypothesis was speculative at best, with no supporting evidence— beyond the observation that people in Ethiopia were darker than those in England—it was a serious attempt to explain how the world encountered by eighteenth- and nineteenth-century Christians had changed so much since God created it.

The climate hypothesis preserved the veracity of scripture and the doctrine of original sin, but it was hard to square with the facts. Critics noted that identical climates did not always produce identical skin tones. South America had no dark-skinned natives despite having a similar climate to that of Africa. One critic objected that "Several European colonies have subsisted in the torrid zone of America more than two centuries; and yet even that length of time has not familiarized them to the climate: they cannot bear heat like the original inhabitants."[9]

The Royal Navy surgeon John Atkins (1685–1757) challenged monogenesis directly: "I am persuaded the black and white Race have, *ab origine*, sprung from different-colored first Parents."[10] Such polygenetic views took countless forms, some of them sinister.

At a minimum, polygenesis implied for Christians that God had created multiple Adams—a black Adam for Africa, a white Adam for Northern Europe, Native American Adams for the New World, Oriental Asian Adams for the Far East—and accompanying Eves. This view seems like a *reasonable* extrapolation of the creation story that undergirded eighteenth-century explanations of the flora and fauna of the planet. God could have placed different tribes—and plants and animals—in different locations. The wisdom of God would explain why dark-skinned humans flourished in locations where dark skin was beneficial, just as God's wisdom explained why fish were so well adapted for living in the water and birds were so good at flying. European encounters with other tribes, however, led to racist comparisons, and polygenesis fed this tendency in the worst way by providing a natural, divinely ordained template with which to rank the races.

Scientific perspectives, unfortunately, supported racist rankings well into the twentieth century. In 1800 an influential member of the British Royal Society, Edward King (ca. 1734–1807), published a *Dissertation Concerning the Creation of Man*, claiming that human tribes were different *species*. Such classifications raised questions about God's intentions. If God created separate races, would it not be wrong to undermine the separation? Such thinking led to volatile discussions of racial *mixing* and purity of bloodlines. King viewed the Adamic line leading to white Europeans as the "*Transcending Class*, supereminent in all qualifications." Christ, of course, was born into this "unmixed line of pure descent." Cain, on the other hand, had "debased his descent from Adam" by marrying into an "inferior cast, or species of mankind."[11] White Europeans were certain, of course, that Adam looked like them and not like everyone else in the Middle East, as we can see in the portrayals on the Sistine Chapel.

The relationship between Adam and the races that either coexisted with him or descended—deteriorated—from him became a proxy for the moral and political status of exploited tribes. The abolitionist Thomas Clarkson (1760–1846), whose work inspired William Wilberforce (1759–1833), pressed the climate hypothesis to explain race, even arguing for an olive-skinned Adam to make the necessary transformations to white and black easier and remove the primacy of the white tribe. "There is great reason to presume," he wrote in *Essay on Slavery and Commerce*, "that the purest white is as far removed from the primitive colour as the deepest black."[12]

Slavery loomed large in these conversations. The practice seems to have been accepted as a part of the natural order for as long as there have been human tribes. Many cultures believed slave classes or castes to be as natural as the divine right of kings to govern or the right of fathers to give their daughters to political allies. Aristotle taught that some humans were by nature slaves with specifically slavish characteristics. And even the Bible spoke without condemnation of slavery as though it were legitimate. Abolitionists like Wilberforce in England and William Lloyd Garrison in the United States were innovative in claiming slavery violated basic Christian principles. Their opposition, however, provided ever more disturbing reasons—some of them biblical—for why black Africans were appropriately enslaved. And, I note reluctantly, even the most progressive abolitionists did not argue—or believe, as near as we can tell—that all humans were *equal*. Their charity was that of a "superior" white hand reaching out—down?—to the "inferior" black brother.

The controversy about slavery is striking in the degree to which it was adjudicated by appealing to the story of Adam and Eve. From the first century to the present day, countless Christians have supposed that God set up a social order that we must preserve. Unfortunately, the biblical basis for this claim is so ambiguous, piecemeal, and contradictory that exegetes can seemingly find whatever they want in the Bible. The status of the black man was no exception. When the United States went to war over slavery, both sides claimed a biblical mandate for their position.

In the *History of Jamaica* (1774), a Christian apologist for slavery appears to have attacked the climate hypothesis because he found polygenesis more congenial to his belief that Africans deserved to be enslaved. They were, he wrote, subhuman and "brutish, ignorant, idle, crafty, treacherous, bloody, thievish, mistrustful and superstitious," as well as "incestuous, savage, cruel and vindictive, devourers of human flesh, and quaffers of human blood."[13] He compared blacks to orangutans and claimed that African tribes had had sexual relations with primates. "The Negroes themselves," he wrote, "bear witness that such intercourses actually happen."[14]

The reasoning is clear: climate could not possibly have made Africans so different from whites, converting Adam's original tribe into one so dramatically inferior. Thus the black African cannot be a part of the human race; he must have been separately created. And here the conclusion becomes chilling. If the Negro was neither descended from Adam nor part of a human tribe created by God, then what was he? When was he created? The only option—and what a convenient one it was—is that, like the animals, the Negro was one of the creatures God placed in Eden to serve Adam. The Negro would thus have been in the line of creatures, queued up with the cow and the dog, brought by God to Adam to name in anticipation of ruling over them. He would later have boarded Noah's ark with the animals.

As evidenced in the quote from Bob Jones that opened this chapter, muted echoes of these troubling views reverberate today. Creative interpretation of the early stories in Genesis justified abuse of the hapless African. Christian slave owners in the United States operated within a tradition that provided biblical justification for owning slaves in the same way that one owned horses. The arguments were manifold. Did not the Ten Commandments instruct us not to "covet our neighbor's manservant (= slave)"? Did not Abraham have slaves? Didn't Paul return a runaway slave to his master? Why didn't Jesus condemn the widespread slavery in the Roman world?[15]

The mark of Cain offered further justification for slavery. In Genesis 4 we read of God placing a "mark" on Cain for murdering his brother and lying about it when God asked what had happened. As early as the fifth century Cain's curse was interpreted as black skin.[16] When the Northern and Southern Baptists split in 1845 over the issue of slavery, Southern Baptists were using Cain's curse to justify slavery.

A human marked with black skin, however, is still a human. The most pernicious claims were those denying Adamic ancestry of blacks implying they have no souls.

An elaborate argument put forth by the Southern clergyman the Reverend Buckner Payne, in his widely read tract *The Negro: What Is His Ethnological Status* (1867), illustrates the uses of biblical literalism and proof-texting to support this kind of claim. Piecing together Old and New Testament texts referring to Noah's ark, Payne notes that since blacks are present with us today, they "must have been in the ark." (This acknowledges the impossibility of climate turning a white man black in four thousand years.) Referencing the New Testament passage 1 Peter 3:20, "God waited in the days of Noah, while the ark was preparing, wherein few, that is, eight souls were saved by water," Payne does the math: if only eight souls were saved in the ark, and they are fully accounted for by Noah's family, then "the negro being in the ark, was not one of those eight souls." If "negroes" were on the ark but were not a part of the eight that have souls, then they must have been on the ark in the same capacity as horses and cows. And so Payne concludes his biblical argument that "The negro was in the ark; and God thus testifies that he has no soul."[17]

In 1900 the American Book and Bible House published *The Negro a Beast*, by Charles Carroll, extending Payne's argument. The book enjoyed a wide readership and helped inspire the contemporary Christian Identity Movement, a small but noisy theological backwater where America's most racist attitudes still flourish. Carroll took aim at the emerging scientific classification scheme that, although clearly racist, still placed Negroes in the same species as whites. "The Atheist," he writes, "takes the negro which God made an ape and thrusts him violently into the family of man as a lower race of the human species, and enlightened Christianity receives him with open arms."[18]

Such explanations justified mistreatment of Africans: perhaps they are not even human; or maybe they are a vast tribe that God has "marked" for slavery; perhaps they are deteriorated into a childlike state and need owners to look after them. Actual equality for the African was, of course, *unthinkable* for Christians convinced that God had ordained the racial distinctions that separated the human tribes. Denominations with Northern and Southern adherents were houses divided. The national Presbyterian Church split first, in 1837, over theological and social issues, including slavery. American Methodists then separated over the slave owners' role in the church. In 1845 the Southern Baptist Convention split from the Northerners, who refused to appoint slave owners as missionaries. In the late 1840s the Mormons barred Africans from their priesthood.[19]

The splits derived from the conviction that God himself was a racist and had ordained a racially separatist socioeconomic order. Regardless of their position on the morality of slavery or the economics of abolitionism, many feared that God's creative intent would be compromised if the white and black races intermingled, interbred, and slowly merged into one. The fear of being "mixed" into the African race terrified many whites. Sending white children to "colored schools" was unimaginable. Carroll and others lamented the burden this imposed on white families in areas where the student population was predominantly black: "Since they have not yet become so negroized as to send their children to the 'colored schools' they must either employ a tutor for them or allow them to grow up in ignorance."[20] The fear of racial mixing—*negroization*—is palpable here and, as our ongoing failure to integrate our communities and institutions makes only too clear, difficult to dislodge.

Biblically based assaults on blacks have waned but never fully disappeared. The Methodist and Presbyterian schisms were officially healed in 1939 and 1983, respectively. Mormon leaders got a timely revelation in 1978 to rescind their priestly racist exclusivism. The Southern Baptists never reconciled, but then Baptists never do. They did apologize in 1995, however, for their endorsement of slavery, segregation, and white supremacism. And in 2012 the sixteen-million-member body elected its first African American president to preside over an encouragingly diverse community.

These arguments and their endorsers, of course, do not disappear when an official pronouncement cancels them or undermines them in some way. In 1998 the influential fundamentalist school Bob Jones University—perhaps the purest expression of educated Southern fundamentalism left in America—denied admission to a white male student on the grounds that he was married to a black woman: "Bob Jones University is opposed to intermarriage of the races because it breaks down the barriers that God has established. It mixes that which God separated and intends to keep separate."[21] The university's longstanding prohibition of interracial dating—considered a gateway to *mixed* marriage—became such a political issue that Bob Jones personally appeared on Larry King in March 2000 to announce that the rule was being suspended, but not because the underlying theological rationale had been rejected. On the same program students from the university were shown saying things like, "I think you should be free to date whoever you want . . . but I wouldn't probably date 'opposite' because of the reactions of other people," and, "God has made races perfect. . . . He hasn't given us any reason to intermix those races. . . . This is not a policy that discriminates."[22] In principle at least, the policy retains the centuries-old belief that God created separate races for a reason, but without the negative view of nonwhites. These graduates of Bob Jones University would be in their thirties as of this writing. The university estimates it has graduated more than thirty-five thousand students since its founding in 1927.[23]

I would love to write at this point that biblically based racism flew in the face of science, just as heliocentricity flew in the face of biblically based astronomy; I wish it were true that if conservative Christians had been better informed the story would have been different. But this is not the case. In interpreting the Bible's story about the first man the reality is that scientific and religious arguments conspired into the middle of the twentieth century and even beyond to rob the black man—and other nonwhite tribes—of whatever intrinsic value he may have possessed in seeming proportion to his extrinsic value as a slave. Rarely have science and religion—uneasy bedfellows at best for the past few centuries—collaborated so effectively to buttress a repulsive economic and moral argument.

Throughout the nineteenth century biblically based racism found an unwitting ally in science. Scientists, in an effort to quantify the intelligence they believed was distributed so unequally among human tribes, administered tests and measured skulls. They established with the certainty that flows from quantitative measurements that their Caucasian brains were bigger and better than those of Africans and Native Americans.[24] Evidence was amassed that the human races were very different and that the superior Caucasians should not intermarry with the inferior races and dilute the white line.

A conviction that such racial mixing was a crime against both God and nature—and eventually the state—took root in America. More than a few black men were lynched in the South on suspicion of having had sex with white women. States passed laws outlawing marriage and even sexual relations between the races. The Supreme Court finally ruled in 1967, when I was in middle school, that such laws were unconstitutional. At the time sixteen states had such laws, and it was not until 2001 that the last holdout—Alabama—repealed their comatose law forbidding interracial marriages.[25]

High school textbooks ranked the races with the same straightforward certainty with which they explained pollination. *Civic Biology*, the textbook from which John Scopes supposedly taught evolution in 1925, encouraged students to choose their mates carefully for the good of the species. In a section headed "The Races of Man," we read the following description:

> At the present time there exist upon the earth five races or varieties of man, each very different from the other in instincts, social customs, and, to an extent, in structure. These are the Ethiopian or negro type, originating in Africa; the Malay or brown race, from the islands of the Pacific; the American Indian; the Mongolian or yellow race, including the natives of China, Japan, and the Eskimos; and finally, the highest race type of all, the Caucasians, represented by the civilized white inhabitants of Europe and America.[26]

Scientifically based racism is not my quarry here, but I cannot help noting that echoes of such views are still with us. In 1994 two elite social scientists published the massive survey *The Bell Curve: Intelligence and Class Structure in American Life* and argued—dispassionately and with copious documentation—for race-based influences on intelligence.[27] The Nobel laureate in physics William Shockley destroyed his career with a clumsy detour into the relationship between race and intelligence, arguing that comparing the children of randomly chosen whites and randomly chosen blacks will reveal that the "black children will be, as far as the IQ tests are concerned, inferior to the white children."[28]

The racist ideas emerging from science have just about run their course. Genetics has all but demolished the very concept of race, and with it the possibility of any kind of racial ranking system.

Fortunately, the positions espoused by Scopes's biology text, William Shockley, and Bob Jones University no longer represent in a conscious way in either science or Christianity as a whole but persist as disturbing echoes of a past that most people are trying to forget. Ironically, John Scopes has become a cultural hero and champion of enlightenment for daring to teach evolution in violation of Tennessee law. And yet the contents of the textbook he used would set off alarm bells in almost every quarter of American society today. That strange and misunderstood trial stands at the center of the next chapter.

CHAPTER 10

THE CREATIONIST *ÜBER*-ADAM
Why the First Son Could Marry His Sister

*It is absolutely safe to say that if you meet somebody who
claims not to believe in evolution, that person is ignorant,
stupid or insane (or wicked, but I'd rather not consider that).*
—RICHARD DAWKINS[1]

The story of how young-earth creationism, often just called creation-ism, eclipsed the far more intellectual—and orthodox—traditional-ism from which it arose is an odd tale. One can be forgiven for thinking—as creationists like to claim—that God was its author. The movement is so popular now that most of America's one hundred million evangelicals embrace it by default, believing it to be the only authentically biblical posi-tion available.

Creationism came out of left field. Its leading authority during the first half of the twentieth century was a Seventh-day Adventist amateur geolo-gist named George McCready Price. His book *The New Geology* was widely read by fundamentalists interested in the topic, but exerted modest influ-ence because the Seventh-day Adventists were considered a marginal part of evangelicalism. Some considered it a cult.

Price's book was a winsome and potent mixture of biblical literalism and cozy pseudoscience. He appealed to the authority of the Bible as the inerrant word of God and claimed that a proper science reinforced everything the Bible said. He collected examples of things that science could not explain very well or that did not fit the prevailing paradigm, and presented them as both typical and evidence that mainstream science was on shaky ground.

He accused the scientific community of hiding the truth of creationism because of their assumption that God was not the creator. His book reads like a friendly popularization of geology, with photos and technical exposition that leaves the reader with the impression that Price is an important scientist. To take one example of his clever pseudoscience, he exploited the fact that geologists had long been working with both fossils and geological layers to construct their model of earth history. He would find an example in the scientific literature where a fossil was assigned a certain age because it was found in, say, the Cambrian period. Then he would find another example where a geological era would be assigned an age because it contained a certain fossil. He would then claim confidently that the dates assigned by geologists were based on circular reasoning—a claim that lives into the present. His argument was straight-up pseudoscience, but one would have to be well informed to figure that out.

One of Price's most enduring claims was that the climate prior to Noah's flood was radically different. He claimed that Adam and Eve raised their family at a time when the earth was a delightful planetwide greenhouse. Echoing the seventeenth-century English theologian and writer on the origins of the world Thomas Burnet, whom we met earlier, Price claimed that the early earth was enveloped in a canopy of water vapor that filtered sunlight in such a way that the "climate was a mantle of springlike loveliness." He offered little explanation for how this worked; it was quite simply "a matter of fact," but it was embedded in extended pseudoscience and looked like a reasonable inference.[2] The favorable climate resulted in plants and animals that were "larger and more thrifty-looking than their corresponding modern representatives."[3] Our modern counterparts are "degenerate dwarfs."[4] And Adam was a superman.

Price's ideas circulated in the backwaters of American religion until 1961 when Old Testament scholar John Whitcomb and hydraulics engineer Henry Morris teamed up to bring Price's ideas to mainstream evangelicalism. Both of them were enthusiastic biblical literalists. Whitcomb and Morris coauthored *The Genesis Flood*, launching the modern creationist movement, bringing Price's strange alternative geology to main street America as though it was real science, and laying a foundation under the understanding of Adam.

The Genesis Flood: The Biblical Record and Its Scientific Implications was powerful. It and its literary offspring have defined antievolution in America since its publication.[5] *The Genesis Flood* defends a literal reading of the biblical stories of the creation, the fall of Adam and Eve, and the flood. A sustained argument is advanced that anything other than this literal reading so compromises the authority of the Bible that it can't be trusted. I once heard leading creationist Kurt Wise, who earned a PhD in paleontology from Harvard studying under the late Stephen Jay Gould, make the argument that "if the earth was not young, then we have no hope of eternal life." He essentially said that a Bible that gets it wrong on the age of the earth can't be trusted when it speaks of how to get to heaven.

Whitcomb was convinced that Christians had gone too far in accommodating the biblical text to science—making ordinary days into epochs and inserting gaps in the chronology of Genesis 1. Convinced that the Bible should be given more authority than science, he called for a new science in harmony with scripture.

Enter Henry Morris, a credentialed hydraulics engineer and expert in floods. Morris was certain that if Christians had not capitulated to science Christian geologists would have developed alternative scientific models that harmonized with the Bible, perhaps along the lines proposed by Price. After all, God had provided a head start for science: "The creation chapters of Genesis are marvelous and accurate accounts of the actual events of the primeval history of the universe. They give data and information far beyond those that science can determine."[6]

Morris was a solid academic, with a faculty appointment at Virginia Poly Tech. He had published in peer-reviewed scientific journals. He understood floods in the real world, and the Princeton-educated Whitcomb understood them in ancient Near Eastern literature. The argument born of their collaboration proved formidable, and millions of evangelicals holding other positions on origins migrated to this articulate young-earth creationism, which became something of an orthodoxy for fundamentalists.[7]

The Genesis Flood contained two arguments woven together in a way that proved incredibly convincing, and encouraging to fundamentalists feeling marginalized. The first was Price's flood geology, updated, documented, and decoupled from its suspect Seventh-day Adventist heritage. The second was an assault on "compromise" biblical interpretation, and, rather, called the faithful to a stance on scripture known as *plenary verbal inspiration*, the view that the texts of the original manuscripts of the Bible were inerrant communications from God. The duo pointed out, for example, that God must have created everything using supernatural processes no longer operating. This made the study of origins an exclusively *theological* exercise, outside science. Science was redefined to exclude anything other than the study of *present* processes. Inferences about the past, they argued, rest on assumptions. If you assume there is no God and the Bible is unreliable, then you have no choice but to embrace long, blind, meandering processes and claim that humans can be created from chemicals. Scientists are thus driven to evolution by their godless worldview; they don't arrive at it by examining the data.

At the same time that Whitcomb and Morris were warning Christians that evolution was a godless worldview, antireligious culture warriors began using evolution as an argument against religion. The truth of evolution implied the falsity of the Christian belief in creation. Richard Dawkins emerged in the latter part of the twentieth century as the primary but not the first or the only champion of this viewpoint. "Darwin," he wrote in 1986, "made it possible to be an intellectually fulfilled atheist."[8] Creationists came to view evolution as an "origins story for atheists" and people like Whitcomb and Morris as heroes in the most important conflict of our time.

Evangelicals loved *The Genesis Flood*—credentialed scholars showing that the Bible and science were in perfect accord and that Christians could use a framework provided by God in Genesis to house a robust "creation model" of origins. This model could be fleshed out with scientific detail by considering the evidence for what God had done, even if the processes could not be investigated.

The creationists began reading the Genesis account *naturally*, like it was just published in English and contained nothing requiring specialized training to understand. They avoided the diverting interference of interpretation, which they critiqued as an unnecessary and entirely human distortion of God's clear message. They did, however, provide scientific supplements to fill in the details. This approach provides a rich narrative of the first man in the true Two Books fashion, but with the book of nature now being read through the lens of scripture. Morris fleshes this out in his popular, seven-hundred-page *Genesis Record: A Scientific and Devotional Commentary on the Book of Beginnings*, published in 1976 with a major update in 2009.[9]

Adam's origin is described in Genesis 2:7, where we read, "And the Lord God formed man of the dust of the ground, and breathed into his nostrils the breath of life." Adam in this account does not originate in an act of creation, says Morris: he is "formed." Notice the scientific detail added and even presumed to have been intended in the original text:

> God used the "dust of the ground" to make man's body, a remarkable phrase conveying the thought that the smallest particles of which the earth was composed (in modern terminology, the basic chemical

elements: nitrogen, oxygen, calcium, etc.) were also to be the basic physical elements of the human body. . . . This fact is not at all obvious to
superficial examination (rocks seem to all appearances to be composed
of totally different substances than human flesh), but it has nevertheless
been verified by modern science.[10]

The discovery of modern science in the Genesis story is clear here. Never
mind that humans are more than 50 percent water, with very little "dust."
Morris, convinced that the science is really there, simply reads the chemists'
periodic table of the elements into this account, implying a remarkable anticipation of modern science. Traditionalists typically recognized that making a man from dust was easily interpreted as poetry, and they would have
seen no need to turn it into an anticipation of modern science. Likewise, as
far back as Augustine we have Christians recognizing that the days of Genesis need not be interpreted literally, since the sun did not even exist for the
first three of them. Morris, however, was convinced that God had provided
glimpses of modern science in his revelation and searched for creative interpretations that would show this. I recall as a teenager being simply thrilled
with the discovery that allusions to modern science could be found in the
Bible. For me it was proof that God had written the Bible, not men.

THE GARDEN OF EDEN

"The whole world," writes Morris, "had been placed under man's dominion,
and all was good in every way." However, a particular region—"Eden,"
from a word meaning "delight"—in what is now Iraq was specially prepared for the first man."[11] This perfect world had no death, for death and
every other lesser evil were not a part of God's original creation. Adam,
Eve, and the animals were created to be vegetarian. Plants could be eaten
since they are not, in the creationist understanding, alive. This world without death was a puzzling, magical place where certain common things could
not happen—a foot could not come down on a bug, a branch could not fall
on a squirrel and kill it, a toddler could not drown under a waterfall. There
could be no death of any sort.

The special garden had trees in it, including one with fruit "of such rich
nourishment as to halt the aging process in a human body." This remarkable fruit is not well understood presently because "gerontologists have no
significant understanding of the aging process."[12] Adam and Eve's access to
this fruit endowed them with vibrant health and eternal youth. In fact, ev-

erything was set up to be eternal—a perfect world of gentle herbivores coexisting peacefully with sinless humans where only one thing could go wrong.

This perfect world came crashing down when a wily serpent beguiled Eve. (In this original creation, before the Fall, the serpent was "a beautiful, upright animal with the ability to speak and converse with other human beings.")[13] The nature of the Fall and the fallen world receive a much fuller treatment in *The Genesis Record*, as the Hebrew scriptures are inspected, often in the original languages, for clues as to how the world was ruined by Adam's sin. This approach, known as scientific creationism, maintains that everything in the *entire* creation was cursed by God, from the asteroids around a distant star to the process by which our stomachs digest food. Helpful bacteria in human intestines turned parasitic at the Fall; plants turned on gardeners as their "smoothly rounded structures deteriorated to thorns"; friendly animals turned vicious as "teeth and nails designed for a herbivorous diet mutated to fangs and claws."[14]

"It may be assumed (as characteristic of most 'decay' processes observed today) that deterioration at first was rapid, later gradually tapering off into a much more gradual process. In terms of modern genetic knowledge, such changes probably were in the form of *mutations*, or random changes in the molecular structure of the genetic systems of the different kinds of organisms."[15]

The decay process precipitated by God's wrath was literally universal. This process was nothing less than the inauguration of "a fundamental scientific law, now called the Second Law of Thermodynamics. This law," writes Morris, "states that all systems, if left to themselves, tend to become degraded or disordered." Everything that was made was now being unmade. "Instead of life and growth, there comes decay and death; instead of evolution, there is degeneration."[16]

Adam and Eve were cast out of the Garden of Eden into a world becoming unfamiliar and unfriendly. Weeds began interfering with their crops; harmful parasites made them sick; predators threatened their lives; everyone grew old and eventually died. But all this took time. Like anything that runs down the hill, the starting point is at the top, and the first humans began their life outside the garden in a world just becoming imperfect. The Bible makes no such suggestion, of course, but the interpretation is not unreasonable. And, by reading gradualism into the Bible story, the creationists solve a few problems with the biblical accounts.

The slow arrival of the full effects of the curse meant that there would be vestiges of perfection that would persist into the fallen and cursed era.

The creationists' favorite example is the original human genome. Before the curse, Adam and Eve would have had perfect genomes—no mutations, no junk DNA, nothing to interfere with the production of perfect children. By imagining the curse as the inauguration of the second law of thermodynamics, rather than a simple and immediate transformation of the created order, the curse begins to work slowly and naturally on a largely perfect order. In the case of the genomes, this means that mutations would begin to occur and genetic problems would gradually appear over time.

By making the first humans' genomes free of mutations for a few generations, the old conundrum of Cain's wife is mitigated. We read in Genesis 4:17, "And Cain knew his wife, and she conceived and bore Enoch." Where Cain found his wife has long been fodder for everything from speculation about pre-Adamites to village-atheist assaults on the Bible. Clarence Darrow, at the Scopes trial in 1925, asked William Jennings Bryan where "Mrs. Cain" came from, to which Bryan responded, "I leave the agnostics to hunt for her."[17]

There are two issues here. The lesser issue is Mrs. Cain. For literalists, Adam and Eve could certainly have had many children, living as they did for centuries. Eve, as the healthiest, most perfect woman who ever lived, could have had hundreds of children and one of them could have been Mrs. Cain. This, of course, means that Cain married his sister or a niece, implying incest. What do we make of this? Did God create a world where the continuation of the species required that the children of the first couple marry each other in violation of his moral laws? But, say the creationists, incest was not a problem when siblings had almost perfect genomes. Incest is not prohibited by God until many generations later, when genetic abnormalities had accumulated to the point where marrying a sibling would carry some risk.

This construction of the first human lets Cain marry his sister, and it explains why the laws against incest did not appear until later. But this is also an interpretation of the laws. Creationists need those laws to be new when they are first mentioned in the Bible. They cannot simply be the formal codification of laws that have always existed. Otherwise, Cain was wrong to marry his sister or, even worse, there were other humans in the Middle East besides those descended from Adam and Eve. This, of course, makes the incest laws different from the laws prohibiting murder. When Cain kills his brother Abel, the Bible is clear that he has broken some law and he fears for his life. But, as no laws have yet been formally provided by God, the status of Cain's crime is puzzling. Somehow there has to be an implicit law against killing, to be codified later, but no implicit law against incest.

Creationists respond that incest was not wrong in the beginning. It only *became* a sin later, when God declared it sinful in order to protect his children from genetic disorders. Morris writes:

> Probably, in that first generation, all marriages were brother-sister marriages. In that early time, there were no mutant genes in the genetic systems of any of these children, so that no genetic harm would have resulted from close marriages. Many, many generations later, during the time of Moses, such mutations had accumulated to the point where such unions were genetically dangerous, so that incest was thenceforth prohibited in the Mosaic laws.[18]

Two birds are killed with this well-targeted stone: Cain can marry his sister, or niece, without sinning or worrying about the health of their children (their son Enoch went on to produce grandchildren for the Cains) and an apologetic argument arises, based on the modern science of genetics (known only to God at this time), for the prohibition of incest in Mosaic law.

All this has a certain plausibility within the framework of scientific creationism. But the host of assumptions necessary to construct this particular Adam, as well as the environment in which he lived, makes it clear that this Adam is not based on the plain reading of scripture the creationists trumpet as their interpretive guide.

OUTSIDE THE GARDEN

Creationists claim that Adam and Eve's post-Edenic life was not initially a vale of tears. Several generations lived for centuries, with some of them making it past the age of nine hundred. Their world, in this model, was a lush paradise with a global greenhouse providing countless health benefits.

The pre-flood greenhouse has long been a staple of creationists, invoked to explain several odd features of the early earth mentioned in the Bible, including the longevity of the patriarchs, the absence of rain, the presence of giants, the "firmament" in the heavens, and the source of the water that flooded the entire earth at the time of Noah. The so-called firmament in the heavens is mentioned in Genesis 1:6–8 as the first structure God created after the heavens and the earth: In the King James Version of the Bible, preferred by the creationists, we read, "And God said, let there be a firmament in the midst of the waters, and let it divide the waters from the waters. And

God made the firmament, and divided the waters which were under the firmament from the waters which were above the firmament."

The firmament has occasioned anxious speculation on the part of biblical literalists determined that Genesis agree with modern science. The Hebrew word for firmament is *raqia*, which literally means "that which has been hammered or beaten out," like a bowl or dome. The translators for the New Revised Standard Version of the Bible rendered the word "dome." Almost all Old Testament scholars agree that the *raqia* is a part of the ancient Near Eastern worldview. The sky does look like an inverted bowl, or dome, as anyone who has sat under the actual dome in a planetarium or under the apparent dome of the night sky knows. This inverted dome could hold water and wind and snow "up in the air," to be released through windows (Gen. 7:11; 8:2), when God wanted it to rain or snow. The idea of the dome also appears in references to the apocalypse in Revelation 21:1 where the heavens will be "rolled back like a scroll." For prescientific cultures, unfamiliar with the hydrologic cycle, a mechanical explanation like this makes perfect sense. After all, if rain falls down, it must have been held up by something.

We now know no solid dome holds back water in the sky. So what do we make of this "firmament"? For biblical literalists demanding an inerrant Bible, the firmament cannot be a dome in the heavens. Therefore they have developed a strained and implausible translation. Morris writes:

> The firmament referred to in this particular passage is obviously the atmosphere. Unfortunately the English word has been interpreted by many to refer to a solid dome across the sky; consequently this idea has been used by liberal critics as evidence of the "prescientific" outlook of Genesis. Neither the original Hebrew word nor any of the passages in which it occurs suggest such an idea, however. A "firmament" is simply "thin, stretched-out space."[19]

This creationist reading is simply not possible. The noun *raqia* comes from the verb *raqa*, which refers to the flattening of solid material. For example, one of Job's friends, trying to convince him to accept his sad lot in life, asks him, in Job 37:18, "Can you beat out [*raqa*] the vault of the skies, as he [God] does, hard as a mirror of cast metal?"

Creationists resolve this difficulty by equivocating most curiously on the meaning of *thin*. In this passage from Job, "raqa" clearly refers to a process of the sort that would take a piece of metal and hammer it out until it was "thin like the metal in a bowl." But *thin* can also mean "thin like the air at the top of a mountain." This latter meaning provides their license for turning the "firmament" (*raqia*) into "atmosphere," in opposition to virtually every scholar of Hebrew, who would agree with the NRSV that the term should be translated "dome." This rhetorical sleight of hand, however, introduces the problem of "waters which were above the firmament." Just as there is no solid dome in the heavens, there are no waters above the atmosphere. There is a creative solution to this problem, however, in the form of the very idea that would undergird much of the creationists' understanding of natural history—the *vapor canopy*.

Morris writes:

> The "waters above the firmament" thus probably constituted a vast blanket of water vapor above the troposphere and possibly above the stratosphere as well, in the high temperature region now known as the ionosphere, and extending far into space. They could not have been the clouds of water droplets which now float *in* the atmosphere, because the Scripture says they were "above the firmament." Furthermore, there was no "rain upon the earth" in those days (Genesis 2:5), nor any "bow in the cloud" (Genesis 9:13), both of which must have been present if these upper waters represented merely the regime of clouds which functions in the present hydrologic economy.[20]

This vapor canopy has a revealing history. Price spoke of it, as did Whitcomb and Morris, and virtually every creationist after them. Initially Price proposed the canopy hypothetically with no scientific support. Soon, however, the hypothetical canopy and its effects were mutually supporting each other with curiously circular reasoning. Adam's longevity became evidence for the canopy, and the canopy was an explanation for Adam's longevity.

Typical effects of this canopy include the creation of a global greenhouse with a "uniformly pleasant warm temperature all over the world."[21] Uniform temperatures would prevent the movement of air masses and "windstorms would be unknown," the hydrologic cycle would not work, and the "water vapor in the canopy would have been stable." The canopy would filter out harmful "ultraviolet radiations, cosmic rays, and other destructive energies from outer space."[22] "Everything," wrote Whitcomb and Morris in *The Genesis Flood*, "was conducive to physical health and longevity."

As speculative as these claims may be, they represent the more modest and restrained views of the post-Edenic, preflood Adam. Whitcomb and Morris were both, by creationist standards, careful scholars. Whitcomb believed the Bible was inerrant, but he was not prepared to claim biblical license for everything he could imagine. Likewise, Morris believed that science should be subordinated to the Bible, but he did not suppose that this assumption could lead anywhere.

The creationists who took the baton from Whitcomb and Morris, for the most part, were more imaginative. Take Ken ("Dr. Dino") Hovind, for example. Hovind presides over a creation ministry in Florida, run by his son Eric while he finishes a jail sentence for tax evasion and related crimes.[23] Dr. Dino, before being incarcerated, was an enthusiastic speaker and debater, claiming seven hundred appearances a year. He carried a check for $250,000 that he said he would give to anyone who could provide *any* evidence for evolution. His bogus educational credentials include a doctorate from Patriot Bible University, an unaccredited correspondence school located in Colorado, where he wrote a dissertation claiming that the snake in the Garden of Eden taught Adam and Eve about evolution and that Augustine was a theistic evolutionist.[24]

Hovind becomes quite animated about the preflood paradise under the vapor canopy. In reference to the enhanced air pressure created by the canopy, he claims that "just breathing would be exciting!" Adam, he says, would regularly exclaim to Eve about simply breathing: "Wow! Eve, that was fun, let's do that again, ready?" The oxygen enrichment would mean that "you could run for hundreds of miles without getting tired. Adam and Eve did not need a car; they could run to Grandma's!"[25]

Perhaps the most fascinating creationist is Carl Baugh, who claims to have multiple doctorates and is listed by the Trinity Broadcasting Network as the "foremost doctor on creation science."[26] Baugh hosts the television show *Creation in the 21st Century.*[27] His degrees are from unaccredited institutions, one of which lists him as the president![28] Baugh makes the strange claim that before Noah's flood "radio stars would have sung to man each morning."[29] (Radio stars are celestial objects that emit radio waves. They are silent and invisible. How Adam would have even known they existed is a mystery.) In a literal and idiosyncratic reading of the Genesis account of the firmament (*raqia*), Baugh suggests that the earth was originally surrounded by "thin metal sheets" made of compressed hydrogen and creating a planetwide tropical climate.[30] Adam would have been "about seven feet tall," says Baugh, and "encased in a perfect environment."[31]

Research has indicated that the temperature would have been about seventy-two degrees Fahrenheit at night, and about seventy-eight degrees Fahrenheit during the day. Imagine superior man with a perfect environment, perfect food with complete nutrients, no harmful radiation from space, and disease microbes held in check. The preflood world was, in our understanding today, paradise.[32]

Baugh and Hovind are typical of fundamentalists who put "Dr." in front of their names, pretend to have scientific training that informs their antievolutionary crusades, and grow surprisingly large and influential ministries.

THE ADAM OF THE CREATIONISTS

Creationists read Genesis with the conviction that God has provided enough information to reconstruct two remarkable worlds: the Edenic world where a perfect Adam lived in sinless perfection and the preflood world where a cursed and deteriorating planet was, nevertheless, a paradise for Adam and his extended family. The second paradise ended with the great flood of Noah, after which human life spans declined steadily to their present values.

As mentioned near the beginning of this chapter, this reconstruction of Eden and the preflood world is reminiscent of Burnet's seventeenth-century *Sacred Theory of the Earth*. But the resemblance is superficial. Burnet's work was a scholarly exploration, informed by the best understanding of his day. Even Newton applauded. Burnet believed the book of nature should be the primary authority in understanding the natural world and the Bible should be interpreted in light of that understanding. His generation was prepared to set aside literal interpretations of the Bible when the science made that necessary. The creationists today work in a pseudoscientific, pseudobiblical bubble, rejecting most contemporary science, a large amount of biblical scholarship, and whatever other scholarship doesn't fit their model. Forcing an implausible meaning on the Hebrew word *raqia* is a case in point. Although Hebrew scholars agree it means dome, the creationists say it means atmosphere because it has to, not because that is what the language says it means.

The Adam of creationism is certainly inspired by the concept of the first man, but like the Adam of its predecessors—Augustine, Aquinas, Dante, La Peyrère—the vision is imaginative, meeting specific needs and rooted in time and place. The genetically perfect *Über*-Adam of this chapter is fashioned from the dust of apologetics, created in the image of twentieth-century creationism, and brought to life by the breath of biblical literalism. This Adam also appears in several striking dioramas in the $30 million Creation Museum in Boone County, Kentucky, run by Ken Ham and Answers in Genesis.

And this is the Adam whose supporters are being forced to reject much of contemporary science and biblical scholarship, lest he go extinct. This intellectual disaster is the subject of the next chapter.

CHAPTER 11

_____

SCIENCE, ANTISCIENCE, AND THE EXTINCTION OF ADAM

*A historical Adam and Eve is absolutely central
to the truth claims of the Christian faith.*

FAZALE RANA[1]

The literal—and figurative—centerpiece of America's Roaring Twen-
ties was the celebrated confrontation between William Jennings Bryan
and Clarence Darrow at the Scopes trial in Dayton, Tennessee. It was the
most entertaining public battle of wits in American history.

The trial was a great story, made even more so by the celebrated journalist H. L. Mencken, who came to mock Bryan and the Southern sen-
sibilities he defended. Jerome Lawrence and Robert Edwin Lee further
embellished the story in their classic play *Inherit the Wind*. The film version
of the play appeared in 1961, starring Spencer Tracy and Fredric March.
Tens of millions of Americans consider it the history of the confrontation.
The current TV show *The Simpsons* even parodies it in a satirical look at
the evolution controversy.

The trial was largely about Bryan, a cultural giant long past his prime,
making a final failed foray onto the national stage. His death shortly after
the trial was highly symbolic. For years Bryan had railed against evolution
to Christian, largely Southern audiences. Evolution, he thundered from
pulpits and podia, was an evil theory; survival of the fittest was the morally
bankrupt might makes right philosophy, dressed up in scientific garb. Evolutionary ideas, warned Bryan, had inspired Germany's militarism, leading them into World War I flying Darwin's delusionary flag as the nation

sought the "extermination of the crude, immoral hordes."[2] The death and destruction leveled by that Great War should rest on Darwin's grave, said Bryan, a conviction that still disturbs many antievolutionists.[3] He urged states everywhere to prohibit Darwin's theory being taught to their children, using arguments that have lost none of their force in the century since his voice rolled across America's heartland.

The Scopes trial began as an ACLU-driven test of the law Tennessee passed to keep evolution out of their schools:

> That it shall be unlawful for any teacher in any of the Universities, Normals and all other public schools of the State which are supported in whole or in part by the public school funds of the State, to teach any theory that denies the Story of the Divine Creation of man as taught in the Bible and to teach instead that man has descended from a lower order of animals.[4]

The confrontation that ensued between Bryan and Darrow—two of America's leading public figures at the time—was quite extraordinary. Bryan, the beloved Great Commoner, anticipated that the congenial audience in Dayton, including the jurors, would warm to his well-rehearsed rhetoric. Believing his oratorical skills would enhance his case against John Scopes, he even agreed to testify for the defense at Dayton as an expert on the Bible, which meant he would be cross-examined by his nemesis Darrow. Darrow, notoriously agnostic and controversial, had been needling Bryan in print and was eager to have a go at him, to show just how out of touch with modernity conservative Christians had become.

The confrontation became a symbol of how thoroughly the antievolutionary cause had been marginalized in the first quarter of the twentieth century. Bryan was educated, selectively well read, but had no idea how weak his position had become since he started his populist campaign against evolution. He had graduated from college in 1881, when Darwin's explanation for evolution—natural selection—was not taken seriously. Since then he had kept up only selectively with evolution, largely by reading its critics.

When Darrow asked Bryan to name some scientists who shared his views on origins, he tentatively mentioned George Frederick Wright, who had died four years earlier; he unwisely mentioned George McCready Price, the amateur geologist discussed in the previous chapter. Darrow replied that every scientist in the country knew Price was a "mountebank and pretender and not a scientist at all," a dismissal to which Bryan had no response.[5] The small physical space between Darrow and Bryan, as the former assaulted the latter in Dayton, mocked the divide that grown between them and the cultural constituencies they represented in American life. In an earlier time, they had once worked shoulder to shoulder on liberal political causes, but, as Darrow put it, Bryan now held "fool ideas that no intelligent Christian on earth believes."[6]

Creationists still hail Bryan as a hero—rather disingenuously considering that his embrace of the day-age interpretation is now attacked as a "compromise."[7] Fundamentalists are still trying to "set the record straight," to undo the damage done to Bryan and his cause in *Inherit the Wind*.[8] Amazingly, Bryan's antievolutionary cause has, if anything, grown stronger and more conservative in the past century, even as Darwin's theory of evolution has become an established part of mainstream science with near-universal support in the scientific community. The tension between science and the various antiscience movements—young-earth creationism, old-earth creationism, intelligent design—has never been stronger.

Entrepreneurial antievolutionists have discovered in America's heartlands a vast and ready audience of Christians who no longer want to make peace with the science that has taken over the academy—a science that sometimes appears in public wearing atheistic garb. This audience, now numbering more than a hundred million, continues to read Genesis literally, persuaded by the dubious arguments of "mountebanks and pretenders" that something called true science actually supports the Genesis story or that the Bible is more authoritative about the natural world than science. This audience lives in a zone of science denial, strangely out of touch with contemporary scholarship, like a tribe on an island that has lost contact with the mainland. While I was working on this book, the president of Bryan College spoke for this group when he said, "Scripture always rises above anything else. Scripture rises above science." He admonished Christians to ignore the evidence for evolution as an aberration: "Science at some point will catch up with the scripture."[9]

Bryan's death five days after the trial—portrayed as a collapse in the courtroom in *Inherit the Wind*—opened this cultural fault line in America. Conservative Christians, bewildered by their drift from the shores of intellectual life, responded by growing their own parallel culture. They founded Bible schools, colleges, K–12 and preschool programs. They launched publishing houses to produce evangelical literature. Magazines were started and, as soon as television became popular, Christian networks appeared. By the end of the twentieth century a robust evangelical culture had emerged, one with its own experts on everything from economics and child psychology to history and politics, and, of course, science. Tens of millions of dollars were funneled annually into projects convincing the faithful to reject evolution.

Meanwhile, just as life on earth evolved in fits and starts but moved inexorably in the direction of greater diversity and complexity, so Darwin's theory made its way forward in the twentieth century. The non-Darwinian explanations for evolution (orthogenesis, Lamarckism) disappeared as evidence accumulated that natural selection—proposed by Darwin in *On the Origin of Species*—was right after all.

ADAM IN THE MIDDLE

Adam and Eve were caught, perhaps unnecessarily, in the middle of this struggle. In principle, one can imagine variations on evolution that would permit them to be real historical characters and the source of original sin. One could view evolution, as theistic evolutionists and evolutionary creationists do—as God's method of creation. Adam and Eve by these lights are the end result of a long crafting process, at which time God chose them and gave them his image. Their rebellion happens after this engagement with God. But this process has to be highly constrained to work (for example, the human race has to pass through a bottleneck of just two people so that everyone can descend from the same pair). Of course, if God is directing the entire evolutionary process, he can certainly orchestrate this bottleneck as well. Such proposals, however, cannot be squared with a literal reading of Genesis, which is why so many literalists reject it.

The devil, as they say, is in the details, and those details, as they have emerged since Darwin penned his famous work, have made evolution as God's method of creating increasingly implausible. Take the problem of rampant and instinctive cruelty in nature. Darwin wrote eloquently about the way cats torture mice before they kill them, admitting that he could not imagine God creating creatures that would do this. Take the problem of bad design, which can be found in just about every species, including us. Our knees are easily damaged, for example, because they are not well designed for the various activities they are called to perform—like walking upright. We have back pain for the same reason. We have easily injured tailbones and appendices that can threaten our lives while performing almost no useful function. Childbirth is dangerous to both child and mother. Many people choke to death because of a poorly located windpipe. Hips wear out. A mechanical engineer designing a robot could easily correct these and a host of other design flaws. Did God really create all these second-rate systems? Did Adam and Eve have bad knees or inflamed appendices? Or did those come after the Fall? Or were they inherited from ancestral species? The most telling design flaws are found in our genes or, more specifically, in our broken or "pseudo" genes. Pseudogenes also establish human evolution with a certainty that requires heroic leaps of illogic to overcome. And genes increasingly undergird the arguments against the historicity of Adam and Eve, which is why this controversy is erupting today among conservative Christians in America.

Countless arguments like the one above are emerging from the exploding field of genetics and providing fascinating glimpses into the history of our species. The importance of these arguments cannot be overemphasized. If all humans descended from a newly created pair of humans a few thousand or even many thousand years ago, then there is no reason why *any* of our genes should be *identical* to those in other species. Even important genes for features like eyes that we share with other species need not be identical, any more than all the words for mother in every language have to be spelled the same; the language of genes, like human languages, can produce identical structures in many ways. The genes for human eyes need not match those for bonobo eyes any more than instruction manuals for dishwashers made in Germany must match manuals for Canadian dishwashers. The oft-repeated claim of the antievolutionists that "intelligent causes can generate identical patterns independently" provides no basis whatsoever for understanding why God would reuse the same genetic instructions in different organisms.[10]

But what about once-useful genes that now do nothing? One such gene is used to make vitamin C. This gene works in dogs and cats but does not function in either chimpanzees or humans, due to small molecular rearrangements. We get scurvy when we don't consume fruits or vitamin C supplements.

Our broken gene is the same one possessed by dogs and cats, except theirs is not broken. This example drives home the explanatory power of evolution: How can we *possibly* explain why we—and chimps and bonobos—carry the identical broken gene? Is it just a strange coincidence that those mammals that share the broken gene are the ones that evolutionary theory says are most closely related?

Broken genes keep antievolutionists up at night blogging feverishly to try and explain them away.[11] Such genes raise unanswerable questions about common design: Why would God put the same broken gene in several species? But they also point strongly in the opposite direction—toward evolution from common ancestors. There is nothing illogical about claiming that God gave chimps and humans similar eyes, and virtually everyone in the Western tradition believed this until about two centuries ago. Both species make use of eyes. But apply this to broken genes. The claim that God gave the same gene—broken in the same way—to both humans and chimps seems suspicious to anyone with a traditional view of God as a wise creator. What explains this?

The only plausible explanation is the one provided by evolution: chimps, bonobos, and humans share a common ancestor that possessed this broken gene. The problematic gene is not fatal, so this ancient species survived. The line of descent that led to humans carried this broken gene for millions of years, from one species to the next, and delivered it to us; and the lines of descent leading to chimps and bonobos did the same. Simple.

The problem comes when people try to insert Adam and Eve into this history, as traditionalists have been doing for more than a century. In order for you and me to have this broken gene—or any other gene for that matter—it had to be passed down from Adam and Eve. But where did they get it? It would be odd to claim that God created them with a specific broken gene that was a perfect match for one that existed millions of years earlier in the genomes of other primates. But how exactly did they inherit it from an ancestral species unless they evolved from that species?

And the vitamin C gene is just one of thousands telling the same story.

THE PERFECT STORM

Evolution has gone from a chapter near the back of the biology text to the central organizing principle of the entire field of biology. Pollination and photosynthesis are understood now by their evolutionary history rather than in purely descriptive terms. Evolution could no more be removed from the discussion of biology in textbooks than the vowels could be removed.

As the theory of evolution progressed from its fitful beginnings in the decades before Darwin down to the present, the Bible's authority on natural history declined. Geologists noted that portions of the planet had never been flooded, ruling out a worldwide flood. Zoologists determined that Noah's ark was far too small to house the vast menagerie that inhabits the earth. The oldest human fossils were discovered in Africa, not the Middle East. Evidence for the five-billion-year age for the earth became so strong that claims it was six thousand years old sounded as preposterous as claims it was flat.

The best-educated creationist leaders of today now quietly admit that creationism is "implausible on purely scientific grounds,"[12] and compelling only in the context of an overriding commitment to biblical inerrancy.[13] The term *biblical creationism* is now widely used in place of *scientific creationism*, driving home the point that allegiance to the Bible is why one rejects evolution, not allegiance to the best science, as was claimed a few decades earlier. Antievolutionists of all stripes—from young- and old-earth creationists to intelligent design theorists—have collapsed into scientific irrelevance. Virtually nobody in the scientific community pays attention to them and most scientists don't even know they exist.

Biblical literalists' continuing interest in Adam derives from their view that the Bible must be inerrant. If the Bible says Adam was real, one must believe he was real. If the Bible teaches a worldwide flood or that Jonah lived inside a fish for three days, then one must believe that also. If the Bible says God created the earth before the stars or that Balaam's donkey spoke to him one must believe.[14] No discrimination is made between theologically important notions and irrelevant stories that Christianity does not need. Literalists insist on an inerrant scripture as an infallible foundation for their faith, and a historical first couple is a part of that package.

CREATION, FALL, REDEMPTION

In contrast to literalists, the traditionalists we met in earlier chapters approach the Bible with flexibility. The book of nature need not bow down to the book of scripture every time they disagree. Traditionalists have forever understood that Christianity does not need an inerrant Bible any more than the United States needs an inerrant Constitution. On the other hand, traditionalists consistently protect the central theological notions perceived to be at the heart of Christianity, just as fans of the US Constitution protect its central insights.

Consider, for example, the following seventeenth-century objection to Copernican astronomy—an objection based entirely on the way it disrupts the theological *system* rather than the way it challenges the Bible:

[Copernican heliocentricity] upsets the whole basis of theology. If the earth is a planet, and only one among several planets, it cannot be that any such great things have been done especially for it as the Christian doctrine teaches. If there are other planets, since God makes nothing in vain, they must be inhabited; but how can their inhabitants be descended from Adam? How can they trace back their origin to Noah's ark? How can they have been redeemed by the Savior?[15]

Traditionalist anxiety about the historical Adam takes this form. The literal meaning of the Bible verses about Adam's origin—created from dust in a perfect garden in the Middle East six thousand years ago—is not the issue. For traditionalists the *biblical* Adam is not as important as the *theological* Adam—that is, Adam as the source of sin, death, and the curse is what matters, not when and where he lived or if he was the only male alive at the time. Adam keeps the theological system *coherent* just as a centralized earth kept an earlier system coherent.

The Adam controversy is thus in many ways an extension of the concern about the Copernican Revolution that unsettled Galileo's critics. It raises questions about how the *overall* Christian understanding of the world, its structure, and its history, especially the central theological role played by humans, fits with the reality disclosed by science.

A historical Adam is an essential component in the Christian theological system known as creation, fall, redemption. This system is built on the following theological history: (1) God created a perfect world free from sin, consistent with his nature and omnipotence, and with free creatures; (2) Adam and Eve abused this freedom and sinned; (3) Adam's sin produced all the imperfection, evil, death, and suffering, and God is in no way responsible for it; (4) God, working through Christ, redeems humans from their sin, and eventually redeems all creation. Phrases like the "unified biblical narrative" are often applied to this simple scheme.[16]

This basic Christian worldview entwines naturally with the medieval worldview we considered earlier. God creates the world with two realms—earthly and heavenly—both perfect. When Adam sins, God curses the human part of the creation, inflicting it with thorns, carnivores, pain in childbirth, germs that produce sickness and mortality. God does not curse the heavens.

The location in *space* of the earth and the location in *time* of Adam become entangled when we consider two central, related theological issues: the special role played by humans in the divine drama and the spatial and temporal extent of the Fall. If the earth orbits the sun, what is the *spatial domain* of the curse? God cursed the ground that Adam farmed, but did he curse the clouds that watered his crops or the sky over his head? When Neil Armstrong stepped onto the moon was his footprint on perfect soil? Is the outer solar system photographed by the *Voyager* spacecrafts cursed like the earth? Are aliens on distant planets sinful? Would aliens like *Star Trek*'s Mr. Spock, with one human parent, inherit Adam's original sin? These questions seem strangely out of place in an age of science and yet a curse on the physical creation has long been a central Christian doctrine.

Likewise, the *temporal domain* of the curse cannot be pinned down in time without a historical Adam near the beginning. If death entered the world with Adam's sin, how did so many species go extinct before he sinned? If nature was "red in tooth and claw" before sin, as Tennyson wrote, is God then responsible for suffering? Did God *intend* the lion to chase down the hapless zebra? Or is that grisly scenario a consequence of human sin? But if we evolved from earlier life forms, how did our sinful natures arise? And at what point in the evolution of intelligent primates does the concept of sin begin to make sense? Do we even have sinful natures? If there is no fall from perfection, then what does salvation mean? Is it "all in pieces, all coherence gone," as the poet John Donne wrote of the new order inaugurated by Copernicus?[17]

No Christian thinker has found a satisfactory resolution to the origin of sin, the nature and extent of the curse, and the closely related *problem of evil.* Adam and Eve are part of this mystery. A 2013 edited volume titled *God and Evil,* written largely from the traditionalist perspective, and to which I made a modest contribution, begins by noting that "There are few topics in the history of Christianity—indeed, of Western thought in general—about which more has been discussed than this one."[18] Adam's role in bringing evil into the world figures prominently in all twenty of the discussions.

The challenge of taking God's Two Books seriously has grown dramatically in recent years as genetic evidence has made it clear that Adam and Eve cannot have been historical figures, at least as described in the Bible. More scientifically informed evangelicals within conservative traditions are admitting that the evidence is undermining creation, fall, redemption theology. Traditionalists have struggled to preserve this central Christian understanding in a way that is faithful to both the Bible and science; literalists have tried to preserve it by rejecting science or making increasingly strange claims about the world. The task is beginning to look impossible from any perspective, as we will now see from the implausible and inconsistent proposals that are circulating.

CREATING ADAMS

Not long ago the media buzzed about a new planet discovered far from our solar system, Gliese 581g. The new planet was potentially habitable since its temperature was in the range where water is liquid, the most important consideration for life. The news promoted speculation about possible alien life. Ken Ham, who succeeded Henry Morris as America's leading creationist, responded that the alien planet would have been victimized by Adam's fall: "The Bible makes it clear that Adam's sin affected the whole universe," he said. "This means that any aliens would also be affected by Adam's sin."

Ham is suggesting that the "Gliesans" would have seen their paradise planet mysteriously wrecked about six thousand years ago when God cursed the creation. The Gliesans would have been happy, immortal, surrounded by docile herbivores. Suddenly, because of an act on a planet trillions of miles away, Gliese would have been stricken with inexplicable suffering, death, and different laws of physics. And, although human sin on a distant Earth wrecked their planet, the poor Gliesans "can't have salvation," says Ham. "Only descendants of Adam can be saved." To even "suggest that aliens could respond to the gospel is just totally wrong," he says.[19]

Ham's commitment to the universality of the curse flows directly from the challenge of Copernicus, since fundamentalist theology ties the two together. As long as the heavens and the earth could be separated, the curse could be constrained to an earthly realm. But once the earth is lifted into the heavens, the natural boundary for the influence of sin disappears.

A slightly less strange proposal comes from Hugh Ross and his Reasons to Believe organization, which defends old-earth creationism with a day-age reading of Genesis of the sort discussed earlier. Reasons to Believe denies that the day-age interpretation represents a compromise with science, insisting that a careful reading of the entire Bible—and not just Genesis—points clearly to the days of creation being long epochs.[20] Ross also insists that the Fall inaugurated only human death, accusing the young-earth creationists of misinterpreting Paul's comments in Romans 5:12 on which that claim is based: "Just as sin came into the world through one man, and death came through sin.[21]

Ross goes further. Not only is death a part of the natural order but God also ordained it to provide oil and other raw materials useful for humans.

The benefits to humanity of these earlier life forms, says Ross, renders their suffering, death, and even extinction a good thing, and not an evil to be explained as a consequence of sin.

Ross holds a PhD in astrophysics from the University of Toronto; he is respected by fundamentalists for the ingenious ways he resolves scientific challenges to the Bible. He enlarges the Garden of Eden to reach Africa, for example, to align with the discovery that humans originated there. He pushes Adam and Eve back far enough in history so their origins agree with the fossil record.[22] And he finds a biblical justification for all these moves. His claim that the extinction of millions of species was part of God's "good" intentions, however, is quite strained, like most of his other proposals.

The leading intelligent design theorist William Dembski shares the widely held view that animal death is a real evil caused by human sin and not God's way of making petroleum. Dembski, with a PhD in mathematics from the University of Chicago and a PhD in theology from the University of Illinois at Chicago, is the best-educated antievolutionist in the country. Like Ross he understands that science has proven that the earth is very old. So how does Adam's sin make the dinosaurs go extinct seventy million years before he existed?

Dembski describes his book *The End of Christianity: Finding a Good God in an Evil World* as an attempt "to resolve how the Fall of Adam would be responsible for all evil in the world, both moral and natural IF the earth is old and thus IF a fossil record that bespeaks violence among organisms predates the temporal occurrence of the Fall." The description of the problem is mainstream and one reason why the young-earth creationists are forced to reject so much science. But Dembski's resolution is anything but mainstream.

Dembski proposes that "the effects of the Fall can go *backward in time*." He proposes a "retroactive view of the Fall, in which God by anticipation allows natural evil in consequence of the Fall."[23] One can appreciate the magnitude of the problem being addressed by looking at the strangeness of the solution being proposed.

The British biochemist Denis Alexander offers yet another solution. He accepts the great age of the earth; evolution, including human evolution; and millions of years of death, suffering, and extinction prior to the arrival of humans. He also understands that genetic evidence rules out the possibility that the human race ever consisted of one man and one woman.

However, Alexander is also a traditionalist—unlike Ham, Ross, and Dembski. As such he embraces key biblical ideas that play meaningful roles in Christian theology, but he does not insist on literal interpretations. He seeks historical events that lie "behind the text"—events that undergird the theological content of the biblical accounts, but may be quite different from the accounts themselves. Drawing on a tradition of like-minded thinkers, Alexander suggests that the Genesis account is based on an actual historical episode where God reached into history: "God in his grace chose a couple of Neolithic farmers in the Near East, or maybe a community of farmers, to whom he chose to reveal himself in a special way, calling them into fellowship with himself—so that they might know him as a personal God."[24]

Alexander calls these early humans *Homo divinus*, "the divine humans, those who know the one true God, the Adam and Eve of the Genesis account." "*Homo divinus* were the first humans who were truly spiritually alive in fellowship with God," says Alexander. "*Homo divinus* marked the time at which God chose to reveal himself and his purposes for humankind for the first time."[25] The death brought on by sin was *spiritual*, not physical. The biblical literalists, of course, find all this totally unacceptable: "In Alexander's hands the Bible loses its authority" and is no longer "allowed to dictate the acceptable boundaries for other pursuits; biology is an independent authoritative revelation."[26]

I waded naively into these troubled waters in 2008 with my book *Saving Darwin: How to Be a Christian and Believe in Evolution*. I suggested that what is labeled theologically as sin remains a useful insight into human nature, even after we abandon a historical Adam, his fall, and the original sin he passed on to us. God, however, did not build sin into the natural order. Rather, God endowed the natural order with a genuine freedom—including the freedom to evolve—and the result was an interesting, morally complex, spiritually rich, but ultimately selfish (= sinful) species we call *Homo sapiens*. The story of Adam is thus the story of Everyman, unable to resist temptation, ignoring the better angels of his nature.[27] Few evangelicals liked my proposal. Dembski, in a rather ad hominem review of the book, described me as someone who "got some education, swallowed Darwin hook, line, and sinker, and now spends his days justifying why his move to embrace Darwin was the better part of wisdom—all the while proudly proclaiming that he remains a Christian."[28]

These ways of construing Adam all have adherents claiming the label "evangelical" in America, although, as the most liberal on the brief survey above, I have critics telling me to abandon that designation.[29] Leading fundamentalist gatekeeper Al Mohler was right to describe me as "far outside of the evangelical mainstream."[30] I don't think I am even in the stream any longer—I am certainly not employed by the evangelical college where I once held tenure! Anyone challenging the historicity of Adam should probably abandon evangelicalism, since they are likely to be ejected anyway.

In an ideal world the positions described above could be in conversation, competing for the allegiance of Christians trying with integrity to reconcile their tradition with the advance of science. Christianity, after all, is not a religion about Adam; it is a religion about Christ, and as we have seen throughout this book, Adam can be understood in many ways. Unfortunately, however, the historical Adam has become a line in the sand for many evangelicals who don't want even to engage the conversation.

MARTYRS FOR SCIENCE?

Evangelical institutions that for years encouraged serious engagement with evolutionary science have consistently retreated when that engagement threatens the historicity of Adam.

The most infamous and to my mind most tragic example of this occurred in the mid-1990s at Wheaton College in Illinois, the most academically elite evangelical school in the country. For decades Wheaton had led the conversation between science and Christianity, encouraging open engagement and empowering the conversation about how Christianity should adapt to new scientific discoveries. It was thus appropriate that Wheaton host a major conference at which leading scholars considered the influence of Darwin.

Local attendees at the conference, however, were shocked to discover that Wheaton seemed to be "countenancing evolution." This concern made it into print and became widely known, and concerned constituents bombarded the president of Wheaton with complaints. The result—tragic and typical—was that Wheaton chose not to defend its right to explore science openly within the broad contours of the Christian tradition; instead Wheaton added the following unscientific item to its statement of faith: "Man was created by a direct act of God and not from previously existing forms of life; and that all men are descended from the historical Adam and Eve, first parents of the entire human race."[31]

This familiar pattern was repeated most recently in 2014 at Bryan College. Bryan hosted a conversation about evolution with some scientists from the BioLogos Foundation, which I helped found with Francis Collins in 2009. BioLogos's mission at the time was to help Christians make peace with evolution, and in its early days was led by scientists, Collins, Darrel Falk, and me, and a biblical scholar, Pete Enns, who all agreed that the key to making peace with evolution was learning to do without a historical Adam. (Incidentally, this approach proved politically impossible and the organization has since moved to a more conservative stance, emphasizing dialog.)

The Bryan-BioLogos conversation stimulated the same sort of scrutiny that occurred earlier at Wheaton. Bryan's statement on human origins read as follows: We believe "that the origin of man was by fiat of God in the act of creation as related in the Book of Genesis; that he was created in the image of God; that he sinned and thereby incurred physical and spiritual death."

This statement accomplishes everything theological that needs to happen with human origins, making clear that death is the result of sin, protecting the creation, fall, redemption motif. And it contains enough flexibility to accommodate evolution. Nothing in the statement precludes that God crafted humans through evolution and gave them his image at the appropriate time. This flexibility allowed Bryan science faculty to study human origins without the straitjacket of young-earth creationism. They were free to seek concordist schemes compatible with both science and Bryan's statement on origins.

However, the Bryan-BioLogos conversation rattled the leadership at Bryan so much they decided they needed to specify exactly what was meant by the above language in the statement of faith and remove any flexibility that might be used to accommodate evolution. (Bryan's charter precludes changing its statement of faith.) Over the objections of many faculty—some with professional expertise in human origins—the president and board of trustees decided the above statement could mean only the following: "We believe that all humanity is descended from Adam and Eve. They are historical persons created by God in a special formative act, and not from previously existing life forms." This hardened stance essentially precludes any biologist at Bryan from being active in any part of his or her field related to human origins.

This controversy continues. To date Bryan has lost 25 percent of its faculty, many forced to uproot their families in search of new employment, which is hard to come by when you have been run off for heresy.[32] Three hundred of Bryan's eight hundred students petitioned to reverse the new interpretation.[33] A flexible approach to Adam and Eve that had been acceptable for decades had now become grounds for termination. Two professors who were terminated against their will are suing the college.[34] The faculty voted no confidence in the president. Some trustees objected to the president's decision and resigned. Enrollment is declining, not surprisingly, as students are voting with their feet and taking their tuition dollars elsewhere.

ADAM ENDURES

The stories at Wheaton and Bryan are not unique. They repeat themselves every time traditionalists enter into a conversation with fundamentalists about the historicity of Adam. As long as the conversations occur in quiet classrooms or over lunch things are fine. But when the conversation goes public the gatekeepers of orthodoxy get involved, and call for the heads of the "liberals."

I have many friends and acquaintances in the traditionalist camp who lost their positions at evangelical colleges and seminaries under pressure from fundamentalist power brokers. Traditionalists trying to take scholarship seriously spend their careers under a dark cloud. For more than a quarter century I promoted mainstream science—including evolution and the big bang—to students at Eastern Nazarene College and to the larger community through my writing. I was regularly summoned to the president's office to deal with gatekeeper concerns but never once to be affirmed for my efforts to help Christians make peace with science. The story was always the same: some fundamentalist pastor who knew nothing about science was upset that I was telling students that evolution was true, or that the earth was old, or that the universe began in a big bang—or that Adam and Eve were not historical figures. They rejoiced when they heard that the notorious heretic Karl Giberson had been pushed out, but lamented that "Only God knows how many students have had their faith shaken or shipwrecked because of his unbiblical teachings."[35] In dramatic contrast, I am unaware of a single faculty member who ever lost their job at an evangelical college because they were too conservative.

The fundamentalists always win.

Adam and Eve, as described in Genesis, cannot have been historical figures. Recent work in genetics has established this unsettling truth beyond any reasonable doubt. But Christians have had centuries to prepare. The problem with the historical Adam was anticipated in the seventeenth century and has been growing steadily more apparent with advances in geology, paleontology, evolution, and even biblical studies.

Conservative evangelicals have responded by denying the scholarship on which these conclusions are based and by simply asserting the superiority of their interpretation of Bible—although they deny they are "interpreting"—calling for Christians to embrace God's word rather than the "foolishness" of science.[36] No argument can be raised against such a position, one that grows ever more intransigent and shows no sign of dying out.

Evangelical Christianity is in crisis. The traditionalists in that community struggle to maintain their twin allegiances to God's Two Books while fighting off threats from conservative elements. Scientifically informed members of America's vast community of evangelicals are calling—as Galileo did four centuries earlier—for the church to give up a cherished and traditional notion. This time it is about the first man. Galileo's summons took centuries to work its way into the pews of conservative Christianity. It appears that things are not going much faster this time around.

WISHFUL THINKING
We Are All Original Sinners

Certain new theologians dispute original sin, which is the
only part of Christian theology which can really be proved.
—G. K. CHESTERTON[1]

John Collins, a leading fundamentalist theologian and champion of the historical Adam, ends his book *Did Adam and Eve Really Exist?* with a list of reasons why we should believe in the historicity of the original sinner. I once found these reasons compelling: it saves us from blaming God for sin; it preserves the importance of the atoning death of Jesus; Adamic ancestry "affirms the common dignity of all people"; a literal Adam preserves the authority of the Bible. But missing from Collins's list is any indication that it matters whether or not the evidence suggests that Adam existed. In fact, Collins is quite clear that evidence, at least of the scientific sort, doesn't matter to him.

Collins's arguments—and indeed most of the arguments for the historicity of Adam—ultimately turn out to be wishful thinking. My sense is that most people identify with this tendency to some degree. Do we not all wish for a world that makes sense, as it once made sense before Copernicus uprooted the earth and before the poet John Donne declared that the "new philosophy casts all in doubt" to such a degree that a once-cozy cosmos was "now in pieces, all coherence gone."[2] If we project our longings and fears onto the cosmos, then we have to admit that it would be more comforting if the earth were fixed at the center of the universe, if the earth and all its inhabitants were created about the same time as humans, if the stars were not unimaginably far away, forever out of our reach. It would be comforting if humans were more distinct from animals, if there was a convenient explanation for suffering and death, if we could know that good would ultimately triumph over evil. Setting aside the question of whether medieval Christianity actually provided a truly comforting worldview, we can certainly acknowledge that science has raised troubling questions about who we are, how we should live, why we are here, and where we came from.

In a volume titled *Four Views on the Historical Adam*, young-earth creationist William Barrick concludes, in the same vein of wishful thinking as Collins, that "Denial of the historicity of Adam . . . destroys the foundations of the Christian Faith."[3] I will not weigh in on this claim, other than to note that many traditional Christians have made peace with the extinction of Adam. It does seem to me, however, that we must always be prepared for new knowledge to overturn ancient ideas. No received wisdom from the past—in sacred texts, confessions, creeds, statements of faith, or anywhere else—is immune to challenge from the advancing knowledge of the present. Christianity emerged in a different time and must be prepared to evolve like everything else.

I want to conclude this discussion of the first man, however, on a different note—one of concern. As Adam fades from our conversations about the human condition, something else disappears also: the recognition that our species is deeply troubled.

In the Christian tradition, humanity's problem is referred to as *sin*, blamed on Adam, and said to be present in us all through the inheritance of original sin. I have argued in this book that such a viewpoint is no longer tenable, and we must learn to get along without it. There is no original sin and there was no original sinner. But we must not forget that the Christian tradition's long conversation about sin was primarily about what was wrong with us and only secondarily about how we got to be that way. Augustine was more interested in his own sin than that of Adam. Regardless of how it originated, or whether it even had an origin, something appropriately called sin remains a deeply rooted part of human nature and, given that we are born this way, original sin is not a bad name for it. G. K. Chesterton calls original sin "the only part of Christian theology which can really be proved." I worry that wishful thinking may once again be at work in those who, having abandoned Adam, would now abandon the associated notion that humans are sinful creatures. This, of course, is not an exclusively Christian conversation, as all religious traditions—and indeed all of history— acknowledge human limitations and tendencies toward wrongdoing.

The Nobel laureate in physiology Christian de Duve, a nonbeliever with no investment in Christian doctrine, nevertheless tips his hat to the sacred writers who "perceived the presence in human nature of a fatal flaw."[4] He is quick to dismiss the Christian concept of original sin as the flaw but quite insistent that the flaw is real, serious, and threatening to our species. The culprit is not Adam but the process of natural selection that has shaped our species over the long course of evolution. This selection process, unfortunately, privileged gene traits that were "immediately favorable to the survival and proliferation of our ancestors . . . with no regard for later consequences."[5] Such traits include "selfishness, greed, cunning, aggressiveness, and any other property that ensured immediate personal gain, regardless of later cost to oneself or to others."[6]

Most of the serious problems we face today arise from this deeply rooted and ineradicable part of our evolved human nature. And yet, we propose to solve these problems with trivial rearrangements of the social order. As I write these words the world is recovering from the worst financial disaster since the Great Depression. Major banks are paying billion-dollar fines for their role in the collapse of the economy. And yet one listens in vain for any suggestion that uncontrollable greed on the part of bankers may have caused the collapse. The news is filled with unhappy stories about growing wealth inequality, but nobody seems to think that greedy self-interest might be part of the problem. In the Middle East ISIS (the Islamic State in Iraq and Syria) is slaughtering innocent civilians and publically beheading Western noncombatants. The intensity of their campaign is rooted in the ancient tribalism that took up residence in our genes when defending one's tribe had survival value. We forget that Western Christians waged similar campaigns a few short centuries ago and that it was only in the last century that Hitler was exterminating the Jews. Setting aside tribal differences requires more effort than economic sanctions or high-brow political conversations at Camp David.

Jimmy Carter has written passionately about the global exploitation of women that occurs in every nation, a natural consequence of social structures where powerful men are in control.[7] In the United States young girls develop eating disorders as they strive to look like artificially enhanced versions of what men find attractive. Evolution has programmed men with unhealthy attitudes toward women and, when not checked, these attitudes express themselves in tragic ways.

Climate scientists are trying in vain to awaken the world to gradual changes that are ruining the planet. Natural resources are being used up. But we are programmed by natural selection to care only about the short term. Thinking about people who will be born in the next century seems like a fantasy. How can we possibly owe them anything? Why should we restrain our lifestyles to enhance theirs?

For centuries those of us from the Christian tradition have understood ourselves as fallen, sinful creatures—an understanding that served as a caution by illuminating our dark behaviors. At its best, it checked our worst impulses. Now we understand ourselves as evolved creatures, shaped by natural selection, but unaware of what that means and how hard we will have to work to transcend those limitations.

We are a troubled species, seemingly destined to obliterate ourselves and puzzled about why that is so. Everyone from the fundamentalist Christian to the crusading atheist knows we need some kind of salvation, although we are certainly looking in different places for it. Perhaps that will come from a transformed Christianity, a reenvisioned science, or from another source. It certainly won't come by denying science. But it won't come from pretending that when Adam vanished he took original sin with him.

Acknowledgments

This project began over coffee—actually, many coffees—with my friend Pete Enns, an Old Testament scholar and leading voice in the controversy about Adam raging within evangelical Christianity. Enns had recently been forced out of Westminster Theological Seminary by fundamentalist gatekeepers, upset that he was asking tough questions in print about the Old Testament—questions to which many were paying attention.

We spent a lot of time talking about Adam and Eve. It seemed to both of us that this was the single most important issue driving evangelical Christianity's strong opposition to science. This opposition spills over into Catholicism and into moderate and liberal Christianity to a degree. It has taken up residence in the Republican Party and plays a significant role in America's declining global leadership in science. It plays into a general distrust of science in America that nurtures the rejection of modern cosmology, climate science, and vaccinations.

Pete and I had been in this conversation for much of our careers, and we were particularly struck by the creativity of Christians in coming up with ways to deflect the emerging scientific evidence that Adam and Eve could not have been historical characters. This creativity included all kinds of imaginative new Adams bearing little resemblance to the one in Genesis, but always with a clear place somewhere in history.

These conversations got me thinking more broadly about how Adam and Eve became what some have called the central myth of Western culture, and why so many Christians cannot part with them. *Saving the Original Sinner* is my contribution to this animated conversation.

I want to thank my agent, David Patterson of Foundry Literary + Media, for getting behind this project and securing me contracts with both Beacon Press in Boston and Audible Books. Thanks to my editor at Beacon, Amy Caldwell, for helping me navigate the many unfamiliar waters I encountered in this project, making many helpful suggestions. And thanks to my copy editor, Andrea Lee, for a host of valuable improvements. Good editors are a writer's best friend and mine saved me from a host of literary embarrassments.

My friend John Schneider, who is a part of the story told in this book, read the entire manuscript and made many helpful suggestions. The chapter on Augustine and original sin was completely rewritten at his urging.

I have always thrived intellectually in an academic community, and during the writing of this book, I made a difficult professional transition from Eastern Nazarene College, where these topics are uncomfortably controversial, to Stonehill College, which is more open. I could not be happier in my new position and want to express appreciation to my provost, Joe Favazza, for his creative efforts in bringing me to Stonehill.

Finally, I want to thank my wife, Myrna, for providing encouragement and stability through the course of this project. This is my tenth book, and she has put up with far too many piles of paper, random piles of books, and endless boxes filled with "research materials" arriving from Amazon. I dedicate this book to her and thank her from the bottom of my heart for almost four decades of marriage.

A WORD ABOUT
BIBLICAL TRANSLATIONS

Unless specified otherwise, all biblical quotations come from the New Revised Standard Version of the Bible (*The Holy Bible: New Revised Standard Version* [Division of Christian Education of the National Council of the Churches of Christ, 1989]). The NRSV combines attention to recent scholarship, concern about gender inclusiveness, and readability. In many cases, however, I have elected to use other translations when the passage was either more familiar—as when Jesus says, "What does it profit a man to gain the whole world if he loses his own soul?"—or when other translations made my point a bit easier to understand. In a few cases I have made reference to the original language of the text when the translation itself is controversial, as is the case with the apparent placement of a solid dome overhead in the Genesis creation story, which is denied vigorously by creationists.

NOTES

Introduction

1. R. Albert Mohler, "False Start? The Controversy over Adam and Eve Heats Up," AlbertMohler.com, August 22, 2011, http://www.albertmohler.com /2011/08/22/false-start-the-controversy-over-adam-and-eve-heats-up/.

2. "Prepare to Believe," CreationMuseum.org, accessed May 2012, http://www .creationmuseum.org.

3. Randall J. Stephens and Karl W. Giberson, *The Anointed: Evangelical Truth in a Secular Age* (Cambridge, MA: Belknap Press of Harvard University Press, 2011), 26.

4. Ken Ham, "What Are Nazarene Students Being Taught?," *Around the World with Ken Ham* (blog), 1:1 Answers Outreach, August 15, 2009, http://blogs .answersingenesis.org/blogs/ken-ham/2009/08/15/what-are-nazarene -students-being-taught/.

5. James Scullin, "You Say Toe-May-Toe, I Say Toe-Mah-Toe," *Reformed Naza-rene* (blog), July 23, 2013, http://reformednazarene.wordpress.com/category /karl-giberson/.

6. "OT Scholar Bruce Waltke Resigns Following Evolution Comments," *Glean-ings* (blog), *Christianity Today*, April 9, 2010, http://www.christianitytoday .com/gleanings/2010/april/ot-scholar-bruce-waltke-resigns-following -evolution.html.

7. John R. Schneider, "Recent Genetic Science and Christian Theology on Human Origins: An 'Aesthetic Supralapsarianism,'" *Perspectives on Science and Christian Faith* 62 (2010), http://www.asa3.org/ASA/PSCF/2010 /PSCF9–10Schneider.pdf.

8. John R. Schneider, communication with author, October 23, 2013.

9. Schneider, "Recent Genetic Science."

10. Calvin College Office of the Provost, "Faculty Membership Requirements: A Guide for Prospective Faculty," http://www.calvin.edu/admin/provost /facdocs/fac-requirements.htm.

11. John Byl, "The Evolution of Calvin College," *Christian Renewal*, November 24, 2010, http://crmag.com/TheEvolutionofCalvinCollege.

12. Michael Ruse, "Calvin College and Original Sin," *HuffPost Religion* (blog), December 16, 2010, updated May 25, 2011, http://www.huffingtonpost.com /michael-ruse/calvin-college-and-origin_b_796747.html.

13. Mohler, "False Start?"

14. "An Unbelieving Professor at Calvin College," *Doctrine Unites!* (blog), October 10, 2012, http://www.twoagespilgrims.com/doctrine/an-unbelieving -professor-at-calvin-college/.

15. "No Adam, No Eve, No Gospel," *Christianity Today*, June 6, 2011, http:// www.christianitytoday.com/ct/2011/june/noadamevenogospel.html?paging =off.

16. Barbara Bradley Hagerty, "Evangelicals Question the Existence of Adam and Eve," *Morning Edition*, NPR, August 9, 2011, audio, 7:44, http://www.npr .org/2011/08/09/138957812/evangelicals-question-the-existence-of-adam -and-eve.

17. "Statement of Faith and Educational Purpose," Wheaton College, 1924, http:// www.wheaton.edu/About-Wheaton/Statement-of-Faith-and-Educational -Purpose.

18. "Evolution, Creationism, Intelligent Design," Gallup, accessed September 20, 2014, http://www.gallup.com/poll/21814/evolution-creationism-intelligent -design.aspx.

19. "Photo: Evolution Less Accepted in U.S. Than Other Western Countries, Study Finds," *National Geographic News*, October 28, 2010, http://news .nationalgeographic.com/news/bigphotos/21329204.html.

20. Matthew 19:5.

21. J. Gerald Harris, "Answers Really Are in Genesis, Ken Ham Says," *Baptist Press* (blog), January 23, 2012, http://www.bpnews.net/37016.

22. Kate McCarthy, "John Quincy Adams a Founding Father? Michele Bachmann Says Yes," ABCNews.com, June 28, 2011, http://abcnews.go.com/blogs /politics/2011/06/john-quincy-adams-a-founding-father-michele-bachmann -says-yes/.

23. Elaine Pagels, *Adam, Eve, and the Serpent* (New York: Random House, 1988), xxviii. Emphasis added.

24. Sarah Ruden, *Paul Among the People: The Apostle Reinterpreted and Reimagined in His Own Time* (New York: Image Books, 2010), xix.

25. Glenn Tinder, *Against Fate: An Essay on Personal Dignity* (Chicago: University of Notre Dame Press, 1984).

26. Denis Alexander, *Creation or Evolution: Do We Have to Choose?* (Grand Rapids: Monarch Books, 2008).

27. Fazale Rana and Hugh Ross, *Who Was Adam? A Creation Model Approach to the Origin of Man* (Canada: NavPress, 2005).

Chapter 1

1. Robert South, "The Happiness of Adam," *English Prose*, ed. Henry Craike (New York: Macmillan, 1916), Bartleby.com, http://www.bartleby.com/209/571.html.

2. "Philo and Origen Are Not Your Friends, Dr. Alexander: A Short Survey of What Two Biblical Allegorists Taught about Adam and Eve," *Uncommon Descent* (blog), December 27, 2011, http://www.uncommondescent.com/intelligent-design/philo-and-origen-are-not-your-friends-dr-alexander-a-short-survey-of-what-two-biblical-allegorists-taught-about-adam-and-eve/.

3. E. T. Babinski, ed., "Men Over Ten Feet Tall?," *Cretinism or Evilution?* No. 3, accessed November 4, 2013, http://www.talkorigins.org/faqs/ce/3/part2.html.

4. Mike Parsons with Jeremy Westcott, "The Supernatural Kingdom of God," *Sons of Issachar,* March 16, 2012, http://freedomarc.wordpress.com/2012/03/16/the-supernatural-kingdom-of-god/.

5. "What Is 'The Serpent Seed'?," *The Serpent Seed*, accessed November 4, 2013, http://serpent-seed.com/.

6. Psalm 127:3–5.

7. Genesis 4:20.

8. Genesis 6:5.

9. Genesis 6:6.

10. Genesis 7:22–23.

11. Genesis 9:12–15.

12. Genesis 9:25–27.

13. Genesis 10:9.

14. Deuteronomy 18:15–16.

15. Lydia Saad, "Three in Four in U.S. Still See the Bible as Word of God," Gallup.com, June 4, 2014, http://www.gallup.com/poll/170834/three-four-bible-word-god.aspx.

16. 2 Timothy 3:16.

17. Teresa McBean, "April 2," *National Association for Christian Recovery*, September 24, 2012, http://www.nacr.org/wordpress/3242/april-2.

18. Numbers 31:2.

19. Numbers 31:17–18.

20. Richard Dawkins, *The God Delusion* (New York: Houghton Mifflin, 2006), 51.

Chapter 2

1. Krister Stendahl, "The Apostle Paul and the Introspective Conscience of the West," *The Harvard Theological Review* 56, no. 3 (July 1963): 199. Available online at http://www.dburnett.com/wp-content/uploads/2011/07/The-Apostle-Paul-and-the-Introspective-Conscience-of-the-West.pdf.

2. Acts 9:1.

3. Krister Stendahl, *Paul Among Jews and Gentiles and Other Essays* (Minneapolis: Fortress Press, 1976), 78.

4. "Major Religions of the World Ranked by Number of Adherents," Adherents.com, accessed April 2, 2012, http://www.adherents.com/Religions_By_Adherents.html.

5. Michael H. Hart, *The 100: A Ranking of the Most Influential Persons in History* (New York: Kensington, 1992), vii.

6. Galatians 1:11–17a. Emphasis added.

7. Jeremiah 1:4–5.

8. Psalm 137:1–4.

9. Isaac Newton, "A Description of the Temple of Solomon," *The Chronology of Ancient Kingdoms Amended* (London: Kessinger, 2004).

10. For an engaging treatment of this topic and the challenges it poses, see Peter Enns, *Incarnation and Inspiration: Evangelicals and the Problem of the Old Testament* (Grand Rapids, MI: Baker Academic, 2005).

11. Peter Enns, *The Evolution of Adam: What the Bible Does and Doesn't Say About Human Origins* (Grand Rapids, MI: Brazos Press, 2012), 97.

12. Bruce M. Metzger and Michael D. Coogan, eds., *The Oxford Companion to the Bible* (New York: Oxford University Press, 1993), 37.

13. "The Angel Dictates to Moses the Primeval History: The Creation of the World and Institution of the Sabbath," Internet Sacred Texts Archive (Santa Cruz, CA: Evinity, 2011), http://www.sacred-texts.com/bib/jub/jub14.htm.

14. William R. G. Loader, *Philo, Josephus, and the Testaments on Sexuality: Attitudes towards Sexuality in the Writings of Philo and Josephus and the Testaments of the Twelve Patriarchs* (Grand Rapids, MI: Eerdmans, 2011), 36.

15. R. H. Charles, ed., *Apocalypsis Mosis* (Oxford, UK: Clarendon Press, 1913), Christian Classics Ethereal Library, http://www.ccel.org/c/charles/otpseudepig/apcmose.htm.

16. Ibid.

17. Ibid.

18. Raphael Patai, "Lilith," *Journal of American Folklore* 77, no. 306 (1964): 295–314, doi: 10.2307/537379.

19. Search results for "Lilith" on BibleGateway.com illustrate that only Isaiah 34:14 makes reference to Lilith directly, but not consistently, across multiple versions of the Bible.

20. Isaiah 34:2.

21. Isaiah 34:13–14.

22. William F. Albright, "An Aramaean Magical Text in Hebrew from the Seventh Century B.C.," *Bulletin of the American Schools of Oriental Research* 76 (1939): 9, doi: 10.2307/1354868.

23. Lauren Kinrich, "Demon at the Doorstep: Lilith as a Reflection of Anxieties and Desires in Ancient, Rabbinic, and Medieval Jewish Sexuality" (senior thesis, paper 4, Pomona College, 2011).

24. Luke 4:18, *The Holy Bible: King James Version* (New York: American Bible Society, 1999).

25. Matthew 10:6.

26. Acts 17:26, *King James Version*.

27. Romans 3:23.

28. Matthew 5:48.

29. Romans 8:22, *King James Version*.

30. Kristen E. Kvam, Linda S. Schearing, and Valarie H. Ziegler, *Eve and Adam: Jewish, Christian, and Muslim Readings on Genesis and Gender* (Bloomington: Indiana University Press, 1999), 64.

31. Romans 5:6–19, *The Holy Bible: New King James Version* (Nashville: Thomas Nelson, 1982).

32. Matthew 15:26.

Chapter 3

1. Alexander Solzhenitsyn, *The Gulag Archipelago Two* (New York: Harper and Row, 1975).

2. 2 Corinthians 11:23–27.

3. Elaine Pagels, *Adam, Eve, and the Serpent* (New York: Random House, 1988), xviii.

4. Dyron Daughrity, "From Sect to Secularization: Understanding the History and Future of the Earth's Largest Faith," *Missio Dei: A Journal of Missional Theology and Praxis* 2, no. 2 (August 2011), http://missiodeijournal.com /article.php?issue=md-2-2&author=md-2-2-daughrity.

5. Ephesians 6:12.

6. Pagels, *Adam, Eve, and the Serpent*, 36.

7. Rodney Stark, *The Rise of Christianity* (Princeton, NJ: Princeton University Press, 1996), 196–215.

8. Elaine Pagels, *The Origin of Satan: How Christians Demonized Jews, Pagans, and Heretics* (New York: Random House, 1995), 119.

9. Pagels, *Adam, Eve, and the Serpent*, 37.

10. Genesis 6:1–7.

11. Peter Kirby, "Justin Martyr," *Early Christian Writings*, accessed July 31, 2013, http://www.earlychristianwritings.com/text/justinmartyr-secondapology .html.

12. Ibid.

13. Peter C. Boutenoff, *Beginnings: Ancient Christian Readings of the Biblical Creation Narratives* (Grand Rapids, MI: Baker Academic, 2008), 45.

14. Pagels, *Adam, Eve, and the Serpent*, 80.

15. Ibid.

16. Mark 8:36, *The Holy Bible: King James Version* (New York: American Bible Society, 1999).

17. 1 John 2:15–17.

18. Mark 10:21.

19. Pagels, *Adam, Eve, and the Serpent*, 83.

20. Matthew 19:12. Emphasis added.

21. Paul Halsall, ed., *Letter to Eustochium*, Internet Medieval Sourcebook, Fordham University website, 1995, http://www.fordham.edu/Halsall/basis/jerome-letter22.asp.

22. E. Gordon Whatley, Anne B. Thompson, and Robert K. Upchurch, eds., "St. Jerome: Introduction," in *Saints' Lives in Middle English Collections* (Kalamazoo, MI: Medieval Institute Publications, 2004).

23. Halsall, *Letter to Eustochium*.

24. Genesis 2:24.

25. Phillip Schaff and Henry Wallace, eds., *Nicene and Post-Nicene Fathers: Second Series*, vol. 6, *Jerome: Letters and Select Works* (New York: Cosimo, 2007), 348.

Chapter 4

1. Lex Loizides, *Church History Blog*, October 15, 2008, http://lexloiz.wordpress.com/2008/10/15/%E2%80%98lord-make-me-pure-but-not-yet%E2%80%99-%E2%80%93-augustine%E2%80%99s-naughty-prayer/.

2. *Stanford Encyclopedia of Philosophy*, s.v. "Saint Augustine," March 24, 2000, rev. November 12, 2010, http://plato.stanford.edu/entries/augustine/.

3. Romans 5:12. Emphasis added.

4. Jesse Couenhoven, "St. Augustine's Doctrine of Original Sin," *Augustinian Studies* 36, no. 2 (2005): 359–96, http://www.academia.edu/1958072/St._Augustines_Doctrine_of_Original_Sin.

5. J. Patout Burns, "The Atmosphere of Election," *Journal of Early Christian Studies* 2, no. 3 (1994): 325–39, doi: 10.1353/earl.0.0152.

6. Gregory, Bishop of Nyssa, "On the Making of Man," in *Writings of the Early Church Fathers*, BibleStudyTools.com, 2003, http://www.biblestudytools.com/history/early-church-fathers/post-nicene/vol-5-gregory-of-nyssa/gregory-of-nyssa/making-of-man.html.

7. Elaine Pagels, *Adam, Eve, and the Serpent* (New York: Random House, 1988), 90.

8. Interested readers are encouraged to consult Jaroslav Pelikan's five-volume work *The Christian Tradition: A History of the Development of Doctrine* (Chicago: University of Chicago Press, 1971–1989).

9. Augustine of Hippo, *The Confessions of St. Augustine*, trans. Rex Warner (New York: New American Library, 1963), 20.

10. Ibid., 23.

11. Ibid., 27–28.

12. Ibid., 41. Emphasis in original.

13. Ibid., 45. Emphasis added.

14. Ibid., 56.

15. Ibid., 243.

16. Ibid., 247.

17. Ibid., 245. Emphasis in original.

18. Ibid., 246.

19. Ibid., 173.

20. Ibid., 177.

21. Ibid., 177–78. Emphasis in original.

22. Ibid., 182.

23. Ibid., 183. Emphasis in original.

24. Ibid.

25. Ibid., 174.

26. Ibid., 102.

27. Romans 7:15–24.

28. "Original Sin," *Religions* (blog), BBC, updated September 17, 2009, http://www.bbc.co.uk/religion/religions/christianity/beliefs/originalsin_1.shtml.

29. Jaroslav Pelikan, *The Christian Tradition: A History of the Development of Doctrine*, vol. 1, *The Emergence of the Catholic Tradition: 100–600* (Chicago: University of Chicago Press, 1971), 313.

30. Alan Jacobs, *Original Sin: A Cultural History* (New York: HarperCollins, 2008), 51.

31. Pelagius, *Letter to Demetrias*, I, quoted in Justin Holcomb, "Pelagius: Know Your Heretics," Justin Holcomb.com, March 15, 2010, http://justinholcomb.com/2010/03/15/pelagius-know-your-heretics/.

32. Pagels, *Adam, Eve, and the Serpent*, 140.

33. Ibid., 139.

34. Ibid.

35. Ibid., 140.

36. Ibid., 130.

Chapter 5

1. E. M. W. Tillyard, *The Elizabethan World Picture: A Study of the Idea of Order in the Age of Shakespeare, Donne and Milton* (New York: Vintage Books, 1959), 5–6.

2. Tim Chaffey, "Feedback: Original Sin," *1:1 Answers in Genesis* (blog), February 18, 2011, http://www.answersingenesis.org/articles/2011/02/18/feedback-original-sin.

3. Bertrand Russell, *A History of Western Philosophy* (New York: Simon & Schuster, 1972), 29.

4. Augustine, *The Confessions*, in *Great Books of the Western World*, vol. 18 (Chicago: Encyclopedia Britannica, 1952), 47–48.

5. Roger Penrose, *Shadows of the Mind: A Search for the Missing Science of Consciousness* (New York: Oxford University Press, 1994), 50–51.

6. Cicero, "The Dream of Scipio: Somnium Scipionis," trans. W. D. Pearman, *De Re Publica*, book 6 (1883), 3–14, http://www.tertullian.org/fathers/cicero_dream_of_scipio_02_trans.htm.

7. The Alexandrian astronomer Ptolemy's famous work is known today by its Arabic title—*The Almagest*.

8. Psalm 93:1.

9. Richard Tarnas, *The Passion of the Western Mind: Understanding the Ideas That Have Shaped Our Worldview* (New York: Ballantine Books, 1991), 195.

10. Tillyard, *Elizabethan World Picture*, 21.

11. Philip C. Almond, *Adam and Eve: In Seventeenth-Century Thought* (New York: Cambridge University Press, 1999), 2.

12. Umberto Eco, best known for his novel *The Name of the Rose*, engages this in *The Search for the Perfect Language* (Oxford, UK: Blackwell, 1995).

13. Eco, *Search for the Perfect Language*, 44.

14. Ibid., 77.

15. Ibid.

16. Ibid., 81.

17. Jean Delumeau, *History of Paradise: The Garden of Eden in Myth and Tradition* (New York: Continuum, 1995), 71.

18. Delumeau, *History of Paradise*, 16.

19. Ibid.

20. Ibid., 19.

21. Ibid.

22. Ibid., 45.

23. Kevin Rushby, *Paradise: A History of the Idea That Rules the World* (New York: Carroll & Graff, 2006), 69.

24. James Hannam, "Deconstructing Copernicus," *Medieval Science and Philosophy*, accessed September 20, 2014, http://jameshannam.com/copernicus.htm.

Chapter 6

1. Ken Ham, "Cain's Wife—Who Was She?," 1:1 *Answers in Genesis* (blog), September 13, 2007, https://answersingenesis.org/bible-characters/cain/cains-wife-who-was-she/.

2. Anthony Grafton, *New Worlds, Ancient Texts: The Power of Tradition and the Shock of Discovery* (Cambridge, MA: Belknap Press of Harvard University Press, 1992), 1.

3. Arthur Koestler, *The Sleepwalkers* (New York: Macmillan, 1963), 119–219.

4. "Andreas Vesalius," *NNDB: Tracking the Entire World*, accessed September 20, 2014, http://www.nndb.com/people/270/000085015/.

5. Paracelsus, *Selected Writings*, trans. Norbert Guterman (New York: Pantheon, 1951), 79–80.

6. Quoted in Arthur S. Peake, *Christianity: Its Nature and Truth* (London: Duckworth, 1908), 116.

7. Philip C. Almond, *Adam and Eve: In Seventeenth-Century Thought* (New York: Cambridge University Press, 1999), 47.

8. Ibid., 48.

9. Ibid., 133–34.

10. Ibid., 50.

11. Anthony Grafton, *New Worlds, Ancient Texts: The Power of Tradition and the Shock of Discovery* (Cambridge, MA: Belknap Press of Harvard University Press, 1992), 32.

12. Timothy Ferris, *Coming of Age in the Milky Way* (New York: William Morrow, 1988).

13. John Milton, "The Argument," in *Great Books of the Western World*, vol. 32 (Chicago: Encyclopedia Britannica, 1952), 233.

14. Ibid., 235.

15. Almond, *Adam and Eve*, 210.

16. Albert Collver, "Copernicus and the Church, Lutherans and the Missouri Synod," *The ABC3s of Miscellany* (blog), August 25, 2011, http://abc3miscellany .blogspot.com/2011/08/copernicus-and-church-lutherans-and.html.

17. Augustine, *The City of God*, in *Great Books of the Western World*, vol. 18 (Chicago: Encyclopedia Britannica, 1952), 495.

18. David N. Livingstone, *Adam's Ancestors: Race, Religion and the Politics of Human Origins* (Baltimore: Johns Hopkins University Press, 2008), 10.

19. Ibid., 17.

20. Almond, *Adam and Eve*, 50.

21. Ibid., 52.

22. Richard H. Popkin, *Isaac La Peyrère (1596–1676): His Life, Work and Influence* (Leiden, Netherlands: E. J. Brill, 1987), 43.

23. Anthony Grafton, *Defenders of the Text: The Traditions of Scholarship in an Age of Science* (Cambridge, MA: Harvard University Press, 1994), 205.

24. Almond, *Adam and Eve*, 57.

25. Ibid.

26. "The Epigram: Part 2," *Southern Literary Messenger* 14, no. 2 (December 1848): 719, Making of America Journal Articles website, http://quod.lib.umich.edu /m/moajrnl/acf2679.0014.012/723:8?page=root;size=100;view=text.

Chapter 7

1. "St. Augustine (354–430)," *St. Augustine's Reserve*, accessed August 22, 2013, http://hyperphysics.phy-astr.gsu.edu/nave-html/faithpathh/augustine.html.

2. Davis A. Young and Ralph F. Stearley, *The Bible, Rocks and Time* (Downers Grove, IL: InterVarsity Press, 2008), 45.

3. James Barr has done extensive analysis of Ussher's chronology and concludes that the 4004 date stands on its own for Ussher, independently of any millennial scheme. The happy convergence of a carefully constructed history and a theologically motivated timeline are exactly what we would expect if God was the author of both the Bible and history. See S. J. Gould, "Fall in the House of Ussher," in *Eight Little Piggies* (New York: Norton Books, 1993), 190.

4. Peter Harrison, *The Bible, Protestantism and the Rise of Natural Science* (New York: Cambridge University Press, 1998), 18–19.

5. Ibid., 19.

6. Ibid., 22.

7. Ibid.

8. Kenneth J. Howell, *God's Two Books: Copernican Cosmology and Biblical Interpretation in Early Modern Science* (Notre Dame, IN: University of Notre Dame Press, 2002), 209.

9. Harrison, *The Bible, Protestantism and the Rise of Natural Science*, 93.

10. Ibid., 103.

11. Ibid., 104.

12. Ibid.

13. Peter Harrison, *The Fall of Man and the Foundations of Science* (New York: Cambridge University Press, 2007), 258.

14. Howell, *God's Two Books*, 110.

15. Roland H. Bainton, *Here I Stand: A Life of Martin Luther* (New York: Penguin Books, 1950), 153–55.

16. Mary Gerhart and Fabian E. Udoh, eds., *The Christianity Reader* (Chicago: University of Chicago Press, 2007), 89.

17. Harrison, *The Bible, Protestantism and the Rise of Natural Science*, 122.

18. Ibid., 211.

19. Stephen J. Gould, *Time's Arrow, Time's Cycle: Myth and Metaphor in the Discovery of Geological Time* (Cambridge, MA: Harvard University Press, 1987), 28.

20. Francis Bacon, *Advancement of Learning* (London: Longman, 1605), Kindle edition.

21. Ibid.

22. Harrison, *The Bible, Protestantism and the Rise of Natural Science*, 144.

23. Ernst Mayr, *The Growth of Biological Thought: Diversity, Evolution, and Inheritance* (Cambridge, MA: Harvard University Press, 1981), 330.

24. "Epochs" for Buffon referred to points in time rather than extended periods. This was the original meaning of the word. See Martin J. S. Rudwick, *Worlds Before Adam: The Reconstruction of Geohistory in the Age of Reform* (Chicago: University of Chicago Press, 2008), 143.

25. John H. Brooke, *Science and Religion: Some Historical Perspectives* (New York: Cambridge University Press, 1991), 236.

26. Brooke, *Science and Religion*, 238.

27. Donald K. McKim, ed., *Encyclopedia of the Reformed Faith* (Louisville, KY: Westminster/John Knox Press, 1992), 61.

28. Genesis 1:1–2. *The Layman's Parallel Bible: Comparing Four Popular Translations in Parallel Columns; Living Bible Version* (Grand Rapids, MI: Zondervan Bible Publishers, 1973).

29. Young and Stearley, *The Bible, Rocks and Time*, 121.

30. Martin J. S. Rudwick, *The Meaning of Fossils: Episodes in the History of Paleontology*, 2nd ed. (Chicago: University of Chicago Press, 1985), 1.

31. Robert Bakewell, *An Introduction to Geology*, 4th ed. (London: A&R Spottiswoode, 1833), 23. Emphasis in original.

32. Young and Stearley, *Bible, Rocks and Time*, 129.

33. George H. Pember, *Earth's Earliest Ages* (Crane, MO: Defender, 2012).

34. Young and Stearley, *Bible, Rocks and Time*, 127.

35. "Book Reviews for December 2003," *American Scientific Affiliation: Science in Christian Perspective*, http://www.asa3.org/ASA/BookReviews2000 -present/12–03.html.

36. Pember, *Earth's Earliest Ages*, back cover.

37. Ibid., 23–24.

38. Young and Stearley, *Bible, Rocks and Time*, 129. Hugh Ross defends his position against charges of having capitulated to science in this program. See "Hugh Ross vs. Ken Ham—TBN Debate," YouTube, July 17, 2012, http:// www.youtube.com/watch?v=zgueGotRqbM.

Chapter 8

1. Maureen Gallery Kovacs, trans., The Epic of Gilgamesh, tablet 11, http:// jewishchristianlit.com/Texts/ANEmyths/gilgamesh11.html. Based on print ed., M. G. Kovacs, The Epic of Gilgamesh (Stanford, CA: Stanford University Press, 1989).

2. Walter E. Aufrecht, *Studies in the Book of Job* (Waterloo, ONT: Wilfrid Laurier University Press, 1985), 34.

3. *Encyclopedia Britannica*, s.v. "Enuma Elish," accessed on September 20, 2014, http://www.britannica.com/EBchecked/topic/189085/Enuma-Elish.

4. Steve Ham, "Is Genesis 1–11 a Derivation from Ancient Myths?," *1:1 Answers in Genesis*, March 29, 2011, http://www.answersingenesis.org/articles/2011 /03/29/derivation-from-ancient-myths; Frank Lorey, "The Flood of Noah

and the Flood of Gilgamesh," *Institute for Creation Research, Acts & Facts* 26 (1997), http://www.icr.org/article/noah-flood-gilgamesh/.

5. Historian Jon Roberts provides a thoughtful analysis of the complex reception of Darwinism in America. See Jon Roberts, *Darwinism and the Divine in America: Protestant Intellectuals and Organic Evolution, 1859–1900* (Notre Dame, IN: University of Notre Dame Press, 2001).

6. Charles Lyell, *Principles of Geology,* vols. 1–3 (London: John Murray, 1830).

7. *Theory of Evolution Development,* Age-of-the-Sage.org, accessed September 20, 2014, http://www.age-of-the sage.org/evolution/theory_of_evolution _development.html.

8. Adam Sedgwick, *The Life and Letters of the Reverend Adam Sedgwick,* vol. 2 (1845; repr., Google Books), 84–85.

9. Sedgwick, *Life and Letters,* 3.

10. Adam Sedgwick, "Natural History of Creation," *Edinburgh Review* 82 (July 1845): 3. Available online at https://www.srcf.ucam.org/acs/data/archive /2009/200904-article3.pdf.

11. Louis Agassiz, *The Structure of Animal Life* (1866; repr., Charleston, SC: Bibliolife, 2008), 2–3.

12. John V. Wyhe, ed., "Prof. Agassiz on the Origin of Species," part 5, Book Notices, *The Complete Work of Charles Darwin Online,* accessed August 26, 2013, http://darwin-online.org.uk/content/frameset?pageseq=1&itemID=A45& viewtype=text.

13. David B. Williams, "A Wrangle over Darwin," *Harvard Magazine,* September 1998, http://www.harvardmagazine.com/1998/09/darwin.html.

14. Roberts, *Darwinism and the Divine in America.*

15. Ibid., 184.

16. Ibid.

17. Ibid., 199.

18. Thomas G. Apple and John M. Titzel, eds., *Reformed Quarterly Review: Reformed Church in the United States* 35 (Philadelphia: Reformed Church Publication House, 1888), accessed August 26, 2013, Google Books.

19. Peter Bowler, *The Eclipse of Darwinism* (Baltimore: Johns Hopkins University Press, 1992), 180.

20. A. N. Wilson, *God's Funeral* (New York: W. W. Norton, 1999), 130.

21. Frank Newport, "In U.S., 42% Believe Creationist View of Human Origins," *Gallup Politics*, June 2, 2014, http://www.gallup.com/poll/170822/believe -creationist-view-human-origins.aspx.

22. Alister E. McGrath, *Evangelicalism and the Future of Christianity* (Downers Grove, IL: InterVarsity Press, 1995).

23. Rachel Held Evans, "Why Millennials Are Leaving the Church," *CNN Belief Blog*, July 27, 2013, http://religion.blogs.cnn.com/2013/07/27/why -millennials-are-leaving-the-church/.

24. Richard N. Ostling, "The Search for the Historical Adam," *Christianity Today*, June 3, 2011, http://www.christianitytoday.com/ct/2011/june/historicaladam .html; Barbara Bradley Hagerty, "Evangelicals Question the Existence of Adam and Eve," *Morning Edition*, NPR, August 9, 2011, audio, 7:44, http:// www.npr.org/2011/08/09/138957812/evangelicals-question-the-existence -of-adam-and-eve; "Tip/Wag—Evangelical Scientists and Rick Santorum," *The Colbert Report*, August 17, 2011, http://thecolbertreport.cc.com/video -playlists/ogz166/colbert-report-07109/uiim37.

25. John Ray, *The Wisdom of God Manifested in the Works of the Creation. In Two Parts . . . With Answers to Some Objections*, 13th ed. (1756; reproduction, Cambridge University Library).

26. Cornelius Burges, "The Confession of Faith of the Assembly of Divines at Westminster," *The Confession of Faith of the Assembly of Divines at Westminster*, tercentenary ed. (London: Presbyterian Church of England, 1946), http:// en.wikisource.org/wiki/The_Confession_of_Faith_of_the_Assembly_of _Divines_at_Westminster.

27. David N. Livingstone and Mark A. Noll, "B. B. Warfield on Creation and Evolution: A Biblical Inerrantist as Evolutionist," *Isis* 91, no. 2 (2000), http:// www.jstor.org/stable/236917.

28. Mark A. Noll, ed., *The Princeton Theology, 1812–1921* (Grand Rapids, MI: Baker Book House, 1983), 293.

29. Ibid., 297.

30. Noll, *Princeton Theology*, 298.

31. B. B. Warfield, *Lectures on Anthropology* (Princeton, NJ: Princeton University, 1888), accessed August 26, 2013, http://networkedblogs.com/N7urv.

32. Roberts, *Darwinism and the Divine in America*, 148.

33. Ibid.

34. G. Frederick Wright, *Studies in Science and Religion* (1882; repr., Charleston, SC: Bibliolife, 2012), 225.

35. Ibid., 224–25.

36. R. A. Torrey, "The Passing of Evolution," *Blue Letter Bible*, accessed August 26, 2013, http://www.blueletterbible.org/commentaries/comm_view .cfm?AuthorID=16&contentID=4590&commInfo=20&topic=The %20Fundamentals.

37. George M. Marsden, *Understanding Fundamentalism and Evangelicalism* (Grand Rapids, MI: Wm. B. Eerdmans, 1991), 147.

Chapter 9

1. "Is Segregation Scriptural? By Bob Jones Sr., 1960," *A Time to Laugh*, March 15, 2013, http://www.drslewis.org/camille/2013/03/15/is-segregation -scriptural-by-bob-jones-sr-1960/.

2. John Blake, "Why Sunday Morning Remains America's Most Segregated Hour," *CNN Belief Blog*, October 6, 2010, http://religion.blogs.cnn.com /2010/10/06/why-sunday-morning-remains-americas-most-segregated -hour/.

3. David N. Livingstone, *Adam's Ancestors: Race, Religion and the Politics of Human Origins* (Baltimore: Johns Hopkins University Press, 2008), 53.

4. Ibid.

5. "Or, Creation of the WORLD," in *An Universal History from the Earliest Account of Time*, vol. 1 (1747), 99, https://play.google.com/books/reader?id= 5NcGAAAAcAAJ&printsec=frontcover&output=reader&authuser=0&hl= en&pg=GBS.PA99. Emphasis in original.

6. Livingstone, *Adam's Ancestors*, 55–56.

7. Ibid., 56.

8. Ibid, 57.

9. Ibid., 58–59.

10. Ibid., 61.

11. Ibid., 63.

12. Ibid., 66.

13. Ibid., 69.

14. Ibid.

15. "The Southern Argument for Slavery," *U.S. History Online Textbook,* accessed September 20, 2014, http://www.ushistory.org/us/27f.asp.

16. David M. Goldenberg, *The Curse of Ham: Race and Slavery in Early Judaism, Christianity, and Islam* (Princeton, NJ: Princeton University Press, 2003), 180.

17. Ariel [Buckner Payne], *The Negro: What Is His Ethnological Status?* 2nd ed. (Cincinnati, 1867), 44.

18. Charles Carroll, *The Negro a Beast* (St. Louis: American Book and Bible House, 1900), http://www.scribd.com/doc/135895931/The-Negro-a-Beast.

19. Barry Hankins and Thomas Kidd, "Column: Southern Baptists Cleanse Past," *USA Today News,* updated June 24, 2012, http://usatoday30.usatoday.com /news/opinion/forum/story/2012–06–24/religion-southern-baptist-luter -slavery/55796742/1.

20. Carroll, *The Negro a Beast.*

21. Stephen R. Haynes, *Noah's Curse: The Biblical Justification of American Slavery* (New York: Oxford University Press, 2002), 4.

22. "Bob Jones University's Racist Anti-miscegenation Rule Discussed," *Larry King Live,* March 3, 2000, YouTube, http://www.youtube.com/watch?v =D12A3D3TGE4.

23. *Investing in Lives for Eternity,* advancement brochure, Bob Jones University, 2008, 6, Bob Jones University Archives, Mack Library.

24. Stephen J. Gould, *The Mismeasure of Man* (New York: Norton, 1981), 73–122. This book challenges the objectivity of the measurements that were made and locates several egregious manipulations of the data. Gould's analysis has, unfortunately, also been challenged, although his general conclusions—that cranial measurements do not establish the intellectual superiority of the Caucasian race—still hold.

25. "Alabama Interracial Marriage, Amendment 2 (2000)," *Ballotpedia,* accessed September 20, 2014, http://ballotpedia.org/Alabama_Interracial_Marriage, _Amendment_2_%282000%29.

26. George Hunter, *A Civic Biology: Presented in Problems* (New York: American Book, 1914), 196.

27. Richard J. Hernstein and Charles Murray, *The Bell Curve: Intelligence and Class Structure in American Life* (New York: Free Press, 1994).

28. Joel Shurkin, *Broken Genius: The Rise and Fall of William Shockley, Creator of the Electronic Age* (New York: Macmillan, 2006), 263.

Chapter 10

1. Richard Dawkins, review of *Blueprint* by Donald Johanson and Maitland Edey, *New York Times*, April 9, 1989.

2. George McCready Price, *The New Geology* (Mountain View, CA: Pacific Press, 1923), 652. A preflood paradise climate, which he called the "eternal spring," was a staple in Price's writings, inferred from fossils of some non-Arctic organisms found at the poles. Geological evidence for prehistoric ice at the poles is dismissed as ambiguous. See Price, *Evolutionary Geology and the New Catastrophism* (Mountain View, CA: Pacific Press, 1926), 258–61. The same argument also appears in Price, *The Fundamentals of Geology* (Mountain View, CA: Pacific Press, 1913), 195–98.

3. Price, *New Geology*.

4. Ibid.

5. Karl W. Giberson and Donald A. Yerxa, *Species of Origins: America's Search for a Creation Story* (Lanham, MD: Rowman & Littlefield), 68.

6. Henry M. Morris and John D. Morris, *The Modern Creation Trilogy*, vol. 1, *Scripture and Creation* (Green Forest, AR: Master Books, 1996), 13–14.

7. Ronald Numbers, "The Creationists," in *God and Nature: Historical Essays on the Encounter Between Christianity and Science*, ed. David C. Lindberg and Ronald L. Numbers (Berkeley: University of California Press, 1986), 415.

8. Richard Dawkins, *The Blind Watchmaker: Why the Evidence of Evolution Reveals a Universe Without Design* (New York: Norton, 1986).

9. Henry M. Morris, *The Genesis Record: A Scientific and Devotional Commentary on the Book of Beginnings* (Grand Rapids, MI: Baker Books, 2009).

10. Ibid., 85–86.

11. Ibid., 87.

12. Ibid.

13. Ibid., 109.

14. Ibid., 125.

15. Ibid., 127.

16. Ibid.

17. Clarence Darrow, *Attorney for the Damned: Clarence Darrow in the Courtroom* (Chicago: University of Chicago Press, 1989), 223.

18. Morris, *Genesis Record*, 143.

19. Ibid., 59.

20. Ibid.

21. Ibid., 60.

22. Ibid., 404.

23. Mark O'Brien, "Hard to Believe a Man with a PhD Didn't Know of a Basic Tax Law," *Pensacola (FL) News Journal*, November 3, 2006.

24. Karen Bartelt, "The Dissertation Kent Hovind Doesn't Want You to Read," *No Answers in Genesis* (blog), accessed September 20, 2014, http://noanswersingenesis.org.au/bartelt_dissertation_on_hovind_thesis.htm.

25. "Dr. Hovind's 'Creation Seminar' Part 2," accessed September 20, 2014, http://www.arrivalofthefittest.com/seminar2.html.

26. Glen J. Kuban, "A Matter of Degree: Carl Baugh's Alleged Credentials," *The TalkOrigins Archive: Exploring the Creation/Evolution Controversy* (blog), accessed October 30, 2008, http://www.talkorigins.org/faqs/paluxy/degrees.html. Originally published in *NCSE Reports* 9, no. 6 (November-December 1989).

27. "Watch Us: Our Programs," *Trinity Broadcasting Network*, October 10, 2008, http://www.tbn.org/index.php/2/4/p/3.html.

28. Kuban, "A Matter of Degree."

29. Carl Baugh, *Panorama of Creation* (Oklahoma City: Southwest Radio Church, 1989), 84.

30. Ibid., 53.

31. Ibid., 57.

32. Ibid., 62.

Chapter 11

1. Barbara Bradley Hagerty, "Evangelicals Question the Existence of Adam and Eve," *Morning Edition*, NPR, August 9, 2011, audio, 7:44, http://www.npr.org/2011/08/09/138957812/evangelicals-question-the-existence-of-adam-and-eve.

2. Alfred Kirchoff, *Darwinismus* (Frankfurt, 1910), 86–87, quoted in Richard Weikert, *From Darwin to Hitler: Evolutionary Ethics, Eugenics, and Racism in Germany* (New York: Palgrave Macmillan, 2006), 184.

3. The historian Richard Weikert makes this case in *From Darwin to Hitler*.

4. House Bill No. 185, Public Acts of the State of Tennessee, Tennessee Evolution Statutes. 1925, ch. 27, http://law2.umkc.edu/faculty/projects/ftrials/scopes/tennstat.htm.

5. Ronald L. Numbers, "Creationism in 20th Century America," *Science* 218 (November 5, 1982): 540.

6. Clarence Darrow, *Attorney for the Damned: Clarence Darrow in the Courtroom* (Chicago: University of Chicago Press, 1989), 227.

7. R. Albert Mohler, "Why Does the Universe Look So Old?," *Institute for Creation Research*, accessed September 20, 2014, http://www.icr.org/article/why -does-universe-look-so-old/.

8. Marvin Olasky and John Perry, *Monkey Business: The True Story of the Scopes Trial* (Nashville: B&H Books, 2005).

9. Ruth Moon, "Bryan College Faculty Vote 'No Confidence' in President over Adam and Eve," *Gleanings* (blog), *Christianity Today* March 7, 2014, http:// www.christianitytoday.com/gleanings/2014/march/bryan-college-faculty -vote-no-confidence-president-adam-eve.html?paging=off.

10. Paul Nelson and Jonathan Wells, "Homology in Biology," in *Darwinism, Design, and Public Education*, ed. John Angus Campbell and Stephen C. Meyer (East Lansing: Michigan State University Press, 2003), 316.

11. Jonathan M., "Unitary Pseudogenes and RNA Editing," *Evolution News and Views* (blog), August 28, 2013, http://www.evolutionnews.org/2013/08 /unitary_pseudogo75831.html.

12. Paul Nelson and John Mark Reynolds, "Young Earth Creationism," in *Three Views of Creation and Evolution*, ed. Paul Nelson, Robert C. Newman, and Howard J. Van Till (Grand Rapids, MI: Zondervan, 1999), 51.

13. Robert Schadewald, "The 1998 International Conference on Creationism," *NCSE Reports*, accessed February 13, 2007, www.nsceweb.org/resources /rnsce_content/vol/9954_the_1998_international_confere_12_30_1899.asp.

14. Numbers 22:30.

15. Andrew Dickson White, *A History of the Warfare of Science with Theology in Christendom* (New York: Free Press, 1965), 130.

16. Ed Stetzer, "The Big Story of Scripture (Creation, Fall, Redemption, Restoration) in Pictures: Your Input Requested," *The Exchange*, November 28, 2012, http://www.christianitytoday.com/edstetzer/2012/november/big -story-of-scripture-creation-fall-redemption.html.

17. John Donne, *An Anatomy of the World*, http://www.poetryfoundation.org /poem/173348.

18. Chad Meister and James K. Dew Jr., eds., *God and Evil: The Case for God in a World Filled with Pain* (Downers Grove, IL: InterVarsity Press, 2013), 9.

19. Karl Giberson, "Christianity and Extraterrestrial Life: Are the Gliesans Going to Hell?," *HuffPost Religion*, October 11, 2010, http://www.huffingtonpost.com/karl-giberson-phd/are-the-gliesans-going-to_b_751761.html.

20. J. P. Moreland, "The Age of the Earth," *Reasons to Believe*, February 2, 2002, http://www.reasons.org/articles/the-age-of-earth.

21. Lee Irons, "Animal Death Before the Fall: What Does the Bible Say?," *Reasons to Believe*, January 1, 2001, http://www.reasons.org/articles/animal-death-before-the-fall-what-does-the-bible-say.

22. Fazale Rana with Hugh Ross, *Who Is Adam? A Creation Model Approach to the Origin of Man* (Colorado Springs: NavPress, 2005), 45.

23. Joe Gorra, interview with William Dembski, *Evangelical Philosophical Society*, November 4, 2009, http://blog.epsociety.org/2009/11/interview-with-william-dembski-end-of.asp. Emphasis mine.

24. Denis Alexander, *Creation or Evolution: Do We Have to Choose?* (Oxford, UK: Monarch Books, 2008), 236.

25. Ibid., 237.

26. David Anderson, "Creation or Evolution: Choose Wisely!," *Creation Ministries International*, May 1, 2009, http://creation.com/review-creation-or-evolution-david-anderson.

27. Karl Giberson, *Saving Darwin: How to Be a Christian and Believe in Evolution* (San Francisco: HarperOne, 2008).

28. William Dembski, "'Saving Darwin'—What's the Point?," *Uncommon Descent* (blog), June 19, 2008, http://www.uncommondescent.com/evolution/saving-darwin-whats-the-point/.

29. Karl Giberson, "Is 'American Evangelicalism' Still Christian?," *Respectful Conversation*, December 16, 2013, http://www.respectfulconversation.net/ae-conversation/2013/12/16/is-american-evangelicalism-still-christian.html.

30. R. Albert Mohler, "Total Capitulation: The Evangelical Surrender of Truth," *AlbertMohler.com* (blog), October 25, 2011, http://www.albertmohler.com/2011/10/25/total-capitulation-the-evangelical-surrender-of-truth/.

31. "Statement of Faith," *Wheaton History A to Z*, accessed September 20, 2014, http://a2z.my.wheaton.edu/statement-of-faith.

32. Associated Press, "Bryan College Losing Nearly 25% of Faculty after 'Adam and Eve' Controversy," *Times News* (Kingsport, TN), May 4, 2014, http://www.timesnews.net/article/9076475/bryan-college-losing-nearly-25-of-faculty-after-adam-and-eve-controversy.

33. Mark Andrews, "Defending Adam and Eve Splits Trustees at Christian College," *CharismaNews* (Lake Mary, FL), July 22, 2014, http://www .charismanews.com/us/44740-defending-adam-and-eve-splits-trustees -at-christian-college.

34. Garrett Haley, "Professors Sue Bryan College Over School's Adherence to Bib- lical Creation Account," *Christian News*, May 17, 2014, http://christiannews .net/2014/05/17/professors-sue-bryan-college-over-schools-adherence-to -biblical-creation-account.

35. James Scullin, "You Say Toe-May-Toe, I Say Toe-Mah-Toe," *Reformed Naza- rene* (blog), July 23, 2013, http://reformednazarene.wordpress.com/category /karl-giberson/.

36. Ken Ham, "The Foolishness of Evolutionists," *Around the World with Ken Ham* (blog), October 27, 2012, http://blogs.answersingenesis.org/blogs/ken-ham /2012/10/27/the-foolishness-of-evolutionists/.

Conclusion

1. G. K. Chesterton, "The Maniac," in *Orthodoxy* (1908), http://www .pagebypagebooks.com/Gilbert_K_Chesterton/Orthodoxy/The_Maniac _p1.html.

2. John Donne, *An Anatomy of the World*. http://www.poetryfoundation.org /poem/173348.

3. Matthew Barrett and Ardel B. Caneday, eds., *Four Views on the Historical Adam* (Grand Rapids, MI: Zondervan Books, 2013), 223. Emphasis in original.

4. Christian de Duve, *Genetics of Original Sin: The Impact of Natural Selection on the Future of Humanity* (New Haven, CT: Yale University Press, 2010), xxv.

5. Ibid., 146.

6. Ibid., 147.

7. Jimmy Carter, *A Call to Action: Women, Religion, Violence, and Power* (New York: Simon & Shuster, 2014).

INDEX